Praise for *The Astrology of Self-Discovery*

One of the best of a new generation of astrology writers who emerged in the 1970s, Tracy Marks has won a wide circle of admirers through her rare combination of astrological expertise and literary skill. *Astrology of Self-Discovery* is . . . about as fine a book on astrology as you'll ever encounter: intelligent, clearly written, a pleasure to read.

—Horoscope Magazine

Every once in a while an astrology book comes along that is sure to be a classic. This is one of those books because it reaches across all levels from beginner to professional . . . it bridges traditional astrology with contemporary psychologically-oriented astrology. The author does not hesitate to draw on her experiences with psychosynthesis, meditation and visualization, Jungian psychology and literature. Ms. Marks is a fine, enjoyable writer!

—NCGR Newsletter

THE ASTROLOGY OF
SELF-DISCOVERY

An in-depth exploration of the
potentials revealed in your birth chart

REVISED AND EXPANDED EDITION

TRACY MARKS

IBIS PRESS
Lake Worth, FL

To Alex Kronstadt,

Who stepped softly
Through the corridors
Of my soul,
Lighting candles.

❧

Published in 2008 by
IBIS PRESS
an imprint of Nicolas-Hays, Inc.
P. O. Box 540206 • Lake Worth, FL 33454-0206
www.nicolashays.com
Distributed to the trade by Red Wheel/Weiser, LLC
65 Parker St., Unit 7 • Newburyport, MA 01950-4600
www.redwheelweiser.com

Special thanks to Stephen Arroyo and the staff of CRCS Publications who
published the previous edition of this book, to Yvonne Paglia and the staff
of Ibis Publishing for this revised, updated edition, and to my friend
and astrologer Beverly Feldt of Camden, Maine.

Library of Congress Cataloging-in-Publication Data
Marks, Tracy, 1950-
The astrology of self-discovery : an in-depth exploration of the potentials
revealed in your birth chart / Tracy Marks. -- Rev. and expanded ed.
p. cm.
Includes bibliographical references.
ISBN 978-0-89254-136-2 (alk. paper)
1. Astrology and psychology. I. Title.
BF1729.P8M37 2008
133.5--dc22   2008038723
VG
Cover and text design by Kathryn Sky-Peck
Cover illustration by Meg Takamura, IZA Stock/Getty Images

Printed in the United States of America
12 11 10 09 08 07 06
7 6 5 4 3 2 1

CONTENTS

INTRODUCTION TO THE
REVISED EDITION

The astrological chart is not merely a means for abstractly understanding ourselves as fixed entities in time, or for determining influences affecting our lives. The chart is also a map for discovering who we truly are and who we can become when we decide to take charge of all our disparate parts and all the internal and external energies affecting us. It is also a guide for aligning ourselves with cosmic influences, so that we may more effectively choose paths which help us live in harmony with the universe. Using astrology consciously, actively, constructively and responsibly, we can both discover ourselves and create ourselves in cooperation with universal forces.

This book advocates an active, dynamic, and transformative approach to astrology, one which involves experientially as well as intellectually contacting the planetary personalities within us. By proactively using astrology, we can discover our overall life purpose and current direction. We can commit ourselves to paths of integration which involve bringing our diverse and often conflicting personalities into dialogue, eventually creating a new synthesis.

Utilizing our natal charts in our evolutionary journeys, we can learn how to cooperate with the positive potentials of transits, progressions and synastry rather than passively react to external influences. As we allow our true selves to unfold and blossom, we are also likely to find viable means for making worthwhile contributions to the world in which we live.

The ideas presented in this book are an integration of depth psychology (including psychosynthesis, gestalt therapy, Jungian psychology and object relations), spiritual teachings and traditional astrology, with learnings derived from my own professional work, psychotherapy, and self-therapy through my adult life. I draw from my own experience, intuition, and the knowledge gained through study, inner work, and indepth interactions with other people.

The original edition of this book was published in 1985. Although I am still an astrological counselor, I have been a psychotherapist and licensed mental health counselor now for nearly twenty-five years, and have counseled on an ongoing basis—with or without the aid of astrology—many clients who are committed to their personal and/or transpersonal development. I aim to utilize my transpersonal understanding as a means to help people contact their own inner guidance and to facilitate their process of growth and integration. This is also one of the primary purposes of this book.

The Astrology of Self-Discovery includes ten chapters. Five were originally published as separate booklets in the early 1980s, and were revised and expanded later in order to reflect my own evolving understanding. Four chapters—on the Moon, Moon signs, lunar nodes, and the misuses of astrology—express ideas and experiential learnings which were an integral part of my development at that time, and which still influence me today.

The tenth and final chapter, written for this revised expanded edition, reflects understanding I have gained during the past two decades in regard to free will and fate, and the use of astrology both to maximize personal freedom, and more effectively cope with the ways in which we are limited and/or determined.

This book is not an all-inclusive text covering all facets of chart interpretation. Rather it is a guidebook to some of the facets of astrology of most importance to those of us attempting to integrate our physical, emotional, intellectual, and spiritual natures, liberate ourselves from restricting past patterns, and awaken the inner spirit which can direct our own processes of unfoldment.

In *The Moon: Reparenting the Inner Child*, we will consider how we have denied the feminine principle and repressed the life-affirming energies of our inner child, and will discuss the often painful but usually enlivening process of reowning and reparenting that inner child. In *Moon Signs*, we will interpret our Moon signs in reference to discovering our needs, nourishing and nurturing ourselves, and engaging in the growth-promoting activities of internal reparenting.

In *New Moon, Full Moon*, we will assess the influences of the lunations upon our planetary personalities and how we can utilize that influence to fertilize seed beginnings possible at the new moon and expand our understanding at the full moon. Worksheets and an appendix listing new moons, full moons, and eclipses by degree of the zodiac (newly expanded to 2015) can enable us to determine lunations which have conjuncted and will conjunct our natal planets, so that we can better to prepare ourselves to take advantage of future aspects.

In *Lunar Nodes: Our Life Purpose*, we will take an in-depth look at the South Node as the pull of the past, and the North Node as life purpose, as well as the integration of both polarities. We will reflect upon the meanings of our own nodes, interpret the lessons of the nodal axes by sign, and consider the lunar nodes in relation to transits, progressions, and chart comparisons.

In *Transits: The Next Step in Our Becoming*, we will assess various philosophies in regard to how transits influence us and how we can actively cooperate with them, as well as discover and live the messages they have to teach us. We will learn how to interpret transits, and how to ask the right questions of each outer planet so that may constructively prepare for and make use of its energies. Half a dozen pages of the Transits chapter have been revised in 2007 to reflect upcoming outer planet transits of the next eight years.

In *Neptune: How to Swim through Cosmic Waters*, we will attune ourselves to the elusive, sensitizing qualities of this outer planet, and thoroughly explore the confusions and transitions which Neptune brings into our lives, so that we may find clarity in the midst of Neptunian fog. We will also consider other meanings and lessons of Neptune such as gains possible from visualization, Neptune's call to service, sacrifice, creativity and spiritual experience, and Neptune in relation to romantic love.

The chapter *Pluto: From Darkness into Light* focuses on the deeply transformative Plutonian experiences of energy release, empowerment, and psychological death. We will discuss how we become powerless, misuse power, and can become capable of empowering ourselves in the areas of our lives which Pluto influences. We will also consider Plutonian factors in relationships.

Principles of Depth Astrology is a summarizing chapter which synthesizes ideas presented in previous chapters. It also introduces new ideas and provides an overall philosophy and approach to chart interpretation which is constructive, practical, and growth-promoting. Principles derived from depth psychology, astrology, contemporary physics, and spiritual teachings are included here.

In *Misuses of Astrology*, we will courageously look at the dangers inherent in studying and interpreting astrological charts, and will see how we allow negative factors in our personalities—such as fear of the future, intellectualization, authoritarianism, helplessness, or victimization—to become embedded in our astrology practice. We will briefly explore how we, as astrological counselors, need to be honest with ourselves and true to our highest values if we wish to use astrology as a helping tool.

I wrote the new, final chapter, *Beyond Fate and Free Will*, to express the fruits of my personal struggle to come to terms with the degree to which we are free to forge our own destinies and/or experience the grace of cosmic energies, and the degree to which we are limited by fate, determinism, and our psychological and social conditioning. This chapter draws not only upon my own personal experience, but also upon what I have learned participating in the lives of friends and clients. It reflects my ongoing study in psychology and spirituality, and recent discoveries in quantum physics and quantum psychology.

Coping with ongoing, often incapacitating chronic illness much of my life, fighting against doctors and insurance companies unsuccessfully for my mother's right to die, and experiencing the inevitable painful losses which we all experience more frequently as we age, I have had to rethink again and again the new age belief that we create our own reality. In the process, I have gained considerable respect for Saturn, and the humility which results from learning to acknowledge and accept limitations in myself, others, and the world.

Perhaps, indeed, the universe has a plan for us which is wiser than the weavings of our personal desires and fantasies. Often, we may benefit most not by trying to shape our own realities but by stepping out of the way of ourselves, while listening, always listening, to the silence within.

The final chapter does not in any way negate the previous chapters or the philosophies or paths of development presented there, but rather modulates the focus on self-creation, and provides a larger perspective that is likely to be especially meaningful to those in middle and later adulthood. It also affirms the experience of grace—those rare fortunate times in our lives—usually under the influence of a powerful outer planet transit—in which we transcend ourselves and are transported into a new and larger reality.

From adolescence to our late thirties and perhaps into our forties, we are often exercising our will to shape our circumstances. As we age and face more frequently the inevitable disappointments of life, and discover that we cannot actualize all of our dreams, we may become depressed, disillusioned, and even bitter. But we may also become capable of facing and coming to terms with our midlife experiences and disappointments. We may reshape and refine the philosophies we have held, perhaps in the process becoming less blindly optimistic, but more realistic, and more capable of finding inner peace.

The astrological chart is an amazingly accurate map of the psyche's tendencies and process of unfoldment, but it is only a map, and a sketchy one at best. It operates on the symbolic level. It can point out a variety of possible goals or destinations and the roads which can lead us there; it can tell us the best time to start each journey. But we must determine the destination, the road, the time. We must rev up the engines of our bodily vehicles, refuel ourselves when drained by adversity, and resist the temptations to explore all the tourist traps a few miles off the highway. The chart can help us determine our direction, but it does not by itself indicate whether we will succeed or fail in our aims.

To use our astrological knowledge most beneficially, we need to commit ourselves to taking charge of ourselves—our actions, thoughts, and feelings. We need to learn to listen to our deepest inner guidance rather than be directed primarily by our intellect, ego, or personal desires. We need to learn to contact, accept, and begin to integrate the diverse parts of ourselves which both help and hinder our process of integration and alignment. We need to be willing to continually revise our self-image, attitudes, and philosophies, to let go of expectations and aims which are not in harmony with universal energies, and adapt to the demands of the sometimes harsh but almost always enriching and enlightening circumstances of our lives.

Astrology can help us to intellectually discover who we are and who we can be, but it is up to us to call forth the courage, the will, the love for ourselves, and the dedication to our highest potential and the potential of others, if we are to make our discovery a reality.

PART I

THE MOON & ITS NODES

Chapter One

THE MOON:
REPARENTING THE INNER CHILD

How connected are we to our basic instinctual and emotional natures? How well do we integrate the receptive and nurturing feminine principle within us which enables us to give and receive nourishment? To what extent are we capable of maintaining contact with the deeply feeling and intuitive energies of our inner child, while also functioning as adults and adapting to external reality? In what ways do we experience our lunar nature and express the energies of the Moon in our daily lives?

The Moon in astrology indicates our deepest emotional patterns and needs, our sensitivity and responsiveness, and it shows our relationship to the internal feminine or anima, as well as to female influences outside us. Our rootedness in our being, in our families and personal past, in our homes, and in our community and larger environment is a function of the Moon. The Moon also influences how we form attachments and how we seek to secure and protect ourselves. It shows how we care for and parent ourselves, our children and other people who are important to us. Becoming attuned to the energies of the Moon and to our own individual lunar needs, as suggested by the position and aspects of the Moon in our natal charts, is essential if we seek to befriend ourselves and to create relationships which nourish and sustain ourselves and others. Yet such attunement is exceedingly difficult when the attitudes, institutions, and requirements of society are at odds with the lunar principle.

The Reawakening of Lunar Consciousness

We live in a world in which lunar consciousness has been repeatedly denied and devalued. From the beginning of patriarchal religion,

---

with the worship of the Sun god followed by the Hebraic father god Jehovah, humankind has ardently battled against the Great Mother of early matriarchy and all she represents—the irrational in contrast to the rational, oneness rather than separateness, the yin qualities of being, containing and nurturing instead of the yang energies of active achievement. The vital, potent, life-giving energies of mother goddess figures were appropriated and distorted by patriarchal religion, leaving only a disembodied powerless Virgin Mary to represent the virtues of the feminine. Pagan religions were extinguished; witches were burned. After the discovery of the Sun as the center of the solar system, heliocentric consciousness began to glorify science and to lose its moorings in religion. Religion by now had begun to degenerate into lifeless formalism lacking the heart-centered and gut-centered aliveness which results from attunement to the life force. Mind existed in opposition to rather than in cooperation with feeling, instinct and intuition. The vast impersonal forces of science and technology began to dissolve the personal and communal satisfaction which had provided a secure foundation for many centuries.

If we consider the disintegration of lunar consciousness from a psychological perspective as well as a collective perspective, we are face to face with the reality that a male-dominated world implies that the emotional issues and developmental tasks of males are bound to have a far-ranging impact upon the attitudes and institutions of society as a whole. Boys, in order to separate from their mothers and establish their individuality, have to denigrate the female principle more than girls do. By disdaining all that is soft and sensitive and reminiscent of the early symbiotic bliss of the womb and infancy, as well as by identifying with their fathers and the assertive self-sufficient male principle, boys begin to establish firm identities apart from female influence.

Once masculine identity is established, males in adolescence begin to reunite with the female without the terrifying danger of losing identity by regressing into symbiotic oneness. The female, rediscovered in adolescent girls and young women rather than in the mother, is valued once more. A new kind of emotional and sexual union is sought and experienced, one which preserves rather than destroys identity. If male development is to proceed positively, the feminine principle must be slowly reintegrated into the psyche, so that "female" qualities may now be experienced and expressed without the loss of ego, and woman may become a cooperative partner rather than a mere vehicle for recovering disowned and projected qualities.

Our male-dominated society has indeed been stuck in one of the developmental crises of male maturation—that of reowning and reintegrating the feminine principle. The hero mystique of Nazi Germany, disconnected from feminine values, may have shocked us collectively into the dawning realization of our shadow and the vengeance of the repressed feminine. Mother Nature now rebels against our rape of the environment; women rebel against the concept of male superiority. Although a man rather than a woman first stepped onto the Moon, the first lunar flight of 1969 did create a new bond between Earth and the Moon, one which may be opening a channel for the recovery of lunar consciousness. Edgar Mitchell and Jim Irwin established the High Flight Foundation after their Moon journey, a result of their moving experience of "God's presence" on the Moon.

In addition to physical exploration of the Moon, we witness in the second half of the twentieth century a revival of interest in many domains which the Moon represents—women's liberation, natural childbirth, natural foods, holistic health, witchcraft, communal and country living, ecology and genealogy. Psychology, with its focus on human nature, has developed new offshoots which are even more lunar in orientation than Freudian psychoanalysis. Jungian psychology has become popular, as have primal therapy and rebirthing. The discovery of Eastern religions by the Western world has led to shifts in attitude which have even brought meditation into the business world. The split between science and religion begins to heal as contemporary physics affirms ancient truths of mystical and matriarchal consciousness. The mystic arts enjoy a resurgence of interest by a public disenchanted with the constricting and desolate inner worlds created by technological society.

The reawakening of lunar consciousness is necessary for both physical and emotional survival. Dissociated from the nourishment of our instincts and our spirit, without attunement to inner and outer nature, we destroy ourselves and the world around us. As Carl Jung wrote, "Whatever one has within oneself but does not live grows against one . . . Anyone who overlooks the instincts will be ambuscaded by them."

When the Moon goddess is not worshipped, literally or figuratively, her dark side is released. The more we reject our primal mother, the more distorted she becomes, degenerating into such lower archetypes as the stone cold Saturnian spinster or the dark devouring Plutonian goddess hellbent on devastation rather than creation. As fairy tales have taught us, forgotten goddesses seek revenge; the witch who was not invited to Sleeping Beauty's christening cursed her with the curse of

11

unconsciousness, requiring that she spend twenty years in lunar realms before meeting her prince and uniting with the masculine principle. But when welcomed, the neglected and embittered witch goddesses within transform into fairy princesses, spirit guides who reveal to us inner treasures we may not know we possess.

When we disown our lunar being, we may suffer from a variety of emotional and physical illnesses which drain our energy and prevent us from discovering our true sources of nourishment. We develop stomach or reproductive disorders; we become compulsive about food, overly dependent in our relationships, constantly in search of external satisfactions which promise to fill us but instead numb us and prevent us from awakening to our true internal resources. We develop neuroses and psychoses as we project our unmet Moon needs outward upon persons, substances and experiences which only give temporary respite from the gnawing inner emptiness. The empty vessel of the Moon goddess cannot be filled or nourished from without; we must burrow deep within, through the pain and anger of this mistreated goddess, in both her child and adult manifestations, and discover within that pain and anger the sustenance which can heal us.

Maternal Deprivation and Nurturance

If we as children suffered from maternal deprivation, if our mothers lacked attunement to their own and our own needs and feelings, we most likely internalized a "bad mother" who is in many ways anti-life. Once outside us, she now exists within us. She fears the aliveness of instinct and emotion; she insists upon perfection and self-sacrifice; she uses anger, fear and guilt to compel us to obey her. Whenever we make contact with our true feelings, we experience anxiety at betraying her. Yet unless we separate and discover our own nature apart from her, we are doomed to live a desolate and fearful existence.

Frequently, the internalization of the "bad mother," a distorted form of our feminine archetype or anima, is accompanied by a likewise distorted animus or male energy which seeks to compensate for what is lacking by driving us relentlessly toward achievement and perfection. Together, they function in a devouring, compulsive, wolf-like manner, driven by greed to satisfy the inner hunger and escape from the terrifying pain of unmet need. If we were unable to relax within the bodies of mothers dissociated from their instincts, we are unable to relax in our own bodies and instincts. We seek refuge in our minds and erect walls against feeling. We lose our enthusiasm and creativity. We drive ourselves toward goals which will not fulfill us even when we attain them.

An alternative pattern is that of identifying with the passive, altruistic feminine mother or role model, the female archetype which validates the softer yin energies and devalues the primal potent energy of the Mother Goddess or Earth Mother. Becoming the embodiment of yin apart from yang, we attract exaggerated yang qualities, which are dissociated from yin softness and gentility. We project our animus outward and draw to us overpowering animus people who dominate and exploit us.

One common indication of having internalized the "bad mother" as a result of not having received proper nurturance is compulsiveness in regard to food. When we carry inside an insatiable hunger, food may easily become a mother substitute which we devour and/or reject. Eating may be an attempt to satisfy many needs apart from physical hunger. We may be seeking to nurture the deprived infant within us; we may swallow our anger toward mother and loved ones who fail to nourish us; we may use food to gain contact with our bodies, to dull the screaming pain of unmet needs, to quiet our minds and surrender to the unconsciousness of the digestive processes. We may even be trying to feed a deep soul hunger, a yearning to connect with our essential nature, which we may have unsuccessfully sought apart from the body.

The Moon revolves around the earth and is dependent upon the earth in order to maintain its orbit. Our lunar feelings are likewise dependent upon our earth bodies which house and contain them. Owning or reowning our bodies requires us to accept our wounded instincts and to experience our anger toward those who failed to meet our needs, while slowly learning to relinquish that anger in order to commit ourselves to the task of being our own mothers and our primary source of nourishment. No one but ourselves can heal the wounds of the past; the waters which nurture us now may have to be the waters of our tears as we mourn what we have only minimally experienced or what we have lost. We must decide to recover our feelings and be true to them, even when they carry the distorted emotional charge of unintegrated past experience; we must awaken to our female archetype or internal goddess figures; we must ask ourselves repeatedly what our real needs are, experience them, validate them and restructure our lives so that we may meet them as fully as possible.

Those of us who have internalized more of the "bad mother" than the "good mother," or who have otherwise lacked attunement to life-affirming lunar energies may need to descend into the chaotic realms of infantile feeling and instinct to recover our life source. In contrast to the

THE MOON

POSITIVE EXPRESSION	NEGATIVE EXPRESSION
(qualities related to early nurturance resulting in attunement to feeling and instinct)	*(dominant, distorted, repressed or undeveloped qualities)*

1. basic trust in self and others

2. rootedness in own being and instinctual nature

3. attunement to feelings; emotional depth and stability

4. sensitivity combined with a healthy degree of self-protectiveness

5. receptivity and responsiveness to others' needs; empathic

6. nurturing and maternal attitudes and behaviors

7. capacity to receive nurturance; balanced pattern of giving and receiving

8. capacity to nurture self

9. ability to experience and satisfy needs in relationship without loss of identity and independence

10. closeness and separateness coexisting within family of origin

11. capacity to form close relationships without sacrificing independence or separateness

1. absence of trust in self and others; distortions in trust/ mistrust patterns

2. lack of internal and bodily rootedness; at mercy of instincts or disconnected from them.

3. overly emotional; emotional instability; emotional repression

4. oversensitive; taking everything personally; insensitive; excessive self-protection; lack of self-protection

5. overly solicitous; overly sympathetic; lacking empathy; unaware of and unresponsive to others' needs

6. overly protective or smothering; martyr tendencies; denial of nurturing and maternal qualities

7. dependent upon others for nurturance; unable to give or receive

8. self-indulgence; self-neglect; lack of self-nurturing behaviors

9. denial of need and dependence; meeting false needs and neglecting true needs; dependence

10. overly dependent upon family of origin; lack of familial bonds

11. forming symbiotic relationships; avoiding closeness and intimacy

THE MOON

POSITIVE EXPRESSION	NEGATIVE EXPRESSION
(qualities related to early nurturance resulting in attunement to feeling and instinct)	*(dominant, distorted, repressed or undeveloped qualities)*

12. loyalty and devotion to loved ones	12. overly tenacious and clinging; disloyal; avoids dependency and commitment
13. capacity to satisfy security needs	13. overly preoccupied with security; insecure; denies security needs
14. establishment of a secure home base; enjoyment of family and domestic life	14. clinging to home; reclusive life-style; avoidance of home or, domestic life
15. shrewd; thrifty	15. selfish; miserly; unconcerned with financial security
16. constructive personal habits	16. detrimental or compulsive habits; lack of constructive habit patterns
17. healthy eating habits	17. excessive or unhealthy eating patterns; self-starvation; lack of attention to food
18. capacity to retreat and regroup one's resources	18. compulsive withdrawal and retreat; inability to turn inward
19. childlike openness and spontaneity	19. overly childish and immature; priggish; dissociated from childlike qualities.
20. ability to adapt without loss of self; capable of following as well as leading	20. overly adaptable; passive and compliant; intense drive as a reaction formation to passivity; inability to adapt
21. openness to intuition; psychic sensitivity	21. overwhelmed by or disconnected from intuitive and psychic processes
22. ability to connect with female energy and women	22. overly attached to or disdainful of feminine energy or women

spiritual quests which look upward and seek to ascend into mystical or heart-centered realms, we may regain our lost spirit only by journeying down, descending into primal realms. Such a journey is a dangerous one and needs to be consecrated to a divine purpose if we are to transmute the often untamed and convoluted energies of fear, pain and anger rather than be overwhelmed by them. The Moon goddess which we have denied for half a lifetime or more may have become a raging Gorgon, a Medusa whose anger is often too terrifying to face; the wounded child within us who has been slapped and silenced ever since infancy may emerge from beneath our defenses and expose us to pain greater than we can endure. Surrendering to our lunar nature must be a conscious and sacred act if it is to serve us. To be repeatedly taken over by emotion and instinct without conscious awareness and choice may lead to madness—lunacy. But when we choose a little madness in order to recover the deeper sanity at the core of it, we unite consciousness and unconsciousness and begin to become whole.

If this is our task, we must move slowly, inviting the support of friends and helpers who understand our quest and already possess the empathy and compassion of the Moon goddess. We must cultivate our internal supports of faith and trust. Each lost piece of ourselves, no matter how terrifying or ugly it may seem upon first encounter, is transformed as we welcome it and reown it. Our pain melts us and opens our hearts. Our anger empowers us. Willingly, we experience and surrender to each bout of pain and anger, and choose to let it go so that it may work its magic upon us. By embracing our wounded and raging instincts, by loving the beasts within, we befriend them and awaken their healing capacities. What we have most feared within ourselves becomes our most valued strength and our gateway to full being. In *Woman's Mysteries,* Esther Harding refers to the recovery of instinct as a journey on the boat of the Moon goddess:

> The salvation is to be found by taking a new attitude toward the power of instinct, involving the recognition that it is, in itself, not human, but belongs to the nonhuman or divine realm. To enter the boat of the goddess implies accepting the uprush of instinct in a religious spirit as a manifestation of the creative life force itself. . . . Instinct can no longer be regarded as an asset to be exploited for the advantage of the personal life; instead it must be recognized that the personality, the ego, must submit itself to the demands of the life force as a divine being.

The Healing Power of Lunar Darkness

One of the lessons of the Moon, which has been almost completely ignored by Western society, concerns the healing capacities of consciously chosen unconsciousness. Modem psychotherapy is based upon the practice of making the unconscious conscious, becoming more aware of the emotions and instincts and incorporating this awareness into our experience of identity. Yet lovers who have surrendered to the ecstasies of merging soul and body, women who have experienced the symbiotic union of childbearing, meditators who have relinquished their minds as they became one with their breath or their mantras, and artists who have transcended the thinking processes and allowed their deep creative energies to guide them—all know the profound level of fulfillment and regeneration which can result from ceasing to control, interpret, organize, analyze or understand.

The child is born in the darkness of the womb; the chicken is hatched after dark incubation within the egg. Birth begins in darkness; dawn follows the long night. Often the light of consciousness destroys what it seeks to illumine, as Psyche, in the myth Cupid and Psyche, lost her lover Cupid by lighting a candle to see him rather than trust the love he gave her unseen in the dark. We must not interrupt the incubation period within us, or force it to bear fruit before its time. To pull a seed out of the earth before it has sprouted, to open a chrysalis before the emerging butterfly has formed its wings is to prevent the new growth from occurring or the new life from living at all.

We associate darkness with death, depression, isolation and evil. Black is dark, and all that is black has been suppressed by white consciousness. We forget about the darkness of the womb or the rich fertile blackness of the soil or even the quiet inspirational darkness of the night when the mind is relaxed, and intuitions and visions freely emerge. We cling to the attachment of our waking consciousness and devalue the third of our lives which is sleep, the darkness to which we relinquish ourselves for the sake of the next dawn. Feelings of pain, anger and fear become dark and rejected feelings at odds with the light feelings of joy, peace and love which we gladly embrace. We endure the darkness only for the sake of the light, rather than value it for its own sake. Then we throw up our hands in despair as we confront the pollution in our environment, the nuclear energy threat, the wars, the murders, even the vicious divorce battles in which the enemy is always the other. Who is to blame? We are to blame. Not for becoming conscious, but perhaps for becoming conscious in the wrong way; not for being unconscious, for in some ways we are too unconscious, but for having lost the ability to surrender to the healing dimensions of unconsciousness.

The light of rational consciousness is solar light, the light of the male Sun, the gift of the Sun god, God the Father, the patriarchy, male supremacy. The light of the Sun is incapable of tackling the darkness; it sets to usher in the darkness; it rises to dissolve the dark night. Only the Moon (and stars) can illuminate the darkness, can exist simultaneously and transform the terrifying blackness of the void into the alive, awe-inspiring darkness of the evening sky. Solar light is polarized light—it creates sharp contrasts; it splits dark and light. Where there is Sun, there is shadow, the projections of our disowned unconscious selves. Where there is Moon, there is hope of integrating darkness and light.

When the demons of the unconscious threaten to overwhelm us internally and externally, our rational minds become impotent. Solar consciousness loses its power in the face of darkness. Healing can then come only from lunar consciousness—the deep creativity and fertility of surrender to instinct and feeling, to intuition and imagination, to the ground of our being which is the ground of the mothers who bore us and the earth which still feeds us.

We may need to embrace the darkness, to descend into the chaotic void within ourselves, into our personal and collective underworld, to stretch our roots downward rather than grow our branches upward until we fall. We need to rediscover our foundations, but to do so we may have to relinquish some of our attachments and behaviors in the outer world, some of our goals which depend upon having, striving, achieving and becoming rather than being and resting deeply in the nourishing womb of cur own nature. We need to embrace loneliness and pain and terror; we need to trust and believe in the healing capacities of fully entering feeling. This is not for the sake of glorifying the feeling or wallowing within it, not to hold onto it, but to move fully through it and let it go as we reunite with the warm nurturing watery energies and the solid sustaining earth energies at our core. We need to relinquish our solar attempts at rationality and control, to open to darkness not in order to remain in darkness but to awaken our lunar consciousness and its healing energies.

Mythological Meanings of the Moon

If we consider ancient mythologies, which conceptualized a world view that existed long before the outer planets were discovered, we encounter meanings attributed to the Moon which we now also associate with Uranus, Neptune, and Pluto. We find the Uranian realms of change, intuition, madness, and genius; the Neptunian realms of compassion, vision, imagination, spirit, sacrifice; the Plutonian realms of death, rebirth, the dark devouring mother, destruction, healing, transformation. Perhaps the Moon is indeed the gateway to the outer planets; perhaps how we deal with our basic feelings, needs and instincts influences whether or not our outer planets are enemies which assail us or guides which, like the Moon, illumine our path.

The lunar way is not an easy one; sacrifice is always required. As daughters, we must relinquish our mothers for a time in order to unite with male energies, just as Persephone, abducted by Pluto into the underworld, gave up the innocent oneness of mother love. As mothers, we sacrifice both our sons and daughters to adulthood; we are like Demeter, mourning the loss of Persephone, who in time will return to us, but who will forever share as great a part of herself with her male partner as she does with us. As fathers, we likewise sacrifice our children to their own process of maturation. As sons, we reject the mother in order to forge our male identity so that we may eventually reunite with women and hopefully also make peace with our internal female principle or anima.

Befriending our anima involves entering the realms of the Moon goddess, who has many faces—the maiden Artemis, associated with the waxing Moon; Aphrodite or Selene, the Mother, with the full Moon; Hecate, the Crone and gatekeeper of the underworld, with the waning Moon. Another significant mythological association with the Moon is the three Fates who represent the powers of destiny—knowledge of the past, instinctive power in the present, and insight into the future. Still another important association with the Moon in mythology is the concept of the Virgin goddess. Virgin, in its original meaning, does not refer to chastity in the sexual sense, but rather to being one-in-oneself. She who is virgin has herself, rules herself, and submits not to a male external to her but to her own nature. She who is virgin surrenders herself in union to the divine within, the internal God, her animus or masculine soul.

The female void is filled by the process of self-fertilization, the inner conjunction of Sun and Moon, the integration of solar and lunar energies. We may seek to regain contact with our lunar instincts and with the lunar goddess, but such a quest is not necessarily an end in itself. Lunar consciousness is not to be considered superior to solar consciousness, but rather its partner. We must first experience our archetypal female energies before we can unite both our masculine and feminine nature. Our aim then may be divine marriage, the internal union which enables us to become one with ourselves, complete, whole, and capable of entering true, solid and enduring union with others who are likewise whole.

Reparenting Our Inner Child

We have been considering the reowning of the lunar principle from many perspectives, taking both a mythological Jungian were, and to some extent still are, and to feel compassion for the internal child whose needs were not met and who may have compensated by developing attitudes and behaviors which do not serve us,

From recognition and acceptance, we then progress to considering new attitudes and behaviors which we can implement. Perhaps we need role models to teach us; perhaps we already have the knowledge of new modes of self-parenting, and only need to apply what we know. Whatever our situation, we must usually exert ourselves in order to overcome the secure, familiar tugs of deeply entrenched habits, and to endure the initial anxiety of developing new, unfamiliar but ultimately satisfying modes of being with ourselves.

An important part of this process is contacting our real feelings and needs, validating them, and beginning to find ways to satisfy them without falling into the trap of hopelessness or despair that we will never find fulfillment, or into the other trap of compensation—substituting immediate but ineffective and inappropriate forms of gratification. How can we meet our real needs for contact, nurturance and belonging? For home and family? Simply experiencing our real feelings and needs with acceptance and tenderness is a significant step. What we have suppressed emerges and fills us, creating its own sustenance. We feel less empty when we are filled with our real selves. Only by contacting our real selves can we begin to create a life which genuinely nourishes us.

Creating that life is our responsibility now, not our parents'. One of the greatest obstacles we may encounter is the powerful, stubborn force of our anger and blame—the part of us which resists claiming our adulthood and instead clings to the attitude of "I won't do it. You do it for me." The more we hold onto our anger at our parents for what they did not provide, the more we seek to get from them that which they may be incapable of giving, and the more we demand from others to make up for unmet needs of the past, the more likely we are to experience increased frustration, disappointment and deprivation.

We are our parents now. However distorted and wounded our feelings and instincts may be, only we can make peace with them.

What we reject in ourselves we will attract in others. What we are unable to give ourselves, we will be unable to receive fully from others. When we look to others to complete ourselves, we become dependent upon them and deny facets of ourselves which may threaten our relationships. Losing contact with our being, we begin to lose contact with others as well, and may in the long run find ourselves alone without internal or external supports. We are our parents now. We need to learn to soothe ourselves when we are afraid or in pain, and to feed ourselves with positive, caring messages as well as foods and activities which deeply satisfy us. Becoming an adult does not mean giving up the internal child but rather learning how both to nurture it and to set limits upon its demands.

Answering the following "Reparenting Your Inner Child" questions may help us to begin the process of dialogue with the internal parent/child dimensions of our Moon. Interpreting our Moon positions before internally assessing its meaning in our lives may bias and limit our understanding. The natal chart is only a map and cannot possibly represent the whole, alive reality of our beings. If we are willing to spend an hour or more writing or speaking (alone, into a tape recorder, or to a friend) our answers to these questions about our parent/child patterns, we may understand more about our Moon placement than if we first approach it through astrological symbolism.

REPARENTING YOUR INNER CHILD
Questions

1. Describe your temperament as a child—ages 3-5, 8-10,13-14.
2. Describe your mother or most significant parent figure.
3. What was your experience of your needs and feelings, and how did you deal with them and express them? How did your parent respond to your:
   needs   wants/desires   fear   pain/hurt   anger   joy?
4. Describe your relationship to your parents and how you received love/ approval and rejection/punishment/disapproval. How and when did your parents express approval and disapproval?
5. What did your parents expect from you? What "shoulds" did they place upon you? How did they nurture you or refrain from nurturing you?

6. What was your experience of feeling loved, feeling safe/secure, feeling o.k./worthy?
7. How does your inner child function within you today?
8. How do you parent yourself today as your parents did in the past? What detrimental patterns are you continuing from the past?
9. What new attitudes or behaviors do you wish to develop to replace those detrimental patterns?
10. What real needs aren't being met in your life, and how might you meet them? How else might you more fully love, nourish and affirm yourself?
11. What message or mantra (such as "You are o.k. exactly the way you are" or "You don't have to be perfect" or "It's all right to be afraid") does your inner child most need to hear?

Suggested Activities

1 Repeat your message (#11) to your inner child several times a day. Ask your friends to express it to you frequently.
2. Write or speak to your inner child daily, establishing a dialogue. Get to know him/her. Learn how to win his/her trust. Using a doll or stuffed animal which has special meaning to you may be helpful.
3. Obtain Joe Cocker's song, "You Are so Beautiful to Me," and sing it aloud to your inner child, loudly, at least three times in a row. Do this daily, or several times a week and discover the love and radiance you possess and can experience and express when your inner child feels nurtured and valued.

Chapter Two

MOON SIGNS

O nce we complete our initial reflections upon our relationship to our parents and our process of internal parenting, we may then choose to consider the additional understanding our charts can give us. Our Moon signs indicate particular energies that our internal child needs to experience and to express in order to feel secure and satisfied, as well as the energies by which our internal parent may respond to our feelings and needs. Honoring our Moon sign is important. Moon in Taurus may require beautiful possessions; Moon in Sagittarius may need the freedom to travel in order to feel content.

Our Moon signs, as well as our Moon's placement by house and aspect, indicate the specific individual patterns of our internal child—extensions of such basic needs as emotional and physical contact, belonging, food and home. When basic needs common to all of us are not met, we may then become compulsive in the expression of our Moon signs, such as accumulating vast amounts of money or possession if our Moon is in Taurus or traveling incessantly if our Moon is in Sagittarius. Extreme, compulsive, or inflexible manifestations of our Moon sign, house, and aspects can indicate that we may be compensating for, rather than satisfying, our real needs. If this is true, then we may wish to enter psychotherapy or join a support group which will help us to uncover and regain contact with feelings and needs we have denied, and to discover how to meet needs we have likewise suppressed or discredited.

Due to the limited scope of this chapter, we will only be able to explore here the signs of the Moon, apart from Moon houses and aspects. We therefore need to use our own astrological understanding in order to view our Moon sign in the light of its position in our charts. Because a 3rd house Moon may have some similarities to Moon in Gemini or a Moon/ Uranus square to Moon in Aquarius, we may want to read on the following pages not only about our Moon sign, but also about the Moon sign positions which by rulership have some bearing upon us. If we have Moon in Leo in the 6th house in square to Mars and trine Jupiter, our emotional patterns may reflect those not only of Leo, but also of Virgo (6th house), Aries (Mars), and Sagittarius (Jupiter). The current sign of the progressed Moon is also worth considering, because our progressed Moon expresses our changing and evolving needs throughout the life cycle. The quotations compiled here to illustrate the meaning of each Moon sign may also help us to experience more deeply our intrinsic Moon energies.

Following the assessment of our Moon signs, we may want to commit ourselves even further to the process of self-nurturance. Beginning an "Inner Development Journal," as described at the end of this chapter, may enable us to more effectively experience and fulfill the needs of our inner child, and to experience considerably more emotional nourishment within our lives.

MOON IN ARIES

☽ ♈ Those of us with Moon in Aries need to express ourselves honestly and openly, to assert our individuality, and to be enthusiastically involved in new projects and activities. Aries is not an easy position for the Moon; we are likely to have counter-dependent tendencies, often denying our needs for closeness and intimacy and attempting to be emotionally self-sufficient. When deep feelings and needs emerge, we may unconsciously fend them off with anger, with impulsive action, and sometimes with sexual expression.

Most likely, an Arian parent was quick to respond to our wants and desires, and allowed us the freedom to pursue our own interests. Such a parent encouraged our independent nature, possibly because he or she was independent and/or self-absorbed and did not wish to be burdened with responsibility for our welfare. He or she may have imparted attitudes of "be strong" and "be tough," but such attitudes may have had less to do with an urge to further our development than they had to do with defenses against closeness and the expression of need and vulnerable feelings. Our parent may have encouraged our individuality while simultaneously failing to really affirm and support who we were. Sometimes an Arian Moon indicates a submissive parent who catered to our whims and impulses, but never really acknowledged or met our true needs, or helped us to develop the frustration tolerance we needed in order to mature and adapt effectively.

One of our tasks may therefore be to learn how to differentiate impulse from deeper wants and needs, and to come to know what we really want beyond the thrill of momentary satisfactions. This may also involve learning how to value and fulfill our deeper needs, maintaining our basic independence while also allowing ourselves to experience and come to terms with our own dependence as human beings. Having Moon in Aries also suggests that we need to become rooted in our physical and instinctive natures, experiencing profoundly "I exist" and "I am" in a manner which gives us reality and substance, so that we are not continually in search of excitement and stimulation in order to experience our vitality and aliveness.

Quotations that Illuminate the Moon in Aries

Either I am
The Foremost horse on the team, or I am none. —JOHN FLETCHER

I want what I want when I want it. —HENRY BLOSSOM

Sincerity is my credentials. —MALCOLM X

I can promise to be frank, but I can't promise to be impartial. —GOETHE

I lack a light touch.
I step on my own words,
a garden rake in the weeds,
I sweat and heave when I should slip away . . .
I ram on. —MARGE PIERCY

We DO . . . what we most want to do. We SAY—speak, paint, carve,
write, express ourselves . . . as we damn please. —ROCKWELL KENT

All here is circulation, motion and boiling agitation. Experiment
follows experiment; enterprise succeeds to enterprise.
—MICHEL CHEVALIER

A fierce unrest seethes at the core
This heartbeat hot and strong. — DON MARQUIS

"Now! Now!" cried the Queen. "Faster! Faster!" —LEWIS CARROLL

And he was the sort of Tigger who was always in front when you
were showing him the way anywhere, and was generally out of
sight when at last you came to the place and said proudly,
"Here we are!" —A.A.MILNE

To be alive is to be burning. —NORMAN O. BROWN

It is not so much trying to keep alive
As trying to keep from blowing apart
From inner explosions every day. —MAY SARTON

If at first you don't succeed, try a little ardor. —ANONYMOUS

I am a passion, I am a flame . . .
l am that desire which transcends shame.
—GUSTAVO BEQUER

Obey that impulse. —TOM MASSON

I want a new beginning. —BARRY STEVENS

If at first you don't succeed, try something else. —ANONYMOUS

I think even lying on my bed I can still do something. —DOROTHEA LYNDE

We are angered by people trying to
arrange our lives for us. —DIANE WAKOSKI

I'm going to fight hard. I'm going to give them hell.
—HARRY S. TRUMAN

Without rehearsing, we take risks.
We are spontaneous. —FRITZ PERLS

Look, I can dare to fall down, and look, I can get up, and look,
I'm not too hurt to try again. —DIANA MICHENER

MOON IN TAURUS

We who have Moon in Taurus need to experience a solid base of self-esteem and internal security, to gain confidence in our internal resources and our capacity to earn what we need and utilize what we have, to experience physical and emotional warmth, to know the pleasures and pains of living within our bodies and senses, and to maintain contact with the earth. When our essential Taurean needs have not been met, we are likely to over-compensate by indulging ourselves, compulsively clinging to other bodies, food, money and external sources of satisfaction. We may become indolent, greedy, overmaterialistic, and bound by our insistence upon security to a routine, risk-free and ultimately sterile existence.

A Taurean parent figure may have influenced our security patterns. Positively, our parent may have been earthy and well-grounded, able to provide the warmth, stability and constancy we needed, to comfort us and to help us gain confidence functioning in the physical world. Negatively, our parent may have been enslaved by his or her senses, attempting to chain us likewise to a predominantly physical level of existence. We may have been overindulged rather than deprived, provided with excess food, money or other comforts of living without our needing to ask, so that we came to expect to be provided for; or we may have been dominated by a possessive parent and learned to resist intrusion by dawdling or by turning to possessive and clinging behaviors ourselves.

We may repeatedly give ourselves messages about our lack of value or competence, about holding on rather than letting go, about the necessity of earning more money and maintaining our job security, or about the importance of purchasing and enjoying all the comforts and physical pleasures which soothe us. We may coddle ourselves into too easy a lifestyle or defend against our needs by maintaining too rigid a self-sufficiency. To successfully reparent our Taurean inner child, we may have to reassess those internal messages which keep us bound in unsatisfying habits and behaviors, and to develop new messages which: a) build our self-esteem, helping us to trust and discover our internal resources and internal security base; b) encourage us to experience and satisfy the most essential needs of our bodies rather than become mired in patterns of laziness, sensual gratification and physical or material greed; c) allow us to relax and surrender to our deeper beings, so that we may let go of our possessiveness or compulsive self-sufficiency and experience our capacity truly to give and receive warmth and devotion.

Quotations that Illuminate the Moon in Taurus

My strength lies solely in my tenacity. —LOUIS PASTEUR

Hold on with a bulldog grip and chew and choke as much as possible. —ABRAHAM LINCOLN

Firmness is that admirable quality in ourselves that is detestable stubbornness in others. —ANONYMOUS

It is better to have a permanent income than to be fascinating.
—OSCAR WILDE

Everything you have wants to own you. —REGINA ELBERT

Spend all you have for loveliness. —SARA TEASDALE

I care not so much what I am to others as I respect what I am in myself. I will be rich by myself and not by borrowing.
—MONTAIGNE

Man s chief purpose is the creation and preservation of values.
—LEWIS MUMFORD

The color of the ground was in him, the red earth,
The smack and tang of elemental things. —EDWIN MARKHAM

Get some rest. Be patient. Wait. —TIMOTHY STEELE

If they try to rush me, I always say, "I've only got one other speed—
and it's slower." —GLENN FORD

Think of me
As quiet . . . with a voice of infinite patience,
Gentle until resisted. —W. S. MERWIN

To be idle requires a strong sense of personal identity.
—R. L. STEVENSON

It is better to have loafed and lost than never to have loafed at all.
—JAMES THURBER

I would give all my fame for a pot of ale and safety.
—SHAKESPEARE

Happiness: a good bank account, a good cook, and a good digestion.
—JEAN-JACQUES ROUSSEAU

Security is an invitation to indolence. —ROD McKUEN

I cast my warmth around me and it is reflected in others. —ANAIS NIN

Early or late, he's always the same fellow. Always good-tempered,
always glad to see you, always sorry when you go! . . . So simple, so
good-natured, and so affectionate. —KENNETH GRAHAME

But I am constant as the northern star,
Of whose true fixed and resting quality
There is no fellow in the firmament.
—SHAKESPEARE

Before we can give something of ourselves to others, we must first
possess ourselves. —IGNAZIO SILONE

MOON IN GEMINI

Those of us with Moon in Gemini need to communicate verbally, to interact with a variety of people, to awaken and satisfy our curiosity, to train and utilize our minds, to develop basic skills, and to be open to and engaged by a stimulating environment. The deepest needs of our Gemini Moon pertain to experiencing and expressing our feelings in relationship, and cultivating a network of people and activities which truly nourish us rather than simply pique our interest. We also benefit by feeding our hunger for knowledge and developing our capacities as thinkers and communicators.

When our real needs are not met, we may lose ourselves in compulsive Gemini behaviors—we may talk incessantly and superficially without making real contact; we may scatter our energies widely, shifting from person to person and activity to activity without experiencing fulfillment anywhere. We may seek refuge in knowledge for knowledge's sake and intellectual activity as an escape from feeling.

Negatively, our Gemini Moon suggests that we experienced one or both of our parental figures as changeable or inconstant, as overly identified with the mind and inclined to rationalize and intellectualize rather than directly express feeling. Such a parent may also have been highstrung, nervous, and preoccupied with trivia. Positively, our parent may have encouraged and supported our verbal and intellectual abilities and provided us with considerable stimulation and challenge.

If our parent did not provide the nurturance we needed, we may have internalized messages which incline us to deny or explain away our feelings, and to remain open to too many outside influences at the expense of learning to make commitments or develop an area of expertise. Feeling insecure in our bodies and emotions, we may have exercised our mental capacities to such a degree that we have become adept at rationalization and prone to use words and superficial interactions to defend against our needs for real contact, intimacy and communication. Our task may be to reconnect with our feelings and bodies in such a way that we may think, communicate and structure our lives to make our mental activities and relationships truly nourishing.

Quotations that Illuminate the Moon in Gemini

When I grow up I want to be a little boy. —JOSEPH HELLER

It is impossible to promise
Absolute fidelity. —ERICA JONG

I am rich only in a never-ending unrest. —W. S. GILBERT

Let others toil from year to year. I live from day to day.
—ISAAC BICKERSTAFF

What I love is near at hand,
Always, in earth and air.
—THEODORE ROETHKE

Conversation should touch everything but should concentrate on nothing.
—OSCAR WILDE

"The time has come," the Walrus said,
To talk of many things:
Of shoes—and ships—and sealing wax—
Of cabbages and kings—"
—LEWIS CARROLL

He is winding up the watch of his wit;
By and by it will strike.
—SHAKESPEARE

If you can't baffle them with brilliance, befuddle them with bullshit.
—ANONYMOUS

You sort of glitter rather than glow. Small talk come easy to you.
—GAIL GODWIN

Many a time I have wanted to stop talking and find out what I really
believed. —WALTER LIPPMAN

If other people are going to talk, conversation is simply impossible.
—ANONYMOUS

I think that I think, therefore I think I am. —AMBROSE BIERCE

Get your facts first and then you can distort them as much as you please.
—MARK TWAIN

One goes on asking questions . . . It is an intellect
Of windings round and dodges to and fro. —WALLACE STEVENS

A man should live if only to satisfy his curiosity. —YIDDISH PROVERB

What can give us more sure knowledge than our senses? —LUCRETIUS

It is terribly amusing how many different climates of feeling one
can go through in one day. —ANNE MORROW LINDBERGH

Sometimes people ask me how I can do so many different things and not feel fragmented. I never feel split because everything I do is a communication. —HEPZIBAH MENUHIN

I am not confused. I'm just well mixed. —ROBERT FROST

All of us are constantly being bombarded by particles of misplaced schizophrenia. —ROGER PIERCE

My dilemma is to force the two poles of life together, to transcribe the dual voices into life's melody. —HERMAN HESSE

MOON IN CANCER

If our Moon is in Cancer, coming to terms with our lunar needs is particularly important, since Cancer is the sign of the Moon. Our basic well-being is therefore dependent upon our connection to our lunar source. If we were either deprived or overindulged as children, we may have become excessively attached to food, home or nurturing figures who cared for and comforted us. When we are in touch with our needs and feelings, we may be inclined to: a) eat or seek oral gratification; b) expect others to cater to us; c) cry incessantly, either in self-pity or in an attempt to compel other people to be more responsive to us; d) cling to people or possessions; e) withdraw into a private world.

An alternative pattern is to seek vicarious satisfaction through compulsively nurturing others. It may be easy for us to become helpless little girls or boys or even Big Mommies or Big Daddies, but difficult to experience full satisfaction or to respond to others in ways which do not infantilize them but instead respect their integrity and individuality. If we have squares or oppositions to our Moon, we may have erected powerful defenses against both our needs to nurture and be nurtured, and may as a result experience psychological or physical (often related to the stomach, uterus or breasts) problems which require us to learn to care for ourselves more fully.

Our Cancerian Moon suggests that one or both of our parental figures may have been maternal, protective and empathic, capable of internally perceiving our needs and satisfying them. However, if our Moon is afflicted, our lunar parents may have unconsciously been influenced by their own unmet needs and encouraged us to remain helpless and dependent upon them for gratification. Such parents are frequently martyrs, doing for us what we needed to do for ourselves, or paying excessive attention to their own emotions and physical ills in an attempt to gain from us the sympathy and consideration which we ourselves may have needed to experience.

As a result, we may have learned to give ourselves internal messages which lead us to feel sorry for ourselves, to indulge our pain, to expect too much from others, or to become overly attached to food, home, loved ones or other external forms of security and gratification. One of our most important tasks may be that of fully mourning the symbiosis our inner child never had or inevitably had to relinquish as part of maturation. We may have to experience the depth of our needs to nurture and be nurtured, and as adults to establish patterns of behavior and interaction which fulfill those needs without catering to them. Our lunar lessons may also include: a) contacting and communicating our real needs and feelings; b) building an inner foundation of security; c) overcoming behaviors based on helplessness or which use helplessness and neediness as weapons; d) learning to support the adult as well as the child in other people, and to love without possessing; e) devoting ourselves to self-nourishment rather than giving undue attention to giving and receiving in relationships.

Quotations that Illuminate the Moon in Cancer

I suppose the most absolutely delicious thing in life is to feel someone needs you. —OLIVE SCHREINER

most of us love from our need to love . . .
most of us comfort because we need comforting. —NIKKI GIOVANNI

but what am I?
An infant crying in the night;
An infant crying for the light,
And with no language but a cry.
—ALFRED LORD TENNYSON

I want to crawl into her refuge   lay my head
in the space   between her breasts   and her shoulder
abnegating power for love. —ADRIENNE RICH

when I call on him and then come away,
he grabs me and holds me and begs me to stay. —J. W. RILEY

I never ask the wounded person how he feels; I myself become the wounded person. —WALT WHITMAN

"I weep for you," the Walrus said:
"I deeply sympathize." —LEWIS CARROLL

i am full of mother love
my kindness has always
been my curse
a tender heart is the cross i bear —DON MARQUIS

We can say, like the ancient Chinese, to successive waves of invaders,
Relax, and let us absorb you. —CAROLYN KIZER

The smell of that buttered toast simply talked to Toad, and with
no uncertain voice; talked of warm kitchens, of breakfasts on bright
frosty mornings, of cosy parlour firesides on winter evenings.
—KENNETH GRAHAME

The eldest Oyster winked his eye,
And shook his heavy head
Meaning to say he did not choose
To leave the oyster bed. —LEWIS CARROLL

My home, my love-nest . . .
my shelter from
the hurricane. —ELIZABETH BISHOP

To save themselves
snails shrink to shelter in their shells
where they wait safe and patient
until the elements are gentler. —ISABELLA GARDNER

The glamour
Of childish days is upon me, my manhood is cast
Down in the flood of remembrance, I weep
like a child for the past. —D. H. LAWRENCE

In personal life, we should be governed, I think, by the deep inner
needs of our nature. —SIGMUND FREUD

There is something about holding on to things that I find therapeutic.
—EDNA O'BRIEN

I can't live without that blanket. I can't face life unarmed.
—CHARLES SCHULTZ (LINUS)

MOON IN LEO

 Those of us with Leo Moons particularly need to feel loved and appreciated, to be treated specially, to play, and to express ourselves spontaneously and creatively. We need warmth and devotion, and are able to give abundantly from our hearts as long as we are also being fed with love. Otherwise, our lunar nature may become distorted and compulsive in its insistence upon attention and/or power. Negatively, we may be unable to relinquish center stage, may overdramatize in order to impact others, or may become dominating or bossy in our attempts to maintain command over ourselves and others.

A Leo Moon suggests that we had loving parental figures who prized us highly, became enthusiastically involved in our activities and triumphs, and were capable of encouraging and sharing our playful spirit. However, an afflicted Moon may indicate parents who either overindulged or deprived us. At one extreme are the mothers who spoiled us with too much attention and too many special treats, preparing us to live our adult lives only as princes or princesses. At the other extreme are the narcissistic parents, the tyrant queens or kings who sought only that we become obedient subjects, or who overly identified with us, urging us to live their dreams and adamantly discouraging our individuality.

As a result of our childhood upbringing, we may have internalized messages which support attention-seeking, childish, demanding and/or dominating behavior patterns. We may act as if we deserve to be the center of everyone's universe and not just our own. We may, because of past unmet needs, become compulsive in our desire to prove our value and gain acclaim.

A Leo Moon has much to give provided it is able to bask in the sunlight of warmth and affection. Those of us who have Leo Moons may need to feed ourselves emotionally rather than always expect others to provide for us. We need at times to give ourselves our full attention and appreciation, to be our own audience, and to encourage and delight in the spontaneity and zest of our inner child. If we are to experience emotional satisfaction, we need to keep our hearts open to pain as well as joy, and to become capable of loving others not only because they love us in turn, but also because we truly love ourselves.

Quotations that Illuminate the Moon in Leo

Pretend you're a child, with nothing to hide,
Then we'll join hands and let the universe swing wide.
—CARLY SIMON

Do anything, but let it produce joy. —HENRY MILLER

Life is short; live it up. —NIKITA KRUSCHEV

When I grow up I want to be a little boy. —JOSEPH HELLER

A man can succeed at almost anything for which he has unlimited enthusiasm. —CHARLES SCHWAB

My true center . . . was an enormous capacity for falling in love with everything around me. —MALVINA HOFFMAN

I cast my own warmth around me and it is reflected in others. —ANAIS NIN

To love is to give, to give, to give.
Give more and more and more. —WILLIAM JAY SMITH

When you possess light within, you see it externally. —ANAIS NIN

We are all worms, but I do believe I am a glow worm.
—WINSTON CHURCHILL

I celebrate myself and sing myself.
I dote on myself, there is that lot of me and all so luscious!
—WALT WHITMAN

When you've got it—flaunt it. —GEORGE LOIS

As soon as he woke up he felt important, as if everything depended upon him. —A. A. MILNE

When I walk out, I am a great event.
I do not have to think, or even rehearse. —SYLVIA PLATH

If anybody wants to clap . . . now is the time to do it. —A. A. MILNE

Always star in your own movie. —KEN KESEY

It is a great art to saunter. —HENRY DAVID THOREAU

Everyone has a right to my opinion. —ANONYMOUS

Had I been present at the Creation, I would have given some useful hints for the better ordering of the universe.
—ALFONSO THE LEARNED

I am in earnest—I will not equivocate—I will not excuse—I will not retreat a single inch; and I will be heard. —W. L. GARRISON

If there is a faith that can move mountains, it is faith in your own power.
—MARIE EBNER VON ESCHENBACH

*The Lion . . . sprang upon the bed and rolled himself up like a cat
and purred himself asleep in a minute.* —FRANK BAUM

MOON IN VIRGO

$$\text{☽ ♍}$$ If we have a Virgo Moon, we may be adept at using our minds to defend against unwanted feelings. We need organization and predictability in at least some facets of our lives; we need to experience ourselves as useful, as providers of valued services in our work and our personal activities; we need mentally to assess and structure our experience as well as care for our physical wellbeing. We have high standards for ourselves and others, and must maintain personal integrity at all costs.

If we lose touch with our deeper emotional and instinctual nature, our constructive Virgoan traits may become destructively compulsive. We insist on a degree of order and efficiency which destroys the spontaneity and vitality in and around us; we become workaholics, unable to relax and at the mercy of our compulsion to keep busy at all costs. We fuss, worry, nag and intellectualize incessantly. We subordinate ourselves to others, compelling them to utilize our services. We rip ourselves apart with self-criticism, and likewise are unable to allow imperfection in other people.

Having a Virgoan Moon suggests that we experienced a significant degree of Virgoan energy in one or both of our parent figures. A nourishing Virgoan parent may have encouraged our mental development, taught us constructive personal habits, and enabled us to experience a safe and orderly early environment without crushing the spirit of our inner child. Such a parent may have taught us how to use reason and common sense to master rather than repress our feelings and desires, and was probably helpful to us through providing many of the little but significant services of daily living.

On the other hand, a Virgoan parent who was not a positive influence upon us may have exposed us to a degree of super-efficiency, criticism, analysis, perfectionism and/or pettiness which frustrated and inhibited our emotional growth and fragile self-esteem. The "should system" of our childhood years may have become an internal structure which continues to enslave us as adults. Our sense of not being good enough impairs our ability to function personally and professionally. A subservient slavish parent may have catered to us too frequently; a hypochondriacal parent may have focused so obsessively upon ill health that we ourselves became sickly or hypochondriacal in order to receive attention and care.

We may need to revise the internal messages we give ourselves which continue to keep detrimental Virgoan patterns in operation. Our task may be to learn how to experience and value all our feelings and needs while also utilizing our analytical capabilities and creating order and discipline in our experience. We may need to develop new standards for ourselves and others, standards which fully accept our imperfectly human behaviors while also valuing our occasional moments of superhuman goodness or accomplishment. Choosing to love ourselves, choosing to discover the wondrous perfection of our imperfection may nourish our souls so profoundly that we do indeed become more giving and capable human beings.

Quotations that Illuminate the Moon in Virgo

The purpose of life is not to be happy—but to be productive, to be useful.
—LEO ROSTEN

she carries food to the table and stoops down
—doing this out of love. —STEPHEN SPENDER

Nothing is more likely to help a person overcome or endure . . .
troubles than the consciousness of having a task in life. —VIKTOR FRANKL

She is so industrious, when she has nothing to do she sits and knits
her brows. —ANONYMOUS

He ran on errands, mailed the mail, and even swept the floor,
And when, at night, his work was done he always asked for more.
—ALBERT STILLMAN

Don't agonize. Organize. —ANONYMOUS

you can
Contain a large world in a small strict plan. —MAY SARTON

I have measured out my life with coffee spoons. —T. S. ELIOT

It's the little things that bother us; we can dodge an elephant but not a fly.
—ANONYMOUS

When I am busy with little things, I am not required to do greater things.
—ST. FRANCIS DE SALES

No amount of genius can overcome preoccupation with detail.
—ANONYMOUS

The trouble is I analyze life instead of live it. —HUGH PRATHER

The habit of analysis has a tendency to wear away the feelings.
—JOHN STUART MILL

All my life I have been a witness of things,
Among which I keep witnessing the eternal unfitness of things.
Daily it is my wont
To notice how things that were designed to fit each other, don't.
—OGDEN NASH

In life, nothing below one hundred per cent is passing. —J. P. McEVOY

Oh, wouldn't the world seem dull and flat with nothing whatever
to grumble at. —W. S. GILBERT

If you're a hypochondriac, first class, you awaken each morning
with the firm resolve not to worry; everything is going to turn out
all wrong. —GOODMAN ACE

He had so abnormal and constant a need for purification that actually he
spent a considerable part of his time before the washbasin.
—THOMAS MANN

No one can make you feel inferior without your consent.
—ELEANOR ROOSEVELT

I'm nobody! Who are you?
Are you nobody, too? —EMILY DICKINSON

No! I am not Prince Hamlet, nor was meant to be;
Am an attendant lord . . . no doubt, an easy tool,
Deferential, glad to be of use,
Politic, cautious, and meticulous. —T. S. ELIOT

MOON IN LIBRA

We who have Moon in Libra crave the experience of beauty and peace; we seek to cooperate with others, to please, and to establish one-to-one relationships which are mutually

gratifying. We also find satisfaction in using our minds, particularly our powers of objectivity and synthesis. A parent who valued us highly, who enjoyed pleasing us, who encouraged our aesthetic and intellectual development and who was willing and able to appreciate our points of view may have helped us to become attuned to the constructive dimensions of our Libran Moon.

If, however, our Moon is in difficult aspect, or if its trines or sextiles suggest a parent who was only superficially available to us, we may be attempting to gain from a partner what we were never able to experience from our parents. We may become overly dependent upon others, seeking to win their favor by being indispensable and satisfying their every desire. We may also be inclined to avoid confronting our anger and pain, suppressing emotions because we fear any threat to our relationships, which might force us to acknowledge our separateness and aloneness. These patterns may have been influenced by a parent figure who placed too much emphasis upon appearance or surface harmony, who was unable to tolerate discord, or who led us to believe that relationship always means subordinating oneself to another. Such a mother or father may have brought many unfulfilled needs into parenting, expecting us to compensate for deficiencies he or she experienced in childhood or in marriage.

Although our Libra Moons suggest that our emotional fulfillment requires cooperative relationships with others, we can only build truly satisfying connections by first developing a secure relationship with ourselves, accepting as valid our own feelings and needs, and being willing to assert ourselves, even when it means experiencing temporary discord for the sake of deeper and more authentic contact. We need to apply our open-mindedness and our capacity to identify with many points of view in relation to both ourselves and others—to listen to and affirm each of our internal personalities, willingly entering into disharmony and imbalance when necessary in order to create the more enduring harmony and balance which is so vital to us. At the same time, we need to honor our Libran need for beauty and peace, creating environments and relationships which, whenever possible, soothe and uplift us.

Quotations that Illuminate the Moon in Libra

We cannot live for ourselves alone. —VERNON E. JORDAN JR.

I know that personal relations are the real life, forever and ever.
—E. M. FORSTER

I don't want to live—I want to love first, and live incidentally.
—ZELDA FITZGERALD

"It isn't much fun for One, but Two
Can stick together," says Pooh, says he.
"That's how it is," says Pooh. —A. A. MILNE

She has composed, so long, a self with which to welcome him,
Companion to his self. —WALLACE STEVENS

He needed the eyes of others to see himself, the senses of another to
feel himself. —MALCOLM X

I have spent hours completely involved in what I thought other people
wished to see me doing. I have suppressed my own desires and wishes, and
ever eager to please, have done what I thought was expected of me.
—LIV ULLMAN

The basic thing which contributes to charm is the ability to forget
oneself and be engrossed in other people. —ELEANOR ROOSEVELT

Charm is a way of getting the answer yes without having asked any
clear questions. —ALBERT CAMUS

"All right," said the Cheshire Cat; and this time it vanished quite
slowly, beginning with the end of the tail, and ending with the grin,
which remained some time after the rest of it had gone. —LEWIS CARROLL

If you give him some sugar,
He will love you. —KENNETH REXROTH

I'm giving you a definite maybe. —SAM GOLDWYN

Some people are in favor of compromising, while other people to
compromise are loath.
I cannot plump for either side, I think there is something to be said
for both. —OGDEN NASH

The test of a first-rate intelligence is the ability to hold two opposed ideas in
the mind at the same time, and still retain the ability to function.
—F. SCOTT FITZGERALD

Sometimes even I can't believe how wishy-washy I am.
—CHARLES SCHULTZ (Charlie Brown)

My dilemma is to force the two poles of life together, to transcribe
the dual voices into life's melody. —HERMAN HESSE

"The great art . . . is—to keep your balance properly. Like this, you know—"
. . . this time he fell flat on his back. —LEWIS CARROLL

No animal, according to the rules of animal etiquette, is ever expected
to do anything strenuous, or heroic, or even moderately
active during the off-season. —KENNETH GRAHAME

I cannot live without beauty. —ALBERT CAMUS

The only way to get the best of an argument is to avoid it. —DALE CARNEGIE

But I want first of all . . . to be at peace with myself . . . I want to
live . . . an inner harmony, essentially spiritual, which can be translated
into outward harmony. —ANNE MORROW LINDBERGH

MOON IN SCORPIO

$\math)$ ♏ Having Moon in Scorpio indicates that we value our privacy, that we are capable of considerable emotional intensity and passion, that we need to probe beneath the surface of experience in order to secure a deep and solid foundation for ourselves, and that we need to experience our power to use our own and other people's resources effectively. When our real feelings are denied or our real needs unmet, we may easily resort to detrimental Scorpio behavior patterns—obsessions with sexuality or money, expressions of revenge or destruction, or demanding or manipulative behaviors. One of the difficulties of a Scorpio Moon is related to the fear of losing control or surrendering. Because of this fear, we may deny or conceal the softer, vulnerable facets of ourselves, thereby preventing ourselves from experiencing the real communion or union which we seek.

We may have internalized messages from our parents which enabled us to develop resourcefulness, endurance and strength of character, as well as the capacity to plummet the depths of experience. Our sexuality may have been awakened early through the intensity of family interactions, so that we were forced to come to terms with our own life force and death force. A Scorpionic parent, however, may have negatively influenced our ability to receive nurturance and to nourish ourselves. Perhaps such a parent was hostile and punitive, so that we developed considerable mistrust and learned to hide our feelings. He or she may have been dominating, intrusive or sexually provocative, leading us to fear being possessed or overpowered. Coldness or undue stoicism, as manifested in a "be tough" attitude may have prevented our internal child from receiving the tenderness and care he or she needed. Sometimes a Scorpio Moon suggests the early death of a parent, or a premature confrontation with realities of death or violence.

We who have Moon in Scorpio can reparent ourselves by recovering, accepting and expressing our feelings and emotional needs, not just our sexual desires. We need to contact our own core, to possess ourselves rather than others, and to learn how to constructively channel our passion. One of the tasks of our Scorpionic Moon is that of discovering our inner power and drawing upon our own capacities to meet our needs rather than manipulating others to give us what we are unable or unwilling to give ourselves.

Quotations that Illuminate the Moon in Scorpio

I am interested only in the basement of the human being. —SIGMUND FREUD

My voice is a minor one, but I must raise it;
I come not only to bury privacy, but to praise it. —OGDEN NASH

When truth is buried underground it grows, it chokes, it gathers
such explosive force that on the day it bursts out, it blows up
everything with it. —EMILE ZOLA

Few men . . . come anywhere near exhausting the resources dwelling within
them. There are deep wells of strength which are never used.
—ADMIRAL RICHARD BYRD

I will be harsh as truth and as uncompromising as justice. I do not
wish to use moderation. —WILLIAM LLOYD GARRISON

I resent it if you don't/Give me all and neatly.
I demand that you invest/What you are, completely. —FRITZ PERLS

For everyone who does not know
How to control his inmost self would fain control
His neighbor's will. —GOETHE

What does not destroy me makes me stronger. —FRIEDRICH NIETZSCHE

When you are sure you're right, you have a moral duty to impose your will
upon anyone who disagrees with you. —ROBERT MAYER

I conceived it as my task to create difficulties everywhere.
—SOREN KIRKEGAARDE

The only way to get rid of a temptation is to yield to it. —OSCAR WILDE

Whatever is not nailed down is mine. Whatever I can pry loose is not nailed down. —COLLIS HUNTINTON

For each ecstatic instant/We must in anguish pay
In keen and quivering ratio/To the ecstasy —EMILY DICKINSON

So he sigh'd and pined and ogled,
And his passion boil'd and bubbled. —WILLIAM THACKERAY

Last night I slept in sheets the color of fire
Tonight I die alone again and curse my own desire
Sentenced first to burn and then to freeze. —CARLY SIMON

And fire and ice within me fight
Beneath the suffocating night. —A. E. HOUSMAN

He loved absolutely, that's why he hates . . . absolutely. —FRIEDA LAWRENCE

To err is human; to forgive is not our policy. —ANONYMOUS

What you can't have, abuse. —ITALIAN PROVERB

She was not only ready to accept suffering, she actively desired it.
—MAURICE FRIEDMAN

I know the bottom . . . I know it with my great tap root. It is what
you fear. I do not fear it. I have been there. —SYLVIA PLATH

Some have named this space where we are rooted a place of death.
We fix them with our callous eyes and call it, rather, a terrain of
resurrection. —ROBIN MORGAN

We must be still and still moving
Into another intensity
For a further union, a deeper communion. —T. S. ELIOT

MOON IN SAGITTARIUS

☽ ♐ If we have a Sagittarian Moon, we need to be free to expand our boundaries—to discover and actualize new possibilities, to travel, and/or to develop our understanding.
We have a generous heart and seek to give from our own bounty; we
also seek to rise above our difficulties through humor and enjoyable
companionship.

When our real needs are not met or when we come into contact with feelings or needs which threaten us, we may express our Sagittarian nature in a defensive or distorted manner—procrastinating or avoiding immediate issues by focusing upon the future, abstract realms or escapist activities; becoming preoccupied with ideals or goals rather than current tasks; intellectualizing or philosophizing incessantly; joking inappropriately; or moving restlessly from activity to activity or person to person on an endless quest both to escape from responsibility and to fulfill our inner emptiness.

Most likely, our mother or significant parent figure provided us with a constructive philosophical framework by which to view life, and imbued us with a love of both internal and external exploration. But such a parent may have been fearful of emotional closeness and taken refuge in distant realms rather than responding to our real needs or feelings or to the difficulties or burdens we experienced. She may have indulged us rather than given us real nourishment. She may have preached rather than gently taught, issuing "shoulds" or religious principles which may not have been in keeping with our own nature and development.

Those of us with Moon in Sagittarius may need to reparent ourselves by creating our own philosophy and morality apart from our parents and by using our philosophy to help us come to terms with rather than suppress our feelings and needs. Our tasks may also include learning to give to ourselves as well as others, developing the internal freedom capable of existing within limitations and commitments, and discovering and maintaining contact with the God within or an internal guiding spirit which leads and inspires us.

Quotations that Illuminate the Moon in Sagittarius

I have tried in my time to be a philosopher; but I don't know how, cheerfulness was always breaking in. —OLIVER EDWARDS

She shall be sportive as the fawn.
. . . Wild with glee across the lawn. —WILLIAM WORDSWORTH

She wanted to give life; to warm the blood and kindle the hope of drab and cautious people. —MARGOT ASQUITH

I am a little deaf, a little blind, a little impotent, and on top of this are two or three abominable infirmities, but nothing destroys my hope.
—VOLTAIRE

—listen: there's a hell of a good universe next door; let's go.
—e. e. cummings

I must be moving on. —DONALD DAVIE

—tomorrow is our permanent address. —e. e. cummings

Count not his broken pledges as a crime.
He MEANT them. HOW he meant them—at the time.
—KENSAL GREEN

Life is the art of drawing sufficient conclusions from insufficient premises.
—SAMUEL BUTLER

Harmonious with virtue was his speech,
And gladly would he learn and gladly teach. —GEOFFREY CHAUCER

"Tut, tut, child," said the Duchess. "Everything's got a moral if
only you can find it." —LEWIS CARROLL

Come, my friends,
'Tis not too late to seek a newer world . . .
for my purpose
holds to sail beyond the sunset, and the baths
Of all the western stars, until I die.
—ALFRED LORD TENNYSON

Oh, Lord, I want to be free, want to be free;
Rainbow round my shoulder, wings on my feet.
—AMERICAN NEGRO SPIRITUAL

He wants to tie me and to narrow me down
But I want to expand by being in all the horizons.—ERNEST STADLER

My life was spent in one long effort to escape from the commonplaces
of existence. —SIR ARTHUR CONAN DOYLE

To put meaning in one's life may end in madness,
But life without meaning is the torture
Of restlessness and vague desire. —EDGAR LEE MASTERS

Climb high/Climb far
Your goal the sky/Your aim the star. —ANONYMOUS

The principal thing in this world is to keep one's soul aloft.
—GUSTAVE FLAUBERT

The only true happiness comes from squandering ourselves for a purpose.
—JOHN MASON BROWN

He who has a why to live can bear almost any how.
—FRIEDRICH NIETZSCHE

*And this I do believe above all . . . that I MUST BELIEVE—that I
must believe in my fellow men—that I must believe in myself—
that I must believe in God—if life is to have any meaning.*
—MARGARET CHASE SMITH

MOON IN CAPRICORN

☽ ♑ Those of us with Moon in Capricorn need the security of organization and structure, and the satisfaction of maintaining commitments and achieving our aims. We take pride in our work, and want recognition for our accomplishments. Capricorn is the position of the Moon's detriment, and is therefore a particularly difficult position for experiencing emotional nourishment and developing self-nurturing behaviors. When feelings and needs emerge, we may not even allow them fully to enter our consciousness. We may be too afraid of our vulnerability or weakness, and too judgmental of our inner child. Repression of the deeper facets of ourselves may lead us to wallow in depression, negativity or self-criticism, to work incessantly, or to isolate ourselves from fulfilling connections with other people. We may continually give ourselves "be tough" messages which support our self-sufficiency but prevent the real contact with ourselves which makes close relationships possible.

Most likely, a parental figure helped us to learn to control our emotions, take responsibility for ourselves and make adult rather than childish decisions, and also provided the consistency and safety we needed in order to feel secure. However, having a Capricorn Moon suggests that we were never allowed to give free rein to our feelings, and that we probably did not receive much tender nurturance. Our parent may have been cold and rejecting; he or she may have neglected us or imparted to us that our feelings and needs had little value. Perhaps he or she was also a perfectionist we could not satisfy, and whose acceptance was conditional upon a high degree of achievement and success. As a result, we may feel a sense of worth only for what we accomplish, but not for who we are.

We who have Moon in Capricorn need to create our own standards for ourselves apart from our parents' standards, and to give up compensatory striving which actually does not meet our real needs. Our task involves developing our internal source of security and giving ourselves the validation and recognition we may have originally sought from others. We may only experience the fulfillment we seek when, by accepting our feelings and needs and allowing ourselves to be vulnerable, we discover strength and self-sufficiency which embraces rather than denies the sensitivity of our inner child.

Quotations that Illuminate the Moon in Capricorn

I will be lord over myself. —GOETHE

Always listen to the control tower. —CHARLES SCHULTZ (SNOOPY)

To have what we want is riches; but to be able to do without is power.
—GEORGE McDONALD

Better put a strong fence round the top of the cliff,
Than an ambulance down in the valley. —JOSEPH MALINES

Put all your eggs in one basket, and—watch the basket. —MARK TWAIN

I've built walls, a fortress deep and mighty
That none can penetrate . . .
I am a rock; I am an island. —SIMON AND GARFUNKEL

My feelings can't quite venture out
I'm filled with memories and doubt
I think I'd rather do without
Than take a chance. —CRYER AND FORD

They wait, when they should turn to journeys,
Then stiffen, when they should bend. —LOUISE BOGAN

I am solitary in the vast society of beings . . . I am in the midst of them,
but not OF them. —RALPH WALDO EMERSON

You have taken yourself too seriously. —GOVERNOR DUPONT

Cling to what is difficult. —RAINER MARIA RILKE

What on earth would a man do with himself if something did not
stand in his way? —H. G. WELLS

The ability to withstand frustration is what keeps us alive.
—ABBIE HOFFMAN

Everybody needs a certain level of misery in his life to be happy.
—ANONYMOUS

I wish to preach, not the doctrine of ignoble ease, but the doctrine of the strenuous life. —THEODORE ROOSEVELT

I have no spur
To prick the sides of my intent, but only
Vaulting ambition, which o'erleaps itself. —SHAKESPEARE

I shall be like that tree. I shall die at the top. —JONATHAN SWIFT

The secret of success is constancy to purpose.
—BENJAMIN DISRAELI

In most undertakings, success requires not only initiative, but also finishiative. —ANONYMOUS

A lack of accomplishment is the greatest suffering.
—THE CHOFETZ CHAIM

She is able to build her life around the inner courtyard, as the cedar builds itself upon the seed, and . . . finds her life's fruition within the limits that befit it. —ANTOINE DE St. EXUPERY

What a man has may be dependent upon others, but WHAT HE IS depends upon himself alone. —ANONYMOUS

I was forced to live far beyond my years when just a child; now I have reversed the order and I intend to remain young indefinitely.
—MARY PICKFORD

MOON IN AQUARIUS

 Our Aquarian Moon indicates that we need to experience and express our individuality, to be free to interact with a wide range of people, and to use our intuitive, inventive and abstract mental capacities, as well as to contribute meaningfully to society. The energies of Aquarius do not mesh easily with the Cancerian Moon principle. We may have difficulty acknowledging and validating our needs and feelings, and fear closeness and intimacy. When threatened by emerging emotions or needs, we may rationalize or intellectualize, may rebel or loudly proclaim our self-sufficiency, or may become overly preoccupied with stimulating activities. Sometimes, Moon in Aquarius may lead us to make sudden abrupt changes in our lives in order to overcome the internal suffocation of too much closeness or feeling experience. Cultivating a large network of friends and/or dedicating ourselves to a cause in which we believe may fulfill us, but may also be a compensation for unmet personal needs.

Most likely, a parent encouraged our Aquarian qualities. He or she may have been intellectual, humanitarian and individualistic, and supported these traits in ourselves. We learned to take pride in our uniqueness and originality and in our social and mental skills. However, such a parent may also have been emotionally detached or cold, and unable to nurture us physically or emotionally, while nonetheless remaining responsive to large groups of people and social involvements which were less restrictive and emotionally demanding than ties to family. One or both of our parents may have been unpredictable or erratic when relating to us, so that we were unable to develop trust in secure and stable relationships, and learned at an early age to defend against intimacy.

We who have Aquarian Moons need to experience and value our own uniqueness, while at the same time creating for ourselves our own society of intimates, one in which our emotional needs are respected and met rather than suppressed. We need to develop and trust our intuition, and to use our minds to help us understand our feelings and discover how to meet our needs, rather than escape from them. Other tasks of our Aquarian Moon involve cultivating the internal freedom which results from full openness to our emotional natures, and learning to be our own friend rather than submerging ourselves in social interactions because of our discomfort with ourselves.

Quotations that Illuminate the Moon in Aquarius

You had better be a round peg in a square hole than a square peg in a square hole. —ELBERT HUBBARD

If this is coffee, I want tea; but if this is tea, then I wish for coffee. —PUNCH

Since you weren't born a genius, then be a cantankerous fanatic. —ANONYMOUS

If a man does not keep pace with his companions, perhaps it is because he hears a different drummer. —HENRY DAVID THOREAU

She's gotten into mysterious devotions
She's gotten into zodiac and zen
She's gotten into tarot cards and potions.
—JONI MITCHELL *(from the song "Clouds")*

Two roads diverged in a wood, and I—
took the one less traveled by,
And that has made all the difference. —ROBERT FROST

A foolish consistency is the hobgoblin of little minds.
—RALPH WALDO EMERSON

Come to a limit and transcend it; come to a limit and transcend it.
Our only security is our ability to change.
—SAM KEEN *(paraphrasing* JOHN LILLY*)*

Again and again, a voice commands us to get out of the rut, to leave
bag and baggage, to change cars, change directions. —HENRY MILLER

I want space. —TU FU

What we want is lib and let lib and not just lib service.
—SAM LEVENSON

I wanted to be free, free to do and to give as my whims dictated.
The moment anything was expected or demanded of me I balked.
That was . . . my independence. —HENRY MILLER

Meek wifehood is no part of my profession;
I am your friend, but never your possession. —VERA BRITTAIN

The only way to have a friend is to be one. —RALPH WALDO EMERSON

Love is only chatter,
Friends are all that matter. —GELETT BURGESS

She seems endowed with a strong mind which will protect her from.
excessive emotion. —GEORGE SAND

Circled by fury, we were the unfurious; surrounded by passion, we
were the dispassionate. —GEORGE CLARKE

I must ask truth, and speak truth, and act with truth, now and forever.
—LILLIAN HELLMAN

Broadmindedness is the result of flattening highmindedness out.
—GEORGE SAINTSBURY

I cannot love all humanity except with a vast and somewhat abstract love.
—ALBERT CAMUS

True security is to be found in social solidarity rather than in isolated individual effort. —FYODOR DOSTOYEVSKY

It's co-existence or no existence. —BERTRAND RUSSELL

When you cease to make a contribution you begin to die.
—ELEANOR ROOSEVELT

And now, Humanity, I turn to you;
I consecrate my service to the world! —VOLTARINE DE CLEYRE

MOON IN PISCES

☽ ♓ Having Moon in Pisces means that we need space in our lives to drift and to dream, relationships based upon empathic bonds, and openness to sources of inspiration inside and outside ourselves. The watery energies of the Moon are easily expressed and sometimes overly emphasized by a Pisces Moon placement. When we experience our feelings and needs, we may even indulge them through long bouts of crying, self pity, or elicitations of sympathy from other people. With or without awareness, we may seek to escape from ourselves through fantasy or idealization, or through such addictions as alcohol or drugs. Many of us with Pisces Moons may vicariously experience our feelings and satisfy our needs by continually focusing upon the feelings and needs of others and devoting ourselves to their welfare.

A parent who was a Piscean influence most likely responded sensitively and compassionately to us and encouraged our inspirational temperament. However, if our Moon is afflicted, such a parent may also have had a detrimental influence upon us. He or she may have overindulged us, catering to our aches and pains, or too frequently played the martyr, giving to us wholeheartedly but also invoking guilt or seeking complete dedication in return. He or she may have been hypochondriacal, or of an ethereal nature which could not easily come to terms with physical reality. A Piscean parent may have been victim to his or her own addictions, or tangled in dreams or fantasies and not fully emotionally or physically present.

We who have Moon in Pisces may need to learn how to respond constructively to our own feelings and needs, to serve our selves and give to ourselves rather than attempt to lose ourselves in others. Often, because we suffer from a divine discontent, we may have difficulty accepting and adapting to the realities of an earthly existence; we need to be able to translate our visions into action, to live those dreams which are viable, thereby forging a link between our practical and spiritual or creative natures. We may seek to experience oneness in close relationships, but we are not likely to know wholly that oneness unless we cultivate our attunement to our own creative and/or spiritual source, and open our hearts to the fullness of both the love and pain within us.

Quotations that Illuminate the Moon in Pisces

I can't figure out where I leave off and everyone else begins.
—GEORGE McCABEE

Agonies are one of my changes of garments; I do not ask the wounded person how he feels . . . I myself become the wounded person.
—WALT WHITMAN

I am myself and what is around me, and if I do not save it, it shall not save me. —JOSE ORTEGA Y GASSET

Who's going to rescue the rescuer? —CHARLES SCHULTZ

*my kindness has always
been my curse
a tender heart is the cross I bear* —DON MARQUIS

If you can't help, at least make a sound of sympathy. —ANONYMOUS

I see myself as a sieve. Everyone's feelings flow through me.
—LIV ULLMAN

Is devotion to others a cover for the hungers and needs of the self, of which one is ashamed? I was always ashamed to take. So I gave. It was not a virtue. It was a disguise. —ANAIS NIN

*Tears from the depth of some divine despair
Rose in the heart, and gather to the eyes.*
—ALFRED LORD TENNYSON

If at first you don't succeed, cry, cry again. —ANONYMOUS

See what you have done! . . . In a minute I shall melt away. —FRANK BAUM

She drifts. All she wants to do with her life is lose it somewhere.
—DOROTHY BAKER

I am a feather for each wind that blows. —SHAKESPEARE

A wise man adapts himself to circumstances as water shapes itself to the vessel that contains it. —CHINESE PROVERB

If you wander around in enough confusion, you will soon find enlightenment. —DIGBY DIEHL

"This is serious," said Pooh. "I must have an Escape." —A. A. MILNE

I will certainly elude you.
Already you see I have escaped from you. —WALT WHITMAN

You may be deceived if you trust too much, but you will live in torment unless you trust enough. —FRANK CRANE

We walk by faith, not by sight. —CORINTHIANS

Not I, not I, but the wind that blows through me. —D. H. LAWRENCE

It is only with the heart that one can see rightly; what is essential is invisible to the eye. —ANTOINE DE ST. EXUPERY

My emotions flowered in me like a divine revelation. —ANDRE GIDE

To me every hour of the light and dark is a miracle,
Every cubic inch of space is a miracle. —WALT WHITMAN

To find your own way is to follow your own bliss. —JOSEPH CAMPBELL

I prefer to be a dreamer among the humblest, with visions to be realized, than lord among those without dreams and desires.
—KAHLIL GIBRAN

§&

YOUR INNER DEVELOPMENT JOURNAL

The following pages describe a self-therapy process which I use with several of my weekly clients in order to help them monitor their progress, clarify their aims, develop a nurturing inner parent, and increase their level of emotional satisfaction and wellbeing. The first step involves purchasing a blank book, a simple notebook or a professionally designed journal which may, because of its color, design or texture by aesthetically and emotionally appealing.

Intentions

Change begins with intention, with the process of clearly defining and allowing ourselves to experience fully the intensity of our wanting. The best way to begin YOUR INNER DEVELOPMENT JOURNAL is to use the first few pages to write down and periodically update your intentions in regard to your growth. Before you start, take some time to reflect upon your primary goals in regard to yourself, and which of those goals you most WANT to actualize. Can you really experience the wanting? Unless you can, your intention may not be strong enough to set processes in motion which will lead to fulfillment. The more you can allow yourself to want each goal for yourself, and the more you allow yourself to deeply experience and affirm that desire, the more likely you are to be able to make choices which reflect it.

When writing your list of intentions, begin each statement with "I WANT" in capital letters. Examples might be: "I WANT to be more aware of the negative messages I give myself and substitute positive messages," "I WANT to care for my body by cooking nutritious meals and exercising three times a week," "I WANT to risk sharing my feelings more openly with friends," or "I WANT to turn to myself first when I am in need, before reaching out to others." Be sure you choose goals which are realistic, by which you can gauge your inner movement, rather than goals which are too abstract or related to some distant endpoint in the future (such as "I WANT to be a successful professional" or "I WANT to be a loving human being"). You might also want to reflect upon all the domains of your life—your relationship to your mind, body, feelings, and spirit, as well as to work, love, friendship, leisure time, home, etc.—as you define your primary intentions. Periodically, you may wish to add to your list, or even assess a large number of the intentions you have recorded and rephrase them in order to express succinctly the ten or twelve which are most important to you. You may also wish to read them over or repeat them to yourself each day in order to reinforce them and strengthen your commitment to actualizing them in your life. The more you can clearly envision living them and experiencing the gains which will concretely result from doing so, the more effective you will be at translating them into action.

Credits

The CREDIT section of your journal is your daily record of experiences about which you feel GOOD—in regard to your relationship with yourself, your activities and other people. Allow yourself ½ to one full page each night for recording at least three experiences in which you took inner or outer action in accordance with your values and aims. You will probably most want to pay attention to those experiences which reflect your intentions, whether they be in regard to how you treated yourself or other people, or what you were able to accomplish throughout the day. If you are someone who makes excessive demands upon yourself to live up to perfectionist standards, then allowing yourself to feel o.k. when you fall short may be worth a CREDIT listing—for example, "I watched TV this afternoon instead of studying, and forgave myself for not being more productive," or "I let myself sleep when I felt depressed rather than forcing myself to go to the party." You will both want to reinforce yourself for your gains and forgive yourself for your failures and regressions; mistreating yourself when you fall short of your expectations rarely leads to healthy change.

Periodically, perhaps every few weeks or every month, you may want to read over your list of CREDITS and allow yourself to experience how you are clearly, although perhaps slowly, moving forward in your own growth. It is also important to let yourself FEEL good as you write down your credits—really soak in the positive feelings, as if you are receiving a compliment from a special friend, an acknowledgement of your own capacity to empower yourself and create your own reality. In time, you will become more adept at paying attention to your positive, growth-related experiences and less preoccupied with and discouraged by the negative; you will begin to internalize a nurturing parent who gives you strokes for each of your gains and accomplishments and loves you in spite of your failures and regressions. As a result, you will need less from others, and be able to receive what others have to give you more fully.

Nourishing Experiences

What are the experiences you have had which are truly emotionally satisfying, which leave you with a feeling of fullness or completion, and/or with feelings of love and joy? We NEED nourishing experiences in our lives, yet by habit we often seek and repeat experiences which do not nourish us, which may stimulate us but also leave us feeling empty, wanting and dissatisfied. Part of the process of self-integration is learning how to relinquish desires which are not in alignment with our needs and to direct ourselves toward discovering and fulfilling those desires which lead to satisfaction. As you begin to record CREDITS in your INNER DEVELOPMENT BOOK, you might also want to record in a separate section those experiences which really nourish you. You may choose to use a page for every week or every month for this purpose. Reading over your list of nourishing experiences each month and consulting it when making decisions regarding your use of time can help you to create more of these experiences and to relinquish unsatisfying goals, activities and relationships which do not really nourish you.

You may want to begin your list of nourishing experiences with an inventory of the past: What were the ten or twenty most fulfilling experiences you can remember? What about during the past five years? During the past year? Reflect also upon what you can do to create more of these kinds of experiences, and how you have created them before. You might also want to consider experiences you have not had, but which you believe will be emotionally satisfying to you. Why not try to create them and see what happens? The more capable you become of "filling your own well" and developing a nurturing inner parent who knows how to make wise, fulfilling choices which satisfy both the adult and child parts of yourself, the less you will be inclined to wait for something out there (which might not exist) to rescue you, and the less you will desperately feel the need for others to provide for you. Many of your nourishing experiences may involve giving and receiving with other people, but as you become aware of your role in the process, of your capacity to actively create such contact, you will be less inclined to view yourself as a passive receptacle waiting for the outside world to fill you and will instead experience your own empowerment in relationships. In the future, you might also want to do a similar inventory of experiences which boost your self-esteem—those which may or may not be emotionally satisfying, but which nonetheless increased your self-respect, your sense of competency, and your experience of yourself as a capable, responsible adult, willing to forego some of the satisfactions your inner child may seek in order to live more in accordance with your own values and function more effectively in the world.

Chapter Three

NEW MOON, FULL MOON

How many of us study transits and progressions influencing our charts, and ignore the aspects made by New and Full Moons? Perhaps we hesitate to thumb through our ephemerides, page by page, looking for the positions of each lunation. Perhaps we are not aware of the significant influence these lunations may have upon us, especially when they conjunct natal planets. Perhaps we have not yet discovered how, by being cognizant of forthcoming New Moons and Full Moons as they aspect our planets, we may become more capable of harnessing their potent energy. At the New Moon, we can learn more fully to BE and to generate important new beginnings in our lives. At the Full Moon, we can keep ourselves open to the insights and revelations which we may easily access then. At this time we can allow the light of our consciousness to intensify and expand so that we may clearly perceive our relationships to ourselves, other people and the world around us. When either of these lunations closely aspects planets in our charts, these planets can be empowered and transformed by solar–lunar energy.

The purpose of this chapter is to enable us to understand how these lunations may affect us, and how we may prepare ourselves in order to gain maximum benefit from them. The degree tables in the appendix give exact positions of all New and Full Moons, as well as eclipses, for a fifty-five year time period.[1] By looking up the degrees of our natal planets, angles and nodes (using a 2 degree orb) and reflecting upon our past, we may gain some understanding of how these lunations have influenced each facet of our charts, and the pattern that has been unfolding for us in regard to particular planets, nodes and angles. By noting future influences and reflecting upon how we might wish them to mani-

---

1. The best source of positions for other time periods is *The American Ephemeris of the Twentieth Century*, compiled and published by ACS Publishing Co.

fest, while motivating ourselves to make constructive use of the energy of the planets influenced, we may actively create experiences and events which help to actualize our goals. The worksheets help us to review our past and to prepare ourselves to shape our future more consciously.

Those of us who too often experience the planets as external forces acting upon us, while only passively responding to the events they trigger, may be astonished to realize the extent to which we can experience ourselves as empowered and active individuals, fully capable of directing our lives and cooperating with cosmic energies. All we need to do is to be willing to learn from our past, assess future influences and choose to expend the energy necessary to manifest their most constructive possibilities.

A Personal Experience

Although I have been aware of the influences of lunations for many years, I only recently discovered the potent energy they make available for personal transformation. During the week of a Full Moon on my ascendant/descendant axis, I was studying the effects of New and Full Moons on that axis, as well as to my Uranus, the 7th house focal planet of an exact t-square. As a result of researching my own past, I discovered (and intensively relived) earlier experiences which contributed to patterns of alienation, rebellion and disruption in close relationships, a pattern further clarified by my mother's exact Pluto conjunction to my Uranus. I also discovered that a significant relationship in my life had actually exploded at almost every New or Full Moon conjunction to Uranus. Approaching another New Moon conjunct my Uranus, which is 13 degrees past my descendant, I became aware of how several key relationships in my life were unstable and unsatisfying, and of the distinct possibility that one or more of these would "explode" by the time of the New Moon. With the energy released by the emotional catharsis of reliving crucial past experiences, and with the newfound awareness of my previous patterns, I reflected upon the problems occurring in current relationships, and asked myself how I might alternatively express my Uranian energy: How might I transform these particular interactions? What might I do to liberate myself from past behaviors and dramatically CHANGE these relationships in a way which would be mutually satisfying?

Once I became aware of possible courses of action and mobilized myself to risk the confrontations I knew were necessary, I experienced a confidence and empowerment which astounded me. Within two weeks, by the time the New Moon conjunction had occurred, I was experiencing a deeper communion and fulfillment with these key people in my life than I had ever believed was possible. But most of all, I began to realize more fully my own capacity—and the capacity of all of us—to transcend our most deeply rooted and disturbing inner conflicts. We do not need to know and use astrology to do so, but the combination of astrological insight and motivation can greatly accelerate the process.

Facts and Theories

We live in a patriarchal culture, a society which is male-dominated and which has worshipped a male god. During the twentieth century, the increasing interest in psychiatry and psychotherapy, in drugs, altered states of consciousness, psychic phenomena and Eastern-based forms of spirituality were manifestations of a repressed lunar consciousness attempting to assert itself and restore balance both to our individual psyches and to the collective. As we begin to integrate solar and lunar forces within us— our female and male energies, our conscious and unconscious, our minds and our emotions/bodies—we further the integration of these elements within society, perhaps restoring the delicate balance between mankind and nature which is so precarious at the present time.

In earlier days, lunar influences were considerably more predominant than they are now. The Hebrew calendar, for example, is based upon 13 lunar months; the Hebrew word SABBATTU, translated as Sabbath, actually means lunar month. The calendars and languages of many primitive cultures also reflect the importance the Moon and lunar consciousness had upon primitive people.

Today, scientists studying fossils of the sea animal, the chambered nautilus, theorize that the spiraling lines contained within it pertain to the cycles of the Moon. The most ancient fossils discovered contain 9 lines, more recent fossils contain 17 lines, and the shells of the chambered nautilus today contain 28–29, reflecting the 28:12 days of the Moon's synodic month, the time it takes for the Moon to return to its original place as it orbits around the earth. Many believe that the Moon was once closer to the earth, once able to complete its orbit in as little as the 9 days charted by the 9 lines. If this is true, the rise of patriarchal culture and the increased consciousness which accompanies the development of a complex civilization (with the related growth of science and philosophy at the expense of religion) is a reflection of the

Moon's waning influence upon the earth as it physically distances itself from our planet.

Recently, scientists have begun to study the influence of New and Full Moons upon the earth and upon human behavior. Because the gravitational pull of both bodies is strongest at these lunations, the combined pull of both Sun and Moon in alignment actually causes earth and water to rise. Land literally expands and contracts; the oceans increase and decrease their supply of water. Inevitably, the fluid balance within our bodies is also affected. We manufacture additional serotonin, a chemical which speeds up the beating of the heart, causing blood to circulate more fully. Our chemical balance is altered. The increase in the electric potential of the earth's magnetic field leads also to an abundance of positive ions in the atmosphere, which are linked to alterations and disturbances in human behavior.

Studies of New and Full Moon phenomena indicate that the following circumstances occur at these times:

- a higher than normal amount of electricity contained within the physical body

- muscle and dream action intensified during sleep

- an increase in epileptic convulsions and asthma attacks

- a greater likelihood of excessive bleeding and hemorrhaging during surgery

- tendency for ovulation to occur (with peak fertility)

- peak times for sexual activity, for both humans and animals

- more births (especially at the Full Moon)

- more murders, robberies, cases of arson and assault

- an increase in the number of admissions to psychiatric hospitals (especially at the Full Moon—note that the word LUNATIC means MOON-MAD)

- a tendency for fish to feed en masse and as a result to be more easily caught by fishermen (especially shrimp and herring)

Today, many scientists are speculating upon the nature of lunation influence upon human behavior. Dr. Robert Becker believes that there are amplifier nodes in the nervous system, equivalent to acupuncture points, which reflect fluctuations in the earth's magnetic field, as influenced by solar-lunar positions and phases. Dr. Arnold Lieber hypothesizes that we all move back and forth between psychological states of "negative receptivity" and "positive receptivity." If a Full Moon occurs when we are in "negative receptivity," withdrawing inward, we are not likely to respond to its influence. However, if we are in "positive receptivity" at the time of a Full Moon, our emotional experience is heightened and we may be prone to experience disturbances in feeling and behavior.[2]

Those of us who were born during a New or Full Moon, who have strongly positioned moons in our charts (in Cancer or perhaps on an angle), or who have several Cancer planets, are most inclined to experience psychologically the influence of these lunations, perhaps because we are simply more aware of our internal oscillations than are most people. We in particular can benefit by remaining aware of solar-lunar cycles, altering our attitudes and actions so as to derive maximum benefit from their influence.

At the New Moon

At the New Moon, the Sun and Moon are conjunct in the same sign. The light reflected from the Moon is less than at any other phase of the lunar cycle, and the gravitational pull of the Moon upon the earth is the greatest. At this time, we are instinctively expressing the energy of the lunation sign in accordance with the area of life indicated by the house in which the New Moon occurs within our charts. Our energy is concentrated deep within ourselves. Although we are not likely to be very objective, clear or self-aware, we are able to attain a state of presence or beingness and to focus our attention quite effectively upon the outer world—especially the affairs of the lunation house.

When the New Moon conjuncts a planet, we naturally BECOME that planetary energy, often without being conscious of how we are expressing ourselves. It is as if the combined power of the Sun and Moon opens a channel within us which contacts our very core, our essential being. Whatever planet, by conjunction, is involved in that process is awakened and energized. A seed is planted and begins to germinate. Whatever we discover, whatever energy we contact and express, whatever we begin, whatever we do in accordance with the nature of this

---

2. For more information about the scientific research on lunar influences, see Lieber's *The Lunar Effect: Biological Tides and Human Emotions* (New York: Doubleday, 1978); Paul Katzeff, *Full Moon: Fact and Fantasy About Lunar Influence* (Secaucus, NJ: Citadel Press, 1981); and Robert Becker: *The Body Electric: Electromagnetism and the Foundation of Life* (New York: Harper, 1998).

planet has a greater capacity to develop and manifest outwardly than at any other time.[3]

Therefore, a lunation conjunct a natal planet or angle signifies a very important time to set an intention related to the planet, sign and house being influenced, to make a new beginning in regard to our expression of this energy. New Moon conjunct Sun may be the time to change our name, experiment with an alternate identity, re-own the power we have projected onto our fathers, husbands or key male figures in our lives. New Moon conjunct Moon may be a time to move to a more satisfying location or adopt a child or begin a new pattern of accepting and revealing our emotional needs. During New Moon conjunct Saturn we could start a new career or work phase or commit ourselves to a substantial and/or long-term venture. With New Moon conjunct Neptune we might begin a practice of meditation or express more outwardly our compassion and inspiration. By consciously choosing to harness the power of the New Moon as it influences our planets, we become capable of generating significant new beginnings in all realms of our lives.

At the Full Moon

At the Full Moon, the Sun and Moon are in opposition, at the same degree of opposing signs. The light reflected from the Moon is more than at any other time, and the gravitational pull of the Sun and Moon upon the earth is the strongest, equivalent to that of the New Moon (although the Sun and Moon are now pulling in opposing directions).

At the Full Moon, we may experience an internal division which re-sults in becoming conscious of feeling separated from other people and/or

---

3. At a previous New Moon conjunct my ascendant, followed by a Full Moon conjunct my focal 7th house Uranus, I wrote the following journal entry. This was one week before my discovery of astrology—a discovery that occurred on the exact day of Full Moon conjunct Uranus: "*Vague insights are floating through my consciousness. I can barely grasp them, can only intuit some es-sential change within me which may have the power to alter who I am in relationship. I find myself watching people, observing how they interact, how they respond to each other, how they make and maintain friendships. And as I observe them, I experience a profound desire to put an end to the alienation I have always known. I discover that I am subconsciously imitating them, slowly echo-ing their behaviors, learning to relate as comfortably as they do. It feels as if I am remaking who I am in relationship, learning to BE more fully in the world, rather than apart from it. . . Slowly, vaguely, deep within me I sense that new foundations are being laid now and I want to take advan-tage of what seems like a very potent and fertile time for change. . . . I am haunted by a quote from Gibran: 'Beyond this burdened self lives my freer self. Too young am I and too outraged to be my freer self. But how shall I become my freer self unless I slay my burdened selves?'*"

of an increased urge to relate. Because the Full Moon bridges two signs and two houses in our charts, we may become aware of tension in regard to integrating these facets of ourselves and areas of our lives. Or, we may become infused with insights in regard to how we have functioned here, how we might integrate and harmonize diverse energies, and what meaning these realms of our experience are providing for us. We seem to possess a capacity to transcend ourselves and view ourselves from an objective distance, clearly perceiving our past and current patterns.

When the Full Moon conjuncts a planet, we naturally become aware of this planetary energy, and particularly aware of how we express this planet in relation to other people.[4] We intuit the needs, both fulfilled and unfulfilled, of this planetary self. Frequently, we project the energy, focusing upon our relationship to a particular person or activity represented by that planet. We may at this time make a decision which we will act upon at the following New Moon, or we may experience the internal or external consequences of an action initiated at the previous New Moon.

Therefore, a Full Moon conjunct a natal planet (or even opposing it, as the Sun is then conjunct the natal planet) signifies a very important time to reflect upon who we are in regard to this planetary energy, especially in relation to other people. Now is the time to meditate, to assess our lives, to clarify our relationships, to give ourselves the space we need to remain open to the influx of awareness which we may access at this time. Now is the time to contact our source of inspiration and to become aware of the meaning and purpose of our lives, particularly in regard to this planet.

Because of the somewhat unsettling influence of a Full Moon upon our emotions and bodies, we may need to ground ourselves by physical exercise, body awareness techniques, adequate diet and mundane chores. The Full Moon may lead to experiences of illuminating insight or painful alienation, contact with or separation from our own source and from other people. The more rooted we are in our own bodies and in the physical world, the more likely we are to have experiences which not only awaken and inspire us, but which can also lead to fulfilling and productive activities and relationships.

---

4. For example, at a Full Moon conjunct my 4th house Aries Moon, I decided to start my first cooking course and to begin my first job—as a waitress. At a Full Moon conjunct my 12th house Mars, I became interested in my 12th house issues, studied the 12th house and decided to write a book on the subject. At every Full Moon conjunct my Neptune, I have discovered the work of an inspiring writer who motivated me to write poetry.

Eclipses

Eclipses occur at New and Full Moons, when the Moon is conjunct its own Node. Most years, we experience two sets of solar and lunar eclipses, and each set consists of a solar eclipse (New Moon) followed by a lunar eclipse (Full Moon) 14 days later. During 2009 and most of 2010, the eclipse cycles are occurring first in Leo and Aquarius, and then Cancer and Capricorn.

Both solar and lunar eclipses involve a blockage of the light transmitted by the Sun or the Moon to the earth, and may influence us by actually blocking the "light of consciousness" and forcing us to deal more deeply than usual with subconscious as well as collective forces. Eclipses are generally considered to be Uranian in nature because of the unexpected events that often accompany them. Under their influence, Pandora's box may be opened; whatever emotional and psychic facets of ourselves we have ignored may explode into consciousness and demand our attention—whether directly through confrontation with our own internal demons and angels, or indirectly in projected form, through our confrontation with other people and external realities.

Frequently, we experience a "wipeout" in the house in which an eclipse occurs within our charts—a time of finishing up, ending, cleaning house, losing or ridding ourselves of past attitudes, behaviors, activities or people who have been important to us. A crisis may occur which demands our full attention. Although difficult, a powerful eclipse influence upon our charts may liberate us by compelling us to let go of whatever is keeping us mired in the past, so that we may more freely embrace the future unfolding within us. At such a time, flashes of insight and unexpected opportunities entering our lives may awaken us to new possibilities.

Solar eclipses tend to affect our vitality, either depleting or intensifying our supply of energy in regard to the sign or house being activated. Because the Sun, the "light of consciousness," is extinguished, our awareness may be clouded and incomplete; we may not view our lives from a clear or objective perspective or be able to make wise decisions. Lunar eclipses more directly influence our emotions and the irrational forces within us; we may hold on to a particular facet of ourselves or our experience during this time, as if operating from an afflicted Moon, clinging to a form of sustenance or security which eludes us.

Eclipses in fire signs usually provide challenges pertaining to our emotional and physical energy, as well as our activities; in earth signs, our material and physical existence; in air signs, the mental, interactive and communication-oriented realms of our lives; and in water signs, our feelings, particularly as related to sources of emotional nourishment and security. The sign of the eclipse, as well as the planets aspecting the degree of the eclipse (especially conjunctions, squares and oppositions within 5 degrees) *in the eclipse chart,* will influence the nature of the eclipse. Its placement in our charts and the aspects it makes to our planets will, of course, affect how we experience it.

Astrologers differ in their interpretation of the time span of an eclipse's influence. Certainly, we experience its effects several weeks before it occurs, but are we under its influence: a) until the next New or Full Moon? b) until the next solar or lunar eclipse, approximately six months later? c) for a length of time related to the length of the eclipse itself, with 1 hour = 1 year for solar eclipses and 1 hour = 1 month for lunar eclipses (i.e., a lunar eclipse lasting 5:12 hours would affect us for 5 months and 12/60 days or 5 months and 6 days)? My own experience attests that the primary time of influence is the month preceding the eclipse, and that if the eclipse conjuncts or closely (within 2 degrees) squares or opposes a natal planet, we experience an undercurrent of its influence until the next eclipse cycle. During this time, whenever a transiting planet (especially Mars or an outer planet) conjuncts the eclipse degree, the eclipse is reactivated.

When eclipses conjunct planets (within 2 degrees), their influence upon us is the most significant; squares or oppositions (within 2 degrees) may precipitate crises affecting our relationships to ourselves and other people; sextiles and trines (within 2 degrees) may have less influence, and usually feel quite beneficial, opening dimensions of our higher subconscious or superconscious and bringing people or experiences of a helping nature into our lives.

How can we prepare ourselves for an eclipse, particularly one conjunct a natal planet? First of all, we can orient ourselves toward "cleaning up" the areas of our experience that will be influenced. We can plan to finish what needs to be finished here, whether concretely experiencing an ending, or simply being open to giving up attitudes or habits which no longer contribute to our well-being. Certainly, before a lunar eclipse, we may want to create more time and space for ourselves so that we can effectively deal with our internal process. Usually, however, we will gain more from grounding activities than activities of inner expansion (such as meditation), because our psyches may be emotionally overloaded and may find any additional opening experiences to be counterproductive. Whether solar or lunar, an eclipse aspecting our charts is likely to compel us to deal with unexpected situations; the best preparation, therefore, is to create space for ourselves which will enable us to confront the unexpected without wreaking unnecessary havoc upon a too rigid or overcrowded schedule.

Doris Hebel, who has led many excellent workshops on eclipses, suggests that we fast on the day of an eclipse, that the week of a solar eclipse we eat citrus foods or other foods grown in the sun in order to increase our "solar energy," and that the week of a lunar eclipse we eat root vegetables or foods which are grown beneath the earth in order to increase our "lunar energy."

Using the Lunation Tables

The tables provided in the Appendix (see pages 304 through 312) give the position of New Moons, Full Moons and eclipses from 1960 to 2015, by degree of the zodiac. Their purpose is to enable us to easily research the influence of previous lunations upon our planets, angles and nodes, and to orient ourselves toward future lunations that will be affecting us. The best way for us to use these tables is to begin by looking up the degrees of our planets (or other astrological factors), noting every lunation that occurs within a two degree orb. We may want to pay particular attention to lunations conjuncting our planets during the next year, copying past data pertaining to these planets and lunations onto the Past Study Sheet provided for this purpose, and noting the upcoming conjunctions on the Future Study Sheet. The reader should make photocopies of pages 67 and 68, keeping the book's study sheets blank.

Our next step is to reflect upon and research our past, in terms of the time periods during which lunations conjuncted a chosen planet, angle or node. What was happening then? What were we experiencing? What seeds were sown? What seeds germinated? What common themes or patterns do we observe as we study the influence of seven or eight lunations upon one particular facet of our charts? What can we learn about the previous responses of this planet, node or angle to solar/lunar energies? Reflecting upon the meaning of the planet and house/houses involved may help us to uncover key dynamics of our earlier experiences.

PAST STUDY SHEET:
NEW AND FULL MOONS

List here each conjunction to your planet, angle or node, using a 2 degree orb (3 degrees for angles if your birthtime could be a few minutes in error.) Indicate New Moons, Full Moons and eclipses, and record your memories of earlier experiences associated with the two weeks preceding and two weeks following each lunation. Note also any pattern that emerges. (Photocopy extras.)

PLANET: _____ DEGREE, SIGN AND HOUSE: _____

ASPECTS: _____ MIDPOINTS: _____

DATE   DEGREE   ORB   PHASE   NOTES

1. _____

2. _____

3. _____

4. _____

5. _____

6. _____

7. _____

COMMENTS _____

_____

_____

_____

FUTURE STUDY SHEET:
HARNESSING THE POWER OF FUTURE LUNATIONS
(Photocopy extras.)

New Moon

DATE:_____ DEGREE & SIGN OF SUN & MOON:_____

ASPECTS TO OTHER TRANSITS (3 degrees):_____

HOUSE INFLUENCED IN YOUR CHART: _____

ASPECTS TO YOUR CHART (2 degrees):_____

CONJUNCTIONS:_____

OTHER:_____

What can you do to be/express this energy more fully? What intention might you set for yourself in regard to channelling the energy of this New Moon according to the planet, sign and house influenced?

Full Moon

DATE:_____ DEGREE & SIGN OF MOON:_____ SUN: _____

ASPECTS BY MOON TO OTHER TRANSITS (3 degrees): _____

HOUSE INFLUENCED IN YOUR CHART BY MOON: _____ SUN:_____

ASPECTS BY MOON TO YOUR CHART (2 degrees):_____

CONJUNCTIONS:_____

OPPOSITIONS: _____

OTHER:_____

What can you do to become more conscious of this energy, in terms of its house and the planets it aspects in your chart? How might you constructively use this energy in your relationships, as related to this area of your life? How might you synthesize the two houses being influenced? What new purpose/ meaning would you like to experience here?

As we attempt to perceive patterns unfolding over time, we might also choose to be aware of lunations occurring near the same degree of the zodiac every 9½ and 19 years—for example, a New Moon occurring 9½ years later near the degree of a Full Moon, and often related to it in meaning, or a New or Full Moon repeating itself every 19 years. Another interesting pattern is related to planets in our charts positioned 13–15 degrees apart, especially when they are in the same house. Because New and Full Moons are approximately 14 days apart, we may experience two lunations conjuncting planets in our charts within the same month. If both of these planets are in the same house, the affairs of that house are of primary significance throughout that month.

After using the Past Study Sheets for a planet, angle or node, we may be ready to turn our attention to the Future Study Sheet, in order to prepare ourselves for upcoming lunations. If we are focusing upon a New Moon, the questions on the following pages may be useful to us. Our aim, of course, is to understand the alternatives open to us at the time of the New Moon, and to be able to take advantage of the most constructive possibilities. Later, we may want to study conjunctions to each important facet of our charts, and even the influence of other aspects, particularly the square and opposition. Even these aspects may reveal to us enlightening patterns of behavior that may better enable us to make wise and satisfying choices in the future.

Questions for New Moon Conjunctions

Before we experience a New Moon conjuncting a planet, angle or node, we might want to prepare to gain maximum benefit from the lunation by asking ourselves the following questions. Each question should be related to the house in which the New Moon conjunction occurs in our charts:

NEW MOON CONJUNCT SUN: How might I more fully be who I am? How might I fully experience myself as the center or director of my life? What might I do to increase my confidence in myself? In what ways might I "shine"? (WOMEN: How might I be the center of my world, even in relation to men, rather than revolve around a man or allow him to express the male principle for me?)

NEW MOON CONJUNCT MOON: What might I do to more fully express and satisfy my emotional needs? How might I nurture or be nurtured? What would help me to experience greater rootedness and security in this area of my life? (MEN: How might I further contact and express my feminine energy rather than seek a woman to manifest it for me?)

NEW MOON CONJUNCT MERCURY: What do I need to communicate here? What knowledge might I gain? What thinking do I need to do about this realm of my experience? How might I satisfy my needs for variety and interaction here?

NEW MOON CONJUNCT VENUS: How might I establish more loving relationships here? What values do I need to fulfill and express? How might I satisfy my need for beauty, peace or aesthetic experience? What would enable me to experience a deeper relatedness?

NEW MOON CONJUNCT MARS: What new beginnings do I want to initiate here? What activities would be stimulating? What desires do I seek to gratify? How do I need to assert myself? What risks might I take?

NEW MOON CONJUNCT JUPITER: How might I expand my understanding or social contacts? How might I enrich my life and increase my confidence and sense of wellbeing? What do I wish to give here? What beliefs and philosophies influence my functioning? What are my future goals in regard to this area of my life?

NEW MOON CONJUNCT SATURN: What do I need to complete here? What work or responsibilities might I tackle? What commitments am I willing to make? How might I experience my strength and self-reliance here? How might I exercise my self-discipline and will? What do I need to do to stabilize and solidify this area of my life?

NEW MOON CONJUNCT URANUS: How do I want to change, liberate or transform this realm of my experience? How might I risk expressing my individuality and originality? How might I open myself to alternative ways of thinking and living? What experimenting would I like to do? In what ways might I more fully experience my freedom and independence? How might I contribute to humanity?

NEW MOON CONJUNCT NEPTUNE: What ideals do I wish to realize here? How might I contact and express my source of inspiration and faith? In what ways might I respond compassionately to others or be of service? How would I like to be creative? How might I heighten my experience?

NEW MOON CONJUNCT PLUTO: What life-and-death issues must I confront here? What must be eliminated? How might I die to the past? How might I totally involve myself in this realm of my life and deepen my experience here? How might I constructively express my power and be a healing influence?

NEW MOON CONJUNCT ASCENDANT: What might I do to experience and improve my relationship to my body? Who am I? Who do I wish to be? How might I outwardly express who I am and what I want? How would I like to come across with other people?

NEW MOON CONJUNCT DESCENDANT: What relationships are important to me? What new kinds of relationships do I wish to begin and how might I do so? How might I expand and deepen my connections with other people? What qualities and behaviors do I seek in my partner?

NEW MOON CONJUNCT I.C.: How might I secure my foundations and develop a greater security within myself? What might enable me to experience a more fulfilling home life and personal life? What new beginnings are needed in this realm of my life? How might I more deeply contact my core?

NEW MOON CONJUNCT M.C.: What do I wish to contribute to society now? What public or professional ventures might I begin? What can I do to experience more satisfaction out in the world? How might I experience myself as "on top of the world"?

NEW MOON CONJUNCT SOUTH NODE: How might I complete this phase of my preoccupation with past relationships and activities? What skills and talents have I developed here, and how might I direct them toward a new and life-enriching purpose?

NEW MOON CONJUNCT NORTH NODE: What skills, talents and behaviors might I develop and express now in order to become who I am capable of becoming? What dream do I wish to manifest here? What mission do I wish to accomplish, and how might I do so? How might I allow the love of God and humanity to help me to awaken and revitalize myself?

Although the above questions pertain to New Moon conjunctions and may help us to determine what we wish to begin or actualize at the

New Moon, we might consider them also when a Full Moon conjuncts planets in our charts. The New Moon is a time of *being* and *action*; the Full Moon is a time for *reflection* and *relationship*. Although we are not as likely to initiate a new phase of our lives at the Full Moon as we are the New Moon, we can benefit by reflecting upon our key issues in regard to the planets and houses aspected at this time. Insights and decisions occurring at the New Moon are likely to have a significant influence upon behaviors and actions occurring at subsequent New Moons.

These questions may also be useful to us when a lunation forms aspects other than conjunctions to our natal planets, angles and nodes. At the conjunction, we naturally experience and express a particular energy; at the square, we experience it in an intensified manner, usually in conflict with another facet of ourselves; at the sextile or trine, we easily access that energy and flow with it; at the opposition, we encounter it in relationship to other people, often confronting our own projections as we experience that planetary energy "coming at us" from someone or something external to ourselves. Whatever the aspect, we are nevertheless dealing with the same energy or planetary self, and can use it most beneficially if we become aware of its increasing influence within us and resolve to direct it in accordance with our values and aims.

Other Lunation Influences

HOUSES: New and Full Moons which make no close aspects to our natal planets will nevertheless influence the houses within which they occur in our charts. Although such influences are not as significant as lunations which aspect our planets, they will indicate beneficial times for new beginnings and expanded awareness in these areas of our lives.

MIDPOINTS: When New or Full Moons occur within a degree of our direct midpoints, they trigger the combined influence of the two planets involved. (The direct midpoint, for example, of a Sun at 16:33 Scorpio and a Moon at 14:13 Capricorn is 15:23 Gemini/Sagittarius.) This influence is especially significant if the two planets are natally in aspect, as the aspect which occurs between them will be activated. But whether in aspect or not, these two planets will be empowered by the lunation, and we will have an opportunity to experience, integrate and channel their energies.

If, for example, a New Moon occurs at our Moon/Neptune midpoint, we may feel particularly vulnerable, confused about our feelings and/or inspired and awakened to our higher Self. Foreseeing this New Moon, we might choose to provide ourselves with additional time to meditate, listen to music or express ourselves creatively. This New Moon may be the beginning of a new spiritual or creative phase of our lives.

SABIAN SYMBOLS: Those of us who respond easily to images may discover that the Sabian Symbols and images associated with them for the degrees of New and Full Moon have both personal and universal meaning for us at the time of a lunation. *An Astrological Mandala* by Dane Rudhyar is an excellent guide to the Sabian Symbols.

THE LUNATION CHART: Charts which are calculated for the time of a lunation reveal the influence of the lunation upon the collective and upon a particular locality. (The A.F.A. provides yearly booklets of lunation charts to its members.) Aspects formed by the Sun and Moon to the planets, especially those within 3 degrees, will influence the impact of the lunation upon us. For example, a New Moon closely conjunct transiting Saturn will have a Saturnian impact upon us, even if it conjuncts within our charts such a dissimilar planet as Neptune.

THE PROGRESSED LUNATION CYCLE: The progressed lunation cycle is one of the most important cycles which influences us, and is truly a guide to our individual psychological and spiritual evolution. Within the course of our lives, we are likely to experience between 5–6 progressed New and Full Moons, each marking turning points in regard to our relationship to ourselves, other people, the world and the universe. The progressed New Moon (progressed Sun conjunct progressed Moon) marks a new and often subconscious beginning—a time at which seeds are planets which will germinate throughout the following 14 years; the progressed Full Moon (progressed Sun opposition progressed Moon) marks a time of flowering, of experiencing the rewards and revelations of the previous years, or the alienation, separations and internal conflicts resulting from unwise choices and actions. Here again, the aspects formed by these lunations to our planets, houses and midpoints will color our experience of these key progressions. The Sabian Symbols for the degrees of these lunations are usually replete with meaning.

If we do not choose to invest the time and energy required to study the transiting New and Full Moons in relation to our charts, we can at least begin to fathom the immense importance of the lunation cycle by determining and reflecting upon the time periods associated with our progressed New Moons and Full Moons. We may be astonished to discover that not even the outer planet transits have as deep an impact upon us, or indicate so precisely our most significant experiences and transformations.

Chapter Four

THE LUNAR NODES: OUR LIFE PURPOSE

The North & South Nodes

The lunar nodes' axis in the birthchart is at least as significant as any of the planets, and of particular significance in regard to our psychological and spiritual development. The South Node indicates behavior patterns from the past—most likely early childhood and past lives—which operate compulsively and rigidly and often feel associated with our survival and identity; such patterns may also reveal innate talents and strengths which we utilize frequently. The North Node, on the other hand, points to a new path of growth and expression, a life purpose, or attitudes and behavior patterns which provide us with deep levels of nourishment and open us to experiences of oneness, union and integration.

The nodal axis is an axis, not merely two separate and unrelated points in space. The nodes operate in relationship to each other. Most of us will find that we benefit especially by consciously using the energies of our South Nodes in cooperation with and in order to fulfill the expression of our North Nodes. Whatever nodal placements we have in our birthcharts, we are nevertheless usually faced with the need to rework our South Node modes of being, awaken our North Nodes, *and also* express both nodes in harmonious relationship with each other. The importance of each of these three tasks will depend upon the specific birthchart. Those of us with South Node conjunct one or more planets may need to focus considerably upon working through the issues of the South Node before we can fully express the North Node and integrate the axis. Those of us with North Node conjunct one or more planets may already be attuned to our life task energies, but may need to cultivate the positive expressions of the sign and house involved rather than the negative expression. Those of us with Libra (or sometimes Virgo or Scorpio) rising, who have signs in reverse houses, such as South Node in Taurus in the 8th house and North Node in Scorpio in the 2nd house, or who have a node conjunct the ruler of the opposite node (for example. South Node in Libra and North Node in Aries conjunct Venus), are clearly dealing with issues in regard to bringing opposing energies into alignment.

Before we begin to focus intensively on the meanings of the South and North nodes as well as the process of integrating the nodal axis, let us consider exactly what the nodes are from an astronomical perspective. First, the lunar nodes are the points in space where the Moon crosses the ecliptic of the earth's orbit. The Moon passes from North to South latitude at the South node and from South to North latitude at the North node; its latitude is 0 degrees when it conjuncts one of its nodes. The nodes travel backward at the approximate rate of 3 minutes per day, through a sign in 19 months, and through the entire zodiac in 18½ years. Actually the true nodes (in contrast the mean nodes, which are approximate positions given in some ephemerides, and which may differ from the true nodes by as much as 3 degrees) move backward and forward, but their movement is primarily retrograde. Because of this retrograde motion, when a node is on the cusp at 0 degrees of a sign, it is clearly entering the previous sign and its meaning may be more reflective of that sign than the sign in which it is actually positioned. For example, a node at 0 degrees 10 minutes of Pisces is both Aquarian and Piscean in meaning, whereas a node at 29 degrees 40 minutes Aquarius is definitely considered to be Aquarius. Eclipses occur when the new or full Moon occurs within 10–12 degrees of a lunar node. Therefore, people born the day of an eclipse are likely to have both their Suns and Moons in conjunction with a lunar node.

In our birthcharts, the signs of our nodes indicate HOW we express the nodal energies, and the houses indicate WHERE we express those energies. One frequently overlooked factor in interpreting the nodes is the position of the nodal ruler—the ruler of the sign in which the node occurs. The ruler suggests by its sign and house a further dimension of life through which the node is or can be channeled. For example, someone with a North Node in Libra in the fifth house might experience fulfillment relating to children or engaging in artistic or cultural pursuits. If her Venus, the ruler of Libra, is in Pisces in the tenth house, such involvement or activities may point to a career in the arts or professional service to children. On the other hand, if her Venus is rising in Gemini, then she may physically and emotionally project the aesthetic, creative or playful facets of herself when making contact with other people.

Because we often refer to the lunar nodes as *nodes*, we forget that the planets also have nodes and that the *lunar* nodes are actually the nodes of the *Moon*. Thus, we may not realize how the lunar nodes are related in meaning to the Moon. If we regard the Moon as the chart indicator of mothering and of nourishment, then we can consider the Moon's nodes to suggest mothering on a more universal level. They show how we become attuned to the spiritual and evolutionary forces which guide us and suggest how we find nourishment on a universal level by ingesting and digesting energies which extend in time and space beyond this lifetime and beyond our bodies. The South Node is the gateway to the past and to previous sources of nourishment; the North Node is the gateway to the future and to the emerging energies of nourishment which can feed the self that we are becoming.

The South Node

The position of our South Node reveals the kinds of behaviors which feel most familiar and habitual to us, and in which we usually engage in a compulsive, rigid, or inappropriate manner. Most likely, we developed the expression of our South Node quite remarkably in past lifetimes and began to express this facet of ourselves early in this lifetime as a means of coping with stress and in order to feel secure. We hold on with our South Node; we return to easy unconscious behaviors as a means of restoring our equilibrium and experiencing emotional safety. When we are tired, ill or overburdened, we often experience our South Node as a resting space, a haven, a means of stabilizing ourselves and reconsolidating our energies. Because our South Node may be the primary indicator of qualities we carry from past lifetimes, our sense of identity is likely to be deeply connected with its expression. Our South Node may mean survival to us, and for this reason we may fear letting go of or turning our attention away from the behavior it represents. Because we have developed it so fully, it may indicate considerable talent, skill and strength which we sometimes take for granted, yet which may nevertheless be a primary means by which we contribute to our personal relationships and the world at large. However, because we are usually unconscious and rigid in our South Node behaviors, we may express its energies not only in situations which benefit ourselves and others, but also in inappropriate situations or in an inappropriate, exaggerated or inflexible manner.

Consider, for example, a woman with South Node in Gemini in the second house, who earns her living working part-time at several jobs.

Her diversity of skills may serve her, but she may also be handicapped by her difficulty in putting aside one task in order to focus for an extended period of time upon another. Her North Node in Sagittarius in the 8th house may actually benefit her by attracting into her life opportunities for financial gain through investment, inheritance, grants or gifts, but because of her tendency to cling to the second house concept of self-sufficiency, she may refuse to take advantage of these options and may deprive herself of the freedom they might bring, as well as the new opportunities for growth which they might make possible.

Frequently, we manifest the negative dimension of the sign and house in which our South Node is placed at least as often as we express the positive dimension, because our compulsive grasping here makes it difficult for us to learn from experience and consciously cultivate new and flexible modes of being. Surprisingly enough, in spite of our South Node capacities, we may indeed doubt our capabilities in regard to this sign and house. We rarely seem to feel complete here; we rarely meet our standards. Some internal pull keeps directing us to repeat the same behaviors over and over again, striving for that source of satisfaction which we expect they will provide. Yet no matter how intensively we express our South Node, fulfillment eludes us. Our bodies are craving vitamins and minerals, but we are eating foods with no nutritional value. Perhaps such foods nourished us in the past, and we therefore assume they will nourish us in the present. So we eat more, unable to understand that what we need is not more of the same, but rather another diet altogether.

In *The Astrologer's Node Book,* Donna Van Toen refers to the "yes but" rationalizations which keep us mired in our South Nodes. Perhaps we have South Node in Virgo in the 4th house and are trying to combine caring for a family with starting a career. Our South Node inclines us to remain aware of all the domestic tasks that remain undone or imperfect, and by focusing upon the dust on the windowsills or worrying about the children's health, we are unable to make time to discover or create our professional niche. Wherever we have the South Node, there will always be unfinished tasks; there will always be more we could do. It may be in our best interest to accept that reality, let go, and direct our attention to our North Node rather than allow South Node intellectualizations to keep us from moving forward. Many of us define our growth in terms of our South Node, which may indeed have been our growth indicator in past lifetime. But rather than facilitate the growth we really need, our South Node usually guides us down paths which become dead ends when we choose to wear blinders and are unwilling to explore the intersecting paths that lead in other directions.

Our South Nodes may indeed give us motivation and stability, as well as capabilities that are of real value, but when we spend too much of our time operating from our South Nodes, we are likely to experience disequilibrium, disintegration and suffering. We lose meaning and emotional connectedness; we lose contact with our inner source; we experience separation both from ourselves and others. The South Node provides us with foundations, but when we collapse into those foundations our lives become unconscious, automatic, unfulfilling, and devoid of meaning. We cease to grow.

The symbol of the South Node is reminiscent of upside down earphones; the symbol of the North Node, of earphones right side up. When we turn inward and make daily choices in regard to our focus of energy, we might want to ask ourselves: "Are my earphones right side up? Exactly what am I listening to when I tune into the cosmic channel—the voice of the past, my old self, or the voice of the future, my newly emerging potential?"

The North Node

The North Node is the astrological indicator of our life purpose, the faculty in ourselves which we most need to develop if we are to gain access to energies inside and outside ourselves which fulfill us and promote our growth. When we are expressing our North Node, we draw upon energies greater than ourselves; we contact our inner source; we attract to us people and opportunities which benefit us. The North Node nourishes by providing us with experiences which satisfy and leave us feeling whole and complete. Both our mental and physical health improve. When we are mired in patterns of behavior, relationships and situations which no longer serve us, an awakening of our North Node may shift our feeling experience and perspective and allow previously unrecognized possibilities to come to light. Our North Node activates capabilities within us which may have remained dormant for years because our cosmic generators were unplugged and inoperative.

For many of us, the North Node is also the key to becoming aware of the dreams we have harbored for ourselves but never realized. Peak experiences, moments of joy and fullness that we have known in the past may be directly related to expression of our North Node, or indirectly made possible because we first engaged in North Node attitudes or actions. Whereas the South Node may lead us to dissolution and separation, the North Node guides us to experiences of connectedness and union with ourselves and other people. Feeling whole within and in touch with our own essence, we make contact with the essence in others. We feed ourselves through experiences of union, and such feeding generates energy which can empower all areas of our lives.

Yet expressing our North Node is usually not easy; we must make an effort. Perhaps because our North Node sign and house represent qualities in ourselves and areas of life which we never truly manifested in past lifetimes, we feel like toddlers learning to walk or first graders attempting to read or write. We are hesitant and insecure as we develop our new muscles. We fear our North Node experience because we feel out of control, swept away or forced to relinquish the familiarity of focusing upon our South Node in order to give full attention to our North Node.

We are helped by people whose planets conjunct our North Node and by transits and progressions which likewise form conjunctions. We are also helped when we structure into our lives activities and situations which require us to draw upon our North Node energies. Consider a female professor who has no difficulty making use of her North Node energies. Her North Node is in Virgo in the 9th house; she teaches literary criticism at a university and therefore must access her North Node capabilities daily. Consider also an actor with South Node in Leo in the 10th house who chooses to live in a communal house with a group of people committed to cooperative living and social reform. In such a living situation, his North Node in Aquarius in the fourth house is continually reinforced.

Many people, seeking their life purpose, attempt unsuccessfully to find the career or job which will bring total satisfaction, or expect that their work is to be their primary contribution to humanity. Yet unless our North Node is in the 6th or 10th house or in Virgo or Capricorn, it may have little to do with vocational choice. Our life purpose is our own personal path of evolution. Such a path may involve relinquishing some of our investment in our work if, for example, our North Node is in the 4th or 12th house, and it may mean instead investing that energy into our personal lives.

Every day we are faced with choices in regard to every action that we undertake. Some of our choices are small and have few repercussions; other choices are large and have a major impact upon the rest of our lives. If our choices are aligned with the meaning of our North Node, they are far more likely to serve both ourselves and others than if they are not. Collecting quotations[1] and developing mantras which express our North Node (for example, "I am my own source of power" for Scorpio in the 1st house) can be aids to keeping us attuned to our life direction. When making decisions, we may want to ask ourselves questions which evaluate our alternatives according to North Node standards. If we have North Node in Aries, we might ask, "Does this choice excite and motivate me? Is it what *I* really want to do, apart from the needs and desires of other people?" If we have North Node in Sagittarius, we question: "Will I find meaning and purpose here, and the freedom to explore new horizons and discover my own truths?" Those of us with a Piscean North Node want to know, "Will this choice awaken my compassion and open my sources of inspiration?" A North Node in Leo similarly may lead us to ask: "Is this the path with a heart?" Whatever our North Node position, we can develop guiding questions and mottos which enable us to stay attuned to the direction which will enliven us, nourish us, empower us and help us to express our true nature.

The Node worksheets in this chapter can enable us to become more aware of our South Node patterns and our North Node potentials. (One worksheet is already filled out to illustrate how it can be used.) Because we are frequently blind to some of the possible meanings of our North Node, we might want to ask an objective observer, a fellow astrology student, to complete a North Node worksheet for us, so that we may perceive possibilities which are not immediately evident to us. Feel free to photocopy the worksheets in any quantity.

Integrating the Nodal Axis

The nodal axis is like an alchemical factory within our psyches through which we are capable of transforming the raw material of past lives and deeply engrained behaviors into new sources of energy. When our North and South Nodes operate cooperatively, we experience a continual mobilization of energy which catalyzes our growth. Frequently, however, we may be unable to relinquish the obsessive pull of the South Node, and we may find it difficult to awaken the latent potential of the North Node or to direct South Node abilities toward a North Node purpose.

---

1. Some of the quotations listed for Moon signs in chapter 2 might also be relevant and inspirational for our North Nodes.

NORTH NODE WORKSHEET

YOUR NORTH NODE BY SIGN & HOUSE: _____

ASPECTS TO NORTH NODE: _____

YOUR NORTH NODE RULER, ITS SIGN & HOUSE: _____

ASPECTS TO NORTH NODE RULER: _____

Keywords for North Node Sign	Keywords for North Node House	Keywords for Planets (if any) Conjunct North Node
_____	_____	_____
_____	_____	_____

Give ten or more meanings for your North Node by Sign and House:

1. _____
2. _____
3. _____
4. _____
5. _____
6. _____
7. _____
8. _____
9. _____
10. _____
11. _____

Keywords for North Node Ruler's House: _____

_____

Give five or more meanings for your North Node Ruler by House:

1. _____
2. _____
3. _____
4. _____
5. _____
6. _____
7. _____

NORTH NODE WORKSHEET (*sample*)

YOUR NORTH NODE BY SIGN & HOUSE: Pisces in the 3rd house

ASPECTS TO NORTH NODE: opposition Saturn and Sun, square ASC

YOUR NORTH NODE RULER, ITS SIGN & HOUSE: Neptune in Libra in the 10th house

ASPECTS TO NORTH NODE RULER: opposing moon, square Uranus, sextile Pluto

Keywords for North Node Sign	Keywords for North Node House	Keywords for Planets (if any) Conjunct North Node
imaginative, creative, sensitive, synthesizing, flowing, watery	immediate environment, relatives, perception, communication, writing	no conjunctions

Give ten or more meanings for your North Node by Sign and House:

1. brief trips to inspirational places (on water); weekend getaways

2. caring relationships with siblings and relatives

3. intuitive communication, imaginative communication

4. creative writing, freeflowing writing

5. music in daily environment

6. sensitivity and giving in daily interchanges; daily service

7. going with the flow in daily routine

8. basic learning/study/practice of the arts

9. attending cultural events (concerts, plays, museums, movies)

10. applying spiritual study; trusting intuition

11. sensitivity to/awareness of immediate environment

Keywords for North Node Ruler's House: public image, profession, self-employment, recognition, reputation, standing in society, employer, mother or father

Give five or more meanings for your North Node Ruler by House:

1. inspirational, creative profession—arts or creative writing

2. self-employed, directed by inner guidance or higher self

3. desire to make a meaningful contribution to society professionally

4. going with the flow in career, following inspiration

5. social service profession, gaining recognition for creative/service capacities

6. high ideals in professional commitments

SOUTH NODE WORKSHEET

YOUR SOUTH NODE BY SIGN & HOUSE: _____

ASPECTS TO SOUTH NODE:_____

YOUR SOUTH NODE RULER, ITS SIGN & HOUSE: _____

ASPECTS TO SOUTH NODE RULER: _____

Keywords for South Node Sign	Keywords for South Node House	Keywords for Planets (if any) Conjunct South Node
_____	_____	_____
_____	_____	_____

Give ten or more meanings for your South Node by Sign and House:

1. _____
2. _____
3. _____
4. _____
5. _____
6. _____
7. _____
8. _____
9. _____
10. _____
11. _____

Keywords for South Node Ruler's House: _____

_____

Give five or more meanings for your South Node Ruler by House:

1. _____
2. _____
3. _____
4. _____
5. _____
6. _____
7. _____

Some of us may consciously or unconsciously create lives in which both our South and North nodes function, but without any relationship to each other. Perhaps we have South Node in Libra in the 5th house and North Node in Aries in the 11th house, and we spend our days caring for our children, while during our evenings out of the house, we actively participate in an adult sports club which we have organized. Both activities may serve us, and we may do well to keep these two realms of our lives separate, paying for babysitters when we are not available to our children. Another person, however, might find more satisfaction in organizing a sports club for both children and adults, thus discovering ways simultaneously both to care for her children and to become involved in the physical activities which are important to her. Or consider a Gemini woman with Sun, Mercury and Neptune in Leo in the 10th house, South Node in Virgo in the 11th, and North Node in Pisces in the 5th house conjunct Mars. She chooses to earn her living through two very separate jobs, working part-time as a bookkeeper for a social service agency and performing as a jazz dancer. Another woman who expresses her Virgo/Pisces axis through her professional activities becomes a piano teacher, using her precise attention to technique, her sensitivity to music, and her creative capacities as she composes practice pieces for her students.

When we attempt to attune ourselves to the energies of our North Node without having fully activated that node, we may discover that we are doing our North Node area of life, but in a South Node way. With a Pisces North Node, we use our Virgo South Node to schedule precise, highly structured meditations. With a Gemini South Node and Sagittarius North Node, we dabble with a variety of self-improvement processes or take courses in five different subject areas at a local university, with no regard for developing a specialty in one area. With South Node in Aries and North Node in Libra, we commit ourselves to a marriage, but choose a partner who, with no interests of his own, is content existing only to meet our needs.

Often, when we are operating from our South Node exclusively and neglecting our North Node, we will experience interference in our lives suggestive of the negative dimension of our North Node, which is demanding attention. Working diligently from our Virgo South Node and refusing to take time to relax or awaken our Piscean inspiration, we may become absent-minded or forgetful or feel tempted to drink in excess as our Piscean North Node seeks to remind us of its existence. Some people experience dramatic shifts in their life when, after a long period of time functioning *from* their South Node, they experience increasing frustration and dissatisfaction which leads them to completely withdraw from their South Node area of life to make a North Node new start. Someone with South Node in Gemini in the 7th house and North Node in Sagittarius in the 1st house may leave a long-standing marriage in order to discover herself; several years later, she may shift again, sacrificing her newly explored personal interests for another partner.

Those of us who wish to avoid such pendulum shifts need to consciously decide to create a lifestyle in which the needs of both our South Node and North Node are met, so that one facet of ourselves does not have to be sacrificed to the other. How can we both pursue our interests and maintain a partnership? How can we, if we have a 4th house/10th house axis, combine a fulfilling home life AND a career? The more disconnected one facet of our lives is from the other, the more difficulty we may experience in integrating them. Working at home is, of course, a viable integration of a 4th/10th house axis, whereas pursuing a career as an airline stewardess while attempting to raise small children might present unresolvable problems.

One way to begin to discover methods of integrating a split axis is to become aware of the essence of the needs we are seeking to fulfill with each of our nodes and to relinquish attachments to specific forms which seem to contradict each other and which we might not be able to integrate. If we are determined to become an airline stewardess and desire to have children immediately with our new husband, we may be face to face with an irreconcilable dilemma, unless our husband is willing to tolerate our frequent absences and take full responsibility for childrearing when we are out of town, or unless we are able to procure a regular shift on a daily commuter flight. But if the essence of our desire to become an airline stewardess is the desire to travel, and the essence of our desire to start a family immediately is to have an outlet for our nurturing energies, more options might be available to us. Consider a woman and her husband who operate a summer camp for children in Austria, or who develop a business on-the-road, purchasing a trailer and raising a family while traveling and working throughout the U.S. In order to discover those difficult to discern possibilities for integration, we may first need to value each opposing facet of our nodal axis, become aware of the essence of the needs each is seeking to fulfill, and clearly brainstorm all the ways we might be able to meet both needs in our lives.

The issue of integrating the nodal axis is particularly significant for people who have either of the following patterns: a) the nodes in houses which oppose their natural placement (e.g., North Node in Aries in the 7th house and South Node in Libra in the 1st house) or b) the South Node is conjunct the North Node ruler or the North Node conjunct the South Node ruler (e.g., North Node in Taurus and South Node in Scorpio conjunct Venus, ruler of Taurus). In the first case, we must remember that the signs indicate energies and the houses areas of life; we express the energy of the nodal sign in the realms of life signified by the nodal house. North Node in Aries in the 7th house is not the same as South Node in Libra in the 1st house. Nor is North Node in Libra in the 1st house the same as South Node in Aries in the 7th house. Consider the following interpretations:

SOUTH NODE IN LIBRA IN THE 1ST HOUSE: tendency to project a pleasing image, and to define oneself through interchange with other people;

NORTH NODE IN ARIES IN THE 7TH HOUSE: learning to take initiative in meeting one's own needs in partnership, to initiate activities with one's partner, and to form close relationships with dynamic, motivated people.

SOUTH NODE IN ARIES IN THE 7TH HOUSE: tendency to let one's partner take the initiative, to choose fiery or possibly aggressive partners, and to sacrifice oneself in order to satisfy partner's needs;

NORTH NODE IN LIBRA IN THE 1ST HOUSE: learning how to make harmonious contact with other people and be responsive to their needs, cultivating a pleasing and sociable persona which recognizes one's own needs for beauty, peace, objectivity and relationship.

When the North Node is conjunct the ruler of the South Node, we cannot express our North Node without simultaneously tuning into qualities related to our South Node sign as expressed through its ruler. When we are activating our North Node in Scorpio conjunct Venus, we may carry with us the warmth and security needs of our Taurean South Node. Likewise, when the South Node is conjunct the ruler of the North Node, we cannot express our South Node without also stimulating qualities related, if only indirectly, to our North Node. Having South Node in Pisces and North Node in Virgo conjunct Neptune, we may turn our attention to the detailed analytical work of our North Node, while simultaneously drawing from our compassionate and inspirational nature.

Often we may fear that if we relinquish our focus upon our South Node dimension of life that we will be completely adrift and unable to draw upon the resources and securities we have cultivated at the South Node. But this is usually not the case, particularly if we have laid the South Node groundwork. In my own life, with South Node conjunct Saturn in Virgo in the 9th house, as well as conjunct Sun in early Libra, I have spent arduous hours preparing lecture notes, fearful that if I didn't have every idea clarified and precisely written down that I would go blank, become confused, or not know what to say (the negative dimension of Pisces). My South Node requires that I carefully prepare my talks, but if I am unable to relinquish the South Node when in front of a group, and I read my lectures rather than use my notes as a back-up guide while trusting myself to speak spontaneously, my presentation is far less inspiring than when I rely less upon Virgoan modes of being. Yet in order to develop the Piscean trust as well as to access my intuition in the moment, I must lay the Virgoan groundwork. Once my notes are fully organized and prepared, they serve as an anchor, and I do not have to depend completely upon them.

Another personal example reveals how, once we are open to discovering and learning the lessons of our North Node, we can become aware of numerous daily choices through which we are free either to attend to our South Node, activate our North Node, or discover a means to express them in alignment with each other. The first time I taught the lunar nodes, I awakened early the morning of the workshop to finish preparing numerous worksheets for my students. Time was limited, and I felt pressured to complete every page I deemed important, as well as to walk to the local grocery store to purchase beverages for the lunch break. While walking home from the store, preoccupied with my planning, I became aware of the frightened meowing of a cat nearby, and saw, to my dismay, a cat perched high above me in a tree, clutching the topmost branch and unable to get down. At that moment, I realized that I had a choice—if I took the time to rescue the cat in my neighborhood (North Node in Pisces in the 3rd house), I would not complete the "very important" worksheets I was finishing (South Node in Virgo in the 9th house) for my students. But what was really more important? Aware of the synchronicity of the event, I could only make the North Node choice. I rescued the cat, did not complete the worksheets, and taught the workshop, at which the worksheets proved to be unnecessary. I was able to tell my cat story, which may well have been more inspiring to my students than one more analytical task would have been.

Every day we are faced with North Node choices. When we take the North Node path and experience the anxiety of turning away from South Node familiarity, we usually discover that we still have our South Node capacities to draw upon, but that such capacities are much more beneficial to ourselves and to others when they are channelled through our North Node modes of being.

Aspects, Synastry & Transits:
Aspects to Lunar Nodes

When a planet is conjunct the South Node (within approximately five degrees) and opposing the North Node, that planet is likely to represent a faculty we have developed in a past lifetime and also early in this lifetime, which, like our South Node, signifies an innate talent, but which also can become automatic, compulsive, rigid, and nonadaptive. This planet indicates a subpersonality or internal self which frequently dominates us, although its influence may remain outside our awareness. We are so deeply identified with the function of this planet that we rarely see how it operates. Its hidden influence may actually seem to give it 12th house connotations.

For example, Saturn conjunct the South Node, like Saturn in the 12th house, may suggest omnipresent fears and anxieties which underlie most of our actions, as well as a deep layer of internal holding, sometimes experienced as a kind of internal wall; positively, Saturn conjunct the South Node indicates an innate capacity for hard work, responsibility and commitment. Moon conjunct the South Node may indicate deep-seated dependencies, but also the capacity both to nurture and be nurtured. Whatever planets conjunct the South Node, they tend to act as lenses through which we perceive reality. Their fit is usually so tight and their use so constant that most of the time we are not aware that we are "wearing" them.

Planets conjunct our South Nodes, like the South Nodes themselves, need to be brought to consciousness and reassessed. Often therapeutic experiences involving recollection and reworking of early experiences and attitudes related to these planets, or past life regressions with themes reminiscent of these planets, aid in this process. Those of us with planets conjunct the South Node may need to spend a major part of our lives reprocessing the past; yet such reassessment need not hinder satisfaction and accomplishment, since the virtues and strengths of our South Node planets are readily available. Our greatest difficulty may be to relinquish the grip of that planet when letting go is in our best interest and to access the qualities of our North Node. If several planets conjunct our South Node, or our South Node is involved in a stellium, our task then is a great one. The pull of the South Node patterns may not only generate remarkable energy for achievement or expression in this realm of life, but also provide remarkable motivation for surmounting the regressive pull and thus awaken in us new modes of being.

In my own life, my Mercury/Venus/Saturn/South Node/Sun stellium in the 9th house, with Saturn and the Sun each approximately four degrees from the South Node, has been both a blessing and a burden. My intellectual and philosophical motivation has been constant throughout my life, especially in regard to finding meaning in my experience and sharing my understanding with others; yet the fear associated with Saturn has frequently kept me locked within a 9th house ivory tower of books and papers, unwilling and unable to venture into the larger world.

Two experiences in my life most contributed to my developing the capacity to use my 9th house talents rather than be used by them, as well as to awaken my North Node. One experience was a helping relationship with a man (note my Saturn conjunct South Node conjunct Sun) whose Neptune/North Node conjunction in Virgo conjuncted my Saturn/South Node conjunction. The other experience was the death of my father, which occurred when Neptune (ruler of my Pisces North Node) last transited my ascendant. When the South Node is conjunct a planet representative of one of the parents (Moon, Sun or Saturn), the attachment to and identification with that parent may be so deeply engrained (and often just as deeply unconscious) that the death of that parent can be experienced as the death of the self that one has known. Such an experience can be terrifying because of the degree of disintegration we may encounter; on the other hand, it can also be liberating, because we are at long last given an opportunity to transcend the patterns which have bound us for many years, and perhaps even for many lifetimes.

Planets conjunct our North Nodes (within 5 degrees) aid us in our capacities to develop North Node functions. Such planets will color the meaning of our North Nodes with their own meanings, in both positive and negative manifestations. Having planets conjuncting our North Nodes does not insure that we will be using our North Nodes constructively; indeed, we may too easily become attuned to the most superficial dimensions of the planets, signs and houses in question, rather than cultivate deeper meanings and expressions. A North Node conjunct Venus in Taurus can incline us to place undue emphasis upon physical beauty at the expense of learning to love; a North Node conjunct Pluto in Leo may incline us to cultivate experiences of intensity and/or sexuality without regard for the value or wisdom of such experiences for our overall wellbeing. When the North Node conjuncts several planets or is situated within a stellium, we have an added boost from the universe in terms of utilizing our North Node energies; yet we still have lessons related to reworking and constructively expressing our South Node, integrating both nodes, and discovering the most favorable manifestations of our North Node planets and signs. Those of us with planets conjuncting the North Node are nevertheless fortunate, and are much less likely to become mired in deep-seated patterns from the past. Indeed, such planets in conjunction have considerable potential for helping us find nourishment inside and outside ourselves and for attracting to us opportunities which fulfill us and further our growth.

Planets in trine or sextile (within 3 degrees) to the nodal axis do not seem to have as powerful an influence as planets in conjunction, but may aid us in regard to integrating the polarities of the opposing signs. These planets can guide us to experiences which help resolve the problems related to the nodal opposition. Sometimes, however, they may have a detrimental influence upon us, because trines especially tend to take the path of least resistance, the easy habitual path, and the easy habitual path of the nodal axis is in the direction of the South Node rather than the North Node. We may, because of such trines or sextiles, lack the motivation we need to awaken our North Node capacities.

Squares to the nodal axis, however, may be quite empowering as well as conflicting, creating a kind of t-square pattern which pulls us away from the nodes themselves toward the planet in question. Such a planet is energized by both the past and future dimensions of the nodal axis, with all its karmic manifestations. Because of these squares, it gains strength, but how we use that strength and power is a matter of individual choice. The squaring planet may further complicate the tension of the nodal axis, increasing the amount of conflict we experience, but also motivating us to attempt to resolve it. It may also, as the midpoint of the nodes, introduce us to experiences which will help us transcend our nodal difficulties. This planet deserves special attention and can often be considered the most karmic and transformative planet in the chart. Because the nodal axis is the axis of growth and transformation, squares to the nodes can clearly be considered as far more beneficial from an evolutionary perspective than trines and sextiles.

A few of us, because of two opposing planets squaring our nodal axis, or our nodes in square to our ascendant/descendant axis or midheaven/nadir axis, may have a kind of nodal grand cross. In this situation, we feel pulled in four directions rather than two directions, and may indeed feel powerless in regard to ever "getting ourselves together" and functioning with any degree of internal harmony. Yet the additional squares likewise provide additional motivation, and the additional opposition increases our awareness. The energy contained within this configuration, as well as the capacities of each of the planets or angles involved can lead to understanding and to integrated action that is significant, impactful and growth-promoting.

In my own life, having my ascendant/descendant axis in close square to my nodal axis, I have frequently discovered that expressing either or both of my nodes has interfered with, rather than promoted, my own self-projection at the ascendant and relationship-formation at the descendant. Attempting to bring all four realms of my life together has required considerable investment of time, energy and awareness, yet has also occasionally led to both internal and interpersonal experiences of profound union, communion, understanding, and transformative action.

Synastry: Nodal Aspects Between Charts

Aspects to the lunar nodes between charts operate similarly to aspects within charts. When another person's planet conjuncts our South Node, our South Node is influenced and reinforced by the specific features of that planet. Such links are often accompanied by a deep sense of familiarity and ease with the person in question. We feel like old friends from the start; we gravitate toward each other and feel especially comfortable relating on the level of the planet and sign involved. Perhaps we have been together in past lives and have long been connected in consciousness. If, for example, our South Node in Leo conjuncts a friend's Mercury in Leo, our communication and thought processes are in alignment; together, we are able to playfully, spontaneously, creatively and confidently share our thoughts.

Yet as natural as it may seem to relate to people whose planets conjunct our South Nodes, such relationships are frequently detrimental in the long run to our growth. The other person does, after all, continually reinforce the function within us which is already overly developed. There is no guarantee that he will express his planet constructively, that he will stimulate the most positive dimension of our South Node, or that he will indeed help us to let go of our negative South Node patterns. In fact, he is likely repeatedly to pull us backward into this realm of our lives and away from our North Node lessons. For a short time, such relationships may be enjoyable and validating; our South Node insecurities may evaporate as this facet of ourselves is confirmed by the other. (Although, of course, if the other person's planet is in hard aspect to other planets in his own chart, he may be at odds with it himself, and therefore at odds with the South Node function in us.) But over time, we may begin to feel as if we are being pulled away from our own direction, as if doors are closing within us as we become locked within the narrow, compulsive South Node realms at the expense of other parts of our personalities and other potentials which need to be catalyzed. South Node conjunctions are the most tempting but probably the least beneficial indicators for long-term relationships if we aim to be fully expressing our North Nodes and awakening our larger capacities.

People whose planets trine, sextile or square our nodal axis influence both of our nodes. Trines and sextiles usually, but not always, pull us back to the South Node; squares invoke all our conflicts represented by our nodal axis, and at the same time motivate us to confront and resolve the issues in question. With all aspects between charts, much depends upon the nature of the planet in question, how strong it is, and whether or not the person is utilizing it constructively or destructively. Many variations can occur. One person's Neptune aspecting our South Node in Virgo can indeed help dissolve some of the overly analytical and critical Virgoan compulsions and awaken a Piscean North Node. On the other hand, if the aspecting planet is Mercury, Virgo is likely to be reinforced. Yet Virgo has many ranges of expression, and it is impossible to predict to what degree and in what manner our South Node qualities will be altered by the other person's influence. Indeed, some people may stimulate our South Node more than our North Node, but through contact with them we actually rework and liberate ourselves from the negative dimensions of our South Nodal issues.

Despite the infinite variety of circumstances and aspecting possibilities, there is probably no more favorable indicator for relationships than a North Node conjunct another person's planets. Such an aspecting planet, each time it is expressed, stimulates our North Node energy. Much of course depends upon how the planet manifests; someone who expresses his Mars in Aries in an aggressive, abrasive way may provoke intense anger in us through our Aries North Node. We may choose not to associate at length with this person. Yet we may experience the mobilization we need in his or her presence. Someone caught in the depressive, rejecting facets of Saturn in Pisces may stimulate our North Node in Pisces by opening us to considerable pain and longing, but such emotional opening could lead us to awaken and develop our Piscean sources of inspiration, creativity and compassion.

Most of the time, experiencing a person's planet conjuncting our North Nodes is likely to be a positive experience, especially when such a planet is Sun, Moon, Venus or Jupiter. The Sun helps us to confidently project our North Node energies; the Moon nourishes and nurtures our North Node; Venus feeds it love; Jupiter promotes and expands it. For this reason, many happy marriages involve such planetary conjunctions with the North Node. Even the person with the aspecting planet benefits from such a partnership, because with our North Node we feed our partner's planet an abundance of life-affirming energy.

Reversed Nodal Connections

One other arrangement between charts which is of noteworthy karmic and evolutionary significance is a reverse node connection between charts, especially when the nodes are within five degrees of opposing each other. An example of a nodal reversal connection is a chart with North Node at 2 degrees Gemini and South Node at 2 degrees Sagittarius, in relation to a chart with South Node at 2 degrees Gemini and North Node at 2 degrees Sagittarius. People whose nodes are reverse will always be approximately 9 years 3 months older or younger than each other, or with gaps in age of 27¾, 46¼ or 64¾ years (see ephemeris nodal positions for exact time periods). If any indicators in the chart are indicators of soulmate relationships, probably the North Node conjunction to a planet and the nodal reversal best qualify. Such a "soul" connection, however, may take the form of friend/ friend, teacher/student, parent/child, employer/employee or virtually any other kind of bond; it does not necessarily indicate the potential for marriage or partnership.

When two people have nodes in reverse to each other within a few degrees, then what one person is naturally is what the other person needs to develop and vice versa. Instinctively being our South Nodal self, we stimulate the other's north Nodal self; instinctively being his/her South Nodal self, he/she stimulates our North Nodal self. Simply being in each other's presence sets powerful transformative energies in motion which impact both parties.

Consider, for example, the charts of John and Abigail Adams, both Scorpios, whose lives were portrayed in the 2008 HBO mini-series,

John Adams. Born nine years and several weeks apart, they have reverse nodes within a few degrees. John Adams, who had South Node and Moon in Aries, and Mars conjunct the North Node in Libra, was known for his assertiveness, determination, and often aggressive behavior in helping to establish the United States and serving as its second President. Later in life, however, he actively devoted himself to his marriage. Abigail, his beloved wife and "dearest friend," had South Node in Libra and North Node in Aries. Sacrificing herself to her husband's career, especially during his many long absences, she learned to rely upon her North Node in Aries to support and raise her family, and also to express herself openly and honestly to her husband.

Although the nodal reversal is one of the most dynamic and growth-producing connections which can occur between charts, it also has disadvantages. The first disadvantage is that the other person may not serve as a constructive example of the particular sign in question. We, with our North Node in Leo, may need to learn to open our hearts, express ourselves personally and creatively and develop confidence in our individuality; another person's South Node in Leo may upon occasion stimulate the egotistic, bombastic, or arrogant facets of Leo rather than its warming, spontaneous, and ego-aligning qualities. A second disadvantage, which often becomes evident when two nodal reversal people have formed a relationship and begun to influence each other significantly, is that a push/pull pattern can occur, as each person seeks to move in the direction of his North Node but feels blocked or thwarted by the other who keeps guiding him back in the other direction. For example, if we have North Node in Aquarius and and South Node in Leo, we may relish the company of a North Node in Leo/South Node in Aquarius individual whose nodes conjunct ours because such a person has the detachment and social/political/metaphysical consciousness which helps us overcome our South Node in Leo tendency to become stuck in emotional issues and ego insecurities. However, this person may be attracted to our heart-centered and personally expressive mode of being and seek to guide the interaction toward shared experiences which maximize Leo rather than Aquarius qualities.

Yet despite the push/pull, the nodal reversal between individuals has powerful capabilities for activating the growth potential of both parties. People whose nodes are in reverse signs to us, but not in aspect to our nodes, may also be helpful to us in regard to awakening us to our North nodal energies; likewise people whose nodes are in reverse houses from us, apart from sign, have lessons to teach us about attunement to the house in question.

In my own life, I have experienced the greatest fulfillment and growth in a long-term helping/teaching relationship with a man whose South Node/Moon conjunction in Pisces conjuncted my North Node within two degrees, and whose North Node/Neptune conjunction in Virgo conjuncted my Saturn/South Node conjunction in Virgo within two degrees. This is an example of a nodal reversal, North Node conjunction and South Node conjunction occurring simultaneously, with all the positive and negative factors of each in operation. I have also consistently sent out requests to the universe to bring into my life people whose planets conjuncted my North Node, and whose nodes reversed my own, and have been amazed at the number of people I have met with such aspects to my chart.[2] All such relationships have been growth-promoting for me, although two were painfully short-lived because of the particular mode of expression of the other person's planet conjunct my North Node. In spite of these two difficult experiences, I remain convinced that North Node conjunctions and nodal reversals between charts are keystones for building relationships which will spur us forward on our personal evolutionary paths, and that we can gain enormously through seeking and cultivating such soul connections.

Transits, Progressions and the Nodes

Our lunar nodes are continually stimulated both by our relationships and by the unfolding influences of transits and progressions. Four particular kinds of transit influences deserve special attention because of their capacities to catalyze our nodal axis and force us to confront our unresolved issues from the past and our emerging new developments. These are:

a) transiting planets (as well as lunations and progressed planets) in aspect to our nodes;

b) transiting North and South nodes in aspect to our planets;

c) the aspects formed between transiting and natal nodes;

d) the daily cycle of the chart involving the ascendant in conjunction to our nodes and to the transiting nodes. Let us consider each of these in turn.

---

2. Once in a workshop I mentioned that I had prayed for people with conjunctions to my North Node to enter my life, and that my prayers were answered immediately. A student in the workshop responded, "But you have North Node in Pisces! People with planets in Pisces were listening!"

Transits to the Nodes

When transiting and progressed planets, as well as the new and full Moons conjunct our North and South Nodes, the energy of the nodes is activated by the specific expression of the aspecting planet. Transiting Saturn may consolidate and focus our energy in alignment with a node; transiting Neptune may confuse, sensitize and inspire us. Transiting inner planets and lunations make only brief contacts, whereas transiting outer planets and all but the Moon's progressions may trigger our nodes for months or years. Because of the current cycle of outer planets between Scorpio and Aquarius, those of us with a node in these signs are under the long range influence of many powerful transits conjuncting either our North or South Nodes; we may experience ourselves as existing within a lengthy phase of either reworking the past or developing new functions. It is useful to pay attention even to the monthly passage of the Moon over our North Nodes, as well as Sun, Mercury, Venus and Mars conjunctions and the occasional new and full Moons which occur there, because the awarenesses, actions and opportunities we experience at these times may alert us to our most beneficial modes of being. Consciously engaging in activities represented by our North Nodes and the transiting planet in question at these times is likely to lead to significant breakthroughs of insight and alignment with our particular evolutionary path.

Transits and progressions in square to our nodal axis are empowered by the t-square-like configuration they create. As focal planets, they receive both the conflicting and motivating energy of the nodal opposition. Likewise, they create experiences for us which activate, highlight and spur us to resolve our nodal issues. Indirectly, our North Node and South Node may be influenced by transits of their rulers to planets and angles in our charts. If we have North Node in Aquarius, the transit of Uranus across our ascendant may help us attune to Aquarian energies. If we have South Node in Aquarius, such a transit may indirectly activate issues related to our Aquarian South Node.

The Transiting Nodes

When the transiting nodes change houses in our charts, they direct our attention to new opportunities for growth presented in the house of the transiting North Node; they also warn us about experiences of compulsion and/or disintegration in the house of the transiting

South Node. When the transiting South Node conjuncts a planet, it frequently pulls us back into a regressive, unresolved behavior related to that particular planet in order for us to reassess and rework our expression of that planetary energy. When the transiting North Node conjuncts a planet, it may at first bombard us with negative energies associated with that planet, but such purging usually occurs in order for us to clear out the dross and become aligned to that planet's highest potential. The transiting North Node conjunct a Pluto in Cancer may attract to us experiences of powerlessness or emotional turmoil before awakening our healing and self-empowering energies. A transiting North Node conjunct Uranus in Taurus may bring about a dramatic financial upset before inspiring us to embark independently and intuitively upon a new project. The transiting nodes in square to a natal planet create a t-square-like configuration to the natal planet, funneling into it the intense energy of nodal conflicts and opportunities, so that the planet may indeed be utilized as a potent agent for change and integration.

Aspects Between Natal and Transiting Nodes

At least as significant as transiting planets aspecting nodes and transiting nodes aspecting planets are the aspects the transiting nodes form to the natal nodes, particularly the nodal return occurring every 18½ years, the nodal reversal occurring every 18½ years and the nodal square (transiting nodes square natal nodes) occurring every 9¼ years.

When we are approximately 18½ years old, 37 years 2 months old, 55¾ years old, and 74½ years old, the transiting nodes conjunct our natal nodes, attracting into our lives experiences which are directly related in meaning to our nodal axis, and which usually present us with choices regarding the expression of our South Node, the development of our North Node, and the integration of the two polarities. When we are approximately 9¼, 27¾, 46½, and 65 years old, the transiting North Node conjuncts our natal South Node, and the transiting South Node conjuncts our natal North Node. This nodal reversal is particularly important because it introduces insights, experiences and relationships which may provide us with opportunities for resolving our nodal dilemmas and bringing our North and South nodes into harmony. Every 9¼ years, between the nodal returns and nodal reversals, the transiting nodes square our nodal axis, often dramatizing the issues related to both nodes and opening within us a channel by which some of our conflicts may be resolved or transcended. Frequently, when the nodes aspect each other (as well as when planets aspect the nodes), we may experience internal shifts from either a South Node pattern to a North Node pattern or vice versa, or we may discover previously un-recognized ways of integrating our nodal axis.

Profound breakthroughs can occur for us when the nodes aspect themselves and when transits or progressions conjunct the North Node, especially when we consciously choose to create experiences which may facilitate the occurrence of such breakthroughs. In my own life one such breakthrough occurred at my nodal reversal, when after several years of feeling mired in Virgoan South Node analytical qualities, as well as a long-term relationship with a man who had a t-square to his Moon conjunct my South Node and Saturn, I attended a week-long writing conference. There, I met a children's book writer who had a Sun/Venus conjunction on my North Node in Pisces in the 3rd house. Sparked by her inspiration, I spent the entire week writing a children's fantasy novel, which was also an allegory of my own life venture. The opening I experienced during that week transformed me so profoundly that I ter-minated the relationship I had been in and began an entirely new phase of writing and teaching which drew at least as much from my Piscean modes of being as from my Virgoan intellectual capacities.

I have also witnessed notable breakthroughs in students and cli-ents who, conscious of significant nodal transits, have made timely choices which allowed for highly favorable opportunities to appear in their lives. Consider, for example, a woman with Venus conjunct South Node in Cancer in the 3rd house and North Node in Capricorn in the 9th house who was a beautician by day and a spiritual student by night. Dissatisfied with the superficial chatter of her beauty shop clien-tele when her soul was aspiring to 9th house goals, she was reassessing her professional choices when the progressed Moon approached her North Node in the 9th house. Aware of this progression, she decided to spend a month studying in a spiritual community. She returned a month later with news that she had discovered a beauty parlor for sale on the premises there, had bought it, and was moving immediately to a locale where she could utilize her skills as a beautician, working with clients who were spiritual students. By taking advantage of her North Node aspects, she attracted to herself a situation which clearly fulfilled the need of both her South and North Nodes.

Daily Cycles and the Nodes

Apart from direct aspects between transits or progressions and our natal charts, we can also make use of the transformative potential of the nodal axis by becoming aware of those times of day when our particular nodal patterns are triggered, as well as when the energy of the transiting nodes is activated. When the degree of our South Node crosses the ascendant in our locality, we instinctively attune to our South Node energies. This is a time for retreating into secure and consolidating patterns, making them work for our advantage; it might also be a superb time to engage in a past life regression or a therapeutic experience related to accessing and reworking past issues. When the degree of our North Node crosses the ascendant, we instinctively attune to our North Node energies. This is the ideal time for consciously taking a break from our daily routine and revitalizing ourselves by aligning ourselves with the meaning of our North Node. Those of us with North Node in Gemini in the 11th house might pick up the phone and communicate with a friend; those of us with North Node in Virgo in the 4th house might choose to engage in such domestic organizing behaviors as housecleaning. Having North Node in Pisces suggests using music or meditation to soothe and awaken our spirit; having North Node in Leo suggests personal, spontaneous or creative self-expression.

Perhaps even more noteworthy than the times the degrees of our nodes cross the ascendant are the times and the degrees of the transiting nodes conjuncting the ascendant degree, because these times affect everyone in our locality. Everyone around us is responsive to the South Node for approximately 5–10 minutes each day, and likewise to the North Node twelve hours later. As we become conscious of these North Node times, we may become aware of the alive, transformative energy available to us during this brief time period, and the possibilities available for both individual and group experience. Imagine a group meditation occurring when the transiting Pisces ascendant is conjunct the transiting North Node in Pisces, or the earning capabilities of a group when the transiting North Node in Taurus conjuncts the transiting Taurus ascendant, or the group creativity which can be activated when the daily Leo ascendant and the transiting North Node in Leo coincide. These North Node time periods each day may be brief, but they are times of spiritual power during which our own potentials for growth, healing and integration, at a personal, social and planetary level, are catalyzed.

THE NODAL AXIS BY SIGN

Rather than specifically interpret the nodes by sign and house, which any astrology student can do who understands the meanings of the signs and houses,[3] I suggest that we focus upon the meanings of the nodal signs in polarity and the lessons to be learned in regard to integrating opposing signs. The chapter on oppositions in my book *Planetary Aspects: From Conflict to Cooperation*[4] contains interpretations of the negative and positive dimensions of opposing signs; this material is also valid for the nodal axis. The interpretations which follow here are expansions of this previous work on integrating polarities, with specific application to the nodal axis.

Aries/Libra Lunar Nodes: Lessons

LESSON #1: Only when we have ourselves can we fully meet another human being without losing ourselves. Only through fully knowing our desires, feelings and needs and being able to assert them can we form relationships which consist not of two half people attempting to become one, but rather two whole people forming a bond which includes and transcends them both. Only when we know our true wants and needs and take responsibility for expressing and satisfying them can we really attune to the true wants and needs of others and respond to people in the most constructive ways. We may not always please them superficially, but we are likely at least to please and affirm the facets of them which are committed to real nourishment, integration and growth. We may not always win the love and approval of their lower self, but we do endear ourselves to their higher self.

LESSON #2: Attunement to ourselves is also attunement to others, because within the deepest realms of our subjectivity resides objectivity and collective awareness. As we contact that dimension of ourselves, which is also our connective tissue to others, we begin to develop an "I that includes the We"; the needs and feelings of the other seem as valid and important as our own. From the "I that includes the We," we become able to build a "We that includes the I," a partnership which

---

3. For specific interpretations **on** the nodes by sign, see *The Astrologer's Node Book* by Donna van Toen, and *Karmic Astrology: The Moon's Nodes and Reincarnation* by Martin Schulman.
4. *Planetary Aspects*, published in 1987, was originally published in 1979 under the title *How to Handle Your T-Square*.

values and satisfies the needs of each individual. Because of our "I win, you win" expectation and philosophy, rather than an attitude of "I win, you lose" or "you win, I lose," we learn to negotiate ways in which we can both fulfill our most essential desires and still maintain relationship. In our commitment to the well-being of our partner as well as to our own well-being, we are likely to discover that the other person, feeling acknowledged and respected, seeks to meet our needs and fulfill our desires. Rather than lose ourselves to gain another or gain ourselves at the expense of another, we become more capable of both finding and fulfilling ourselves within the context of relationship.

LESSON #3: When we are willing to experience conflict within ourselves and with others, while retaining the aim of peace, we become capable of creating both inner harmony and harmony in relationship which is active and dynamic. When avoiding conflict for the sake of superficial peace, our lives become like stagnant pools of water, and we have little real relationship to ourselves and others. Likewise, if we are continually generating conflict, we also sacrifice real connectedness. The peace that is capable of confronting and transcending conflict, the peace of the ocean in a storm, soothing and yet surging with movement and feeling, cannot be lost despite moments of anger and stress. It is alive, vital, centering and enduring.

LESSON #4: When our actions follow consideration of alternatives as well as the needs and feeling of other people, when we allow space for reflection about our most essential desires and the desires of others, we are likely to establish balanced and cooperative action which fulfills us rather than separates us from others or leads to frustration. Our Arian nature, through inclusion of Libra, finds its greatest satisfaction. Likewise, our Libran nature benefits by including Aries. If, when assessing various alternatives and perspectives, we maintain our commitment to act, even when it means a risk of making the wrong choice or displeasing others, we are able to discharge the tension locked in the battle between alternatives and to restore our balance and harmony.

Quotations for Aries/Libra Lunar Nodes

I was brought up to be the person others wanted me to be, so that they would like me and not be bothered by my presence. When I began to be ME, I felt that I had more to give. —LIV ULLMAN

To give oneself has no meaning unless one possesses oneself. You can give only what you have. —ALBERT CAMUS

To meet another and hold your own ground is one of the most difficult tasks in the world, and most of us alternate between various forms of non-meeting instead. —MERLE SHAIN

There is one relationship that will always be there for you: your relationship to yourself. —KENNETH WYDRO

Enmeshed in the strands of a dozen alternatives, unable to select one path when so many paths intersect, I have sat for hours here at this resting place, examining and evaluating each option before me, searching for the minute evidence which would enable me to make the perfect choice . . . But when I am unable to find that evidence, when the answers are unknown or unreachable, and one question depends upon another which depends upon the first, I know that I remain paralyzed at this crossroads not because of want of evidence but because I am unwilling to expend the energy to choose and act upon my choice . . . For the source of meaning now lies not in the right decision but the commitment to one action, one person, one path. No path reveals its end at the beginning. A pump must be primed, a fruit must be allowed to ripen, and I, a climber of inner Everests, must follow one path to its conclusion in order to discover that the sweat and struggle climbing can imbue any choice with value, more than days and months and years attempting to make the perfect choice.

—TRACY MARKS *(from an unpublished manuscript,* A Passing of Clouds.*)*

Aries/Libra Concerns:

relationship between self and other • maintaining self in relationships • coping with interpersonal conflict

Aries/Libra Issues:

subjectivity vs. objectivity • action vs. reflection • conflict vs. harmony

Aries/Libra Keywords:

daring to love • active partnership • an alive and dynamic peace • balanced and cooperative action • reflective action • independence in relationship

Taurus/Scorpio Lunar Nodes: Lessons

LESSON #1: The more we possess ourselves and the more we provide for ourselves, the less we need to possess others, and the less we expect others to provide for us. Other people cannot fill the void in our self-esteem; they cannot make up for our inability to respect, value and support ourselves. Through knowing what we have to use and to give, through valuing and utilizing our own resources, we can express our personal power in relationships rather than demand that others empower us.

As we develop our self-worth and self-sufficiency, we become more grounded and capable of functioning effectively in the physical world; as we determine and live by our true values, we become capable of using our power to benefit others rather than control or manipulate them in order to satisfy our own needs. As we begin to possess ourselves and stand on our own ground, we become more able to surrender emotionally and sexually; then we need not fear losing ourselves entirely in the intensity of merging. On the other hand, the development of internal security enables us to take the ultimate risk of losing ourselves, dying to past patterns and behaviors as we allow ourselves to experience the deepest levels of transformation.

LESSON #2: Through integrating the physicality/sensuality of Taurus and the sexuality/passion of Scorpio, we begin to experience an all-embracing sexuality which involves total body fulfillment while affirming our values. Our sexual experiences reinforce and maintain our self-respect and respect for others, while simultaneously enabling us to surrender fully and know complete emotional, spiritual and physical satisfaction.

LESSON #3: The passion and intensity of Scorpio need not lead to self-indulgence or frustrating self-denial, but can be channelled and harnessed in our commitment to concrete practical action, as well as care for our own resources and our physical bodies. Energy which could be destructive to ourselves and others can become constructive when grounded in physical tasks and experience; it can build rather than destroy. Our ability to transform, sublimate and channel our desire nature can feed our self-esteem and self-support as well as lead to intensive and solid productivity in the world.

LESSON #4: Our values, established through Taurus, need to incorporate the awareness of what is really essential, which Scorpio can provide. Scorpio attunes us to that which makes us feel alive, that which resonates with our core energy. As we contact the deeper forces of our being we are able to discover and experience deeper and more substantial satisfactions. Knowing our truest values, we become able to eliminate that which is inessential in our lives, while holding onto what is essential. Taurus has holding power, and Taurus, once it has gained the essential awareness of Scorpio and Scorpio's eliminative capabilities, can enable us to hold to ourselves—to our highest values, and to our commitment to giving them concrete physical form in our lives.

Quotations for Taurus/Scorpio Lunar Nodes

I call neurotic any man
Who uses his potential to
Manipulate others
Instead of growing up himself.
He takes control, gets power-mad
And mobilizes friends and kin
In places where he's impotent
To use his own resources.
—FRITZ PERLS

Courage means the power to LET GO of the familiar and the secure.
—ROLLO MAY

I would have you consider your judgment and your appetite even as you would two guests in your house. Surely you would not honour one guest above the other; for he who is more mindful of one loses the love and faith of both. —KAHLIL GIBRAN

Taurus/Scorpio Concerns:

personal desire • inner power • sensuality and sexuality • money and personal resources • use of own and other's resources • personal will

Taurus/Scorpio Issues:

stability vs. intensity • accumulation vs. elimination • self-indulgence vs. self-denial • holding on vs. letting go

Taurus/Scorpio Keywords:

self-possession • transformed desire • constructive will • stabilized intensity • grounded passion • personal and productive power

Gemini/Sagittarius Lunar Nodes: Lessons

LESSON #1: Our philosophy of life, belief system and sense of purpose are given concrete meaning when we consciously and actively apply them in our daily interactions through our communications, behaviors and activities. By living rather than merely preaching our beliefs, we are able to test and refine them, eventually developing a viable belief system and life philosophy which can withstand stress and change.

LESSON #2: We can expand our awareness and sense of meaning in the present moment by remaining aware of our unique purpose and keeping before us our future visions and goals. By doing and expressing what is meaningful to us and keeping a unifying perspective, we are likely to experience deep fulfillment in our everyday activities, as well as to uplift and inspire the people around us.

Multiplicity and unity can exist side by side. We can have variety and stimulation which unifies rather than scatters our energies when we remain in contact with an overriding sense of meaning and purpose and make choices which consistently reflect that meaning. Whether we aim for love, nourishment, mutuality, self-respect or integration of body, mind and spirit, we can make choices and engage in diverse experiences in all realms of our lives which satisfy our needs for variety, freedom and newness while simultaneously enabling us to move forward in the direction of our goals.

LESSON #3: When we pursue knowledge for knowledge's sake, we may accumulate information which is interesting to us but which does not add to the quality of our lives or is not aligned with a purpose in which we believe. Knowledge can serve ends which are destructive as well as ends which are constructive, When we pursue philosophy for philosophy's sake, we may become enamored with the meaning we discover, but may not be able to apply that meaning in our daily interactions. As a result, our consciousness may expand, but our lives may seem barren and meaningless.

We need to pay attention to the relationship between means and ends. We need to ask ourselves: To what end do we seek knowledge and understanding, and how might we make use of our knowledge and understanding in order to improve the quality of our lives and the lives of others?

LESSON #4: When we are continually seeking outside of ourselves for what is missing, we may become eternal seekers, but never experience being finders. There is no end to our search if we are committed to the search and do not allow ourselves to stop, to fully experience the present moment, to FIND. What we are seeking may not be in the distance or in the future, but may rather exist in our present experience. Only by committing ourselves to discovering and living the meanings implicit in the present moment can we expand the quality of our present lives and become finders as well as seekers.

Quotations for Gemini/Sagittarius Lunar Nodes

We had the experience but missed the meaning.
—ANNE MORROW LINDBERGH

We may realize that what we are seeking so frantically elsewhere may turn out to be the horse we have been riding all along. —HARVEY COX

Our potentialities are, in fact, legion, and until we bring them under the guidance of a personal direction, they are likely to conduct themselves as demons . . . rather than as the angelic bearers of the abundant life.
—MAURICE FRIEDMAN

My business is to teach my aspirations to conform themselves to fact, not to try and make facts harmonize with my aspirations.
—THOMAS HUXLEY

Many a time I have wanted to stop talking and find out what I really believed.
—WALTER LIPPMAN

We shall not cease from exploration
And the end of all our exploring
Will be to arrive where we started
And know the place for the first time.
—T. S. ELIOT

One way in which I prevent myself from fulfilling any one aim is by trying to be everything, do everything, take in everything. But my body and mind become congested when I eat all the cookies on a plate, visit all my friends, read every book which interests me and include all I know in a chapter I am writing . . . I am trying now to weigh the raw materials of my life on a scale of importance, to determine my priorities and slice off the bottom of the list, much as a newspaper editor cuts an article, knowing that what is lost is not as significant as what has already been expressed . . . I must have time in my life to experience the meaningfulness of all that is meaningful to me; I must have space in myself which allows feelings and insights to penetrate the dense surface, so that what I accumulate is not a variegated spectrum of ideas and emotions amounting to nothing but the blankness of a madly spinning color wheel, but rather one hue or two or three, rich in value and intensity.

—TRACY MARKS *(from an unpublished manuscript,* A Passing of Clouds.*)*

Gemini/Sagittarius Concerns:

freedom • reaching out • expansion • interaction with others • learning and communication • mental stimulation

Gemini/Sagittarius Issues:

knowledge vs. understanding • logic vs. intuition • concrete vs. abstract • means vs. ends • diversity vs. unity • the present vs. the future • the here-and-now vs. the faraway

Gemini/Sagittarius Keywords:

multifaceted • purpose • practical wisdom • meaningful diversity • the expanded present • the dissemination of wisdom • inspired reasoning • purposeful interaction

Cancer/Capricorn Lunar Nodes: Lessons

LESSON #1: When Capricornian strength or self-sufficiency denies needs and represses feelings, it is shaky at best and leads to the emotional deprivation which can fuel compulsive attempts to fulfill ambitions and gain recognition. Only when we can allow ourselves to experience our real needs can we hope to meet them; only by experiencing our feelings can we gain emotional satisfaction. When we allow ourselves to be vulnerable, to need, to feel, to care for and be cared for by others, we can discover the inner strength which lies within our vulnerability. Just as our Capricornian walls may have soft Cancer linings, so may our Cancerian softness reveal sturdy Capricorn foundations.

LESSON #2: *As* we take charge of our lives and take responsibility for ourselves, an important task which we face is relinquishing the demands we placed upon our parents or the demands we place upon surrogate parents, and to learn instead to parent ourselves. As we develop the arts of self-nourishment and self-nurturance and learn to care for the feelings and needs of the child within us, we become capable of giving out of true responsiveness to other people's needs and out of respect for their separateness, rather than giving as an indirect means toward satisfying our own needs and creating dependency.

LESSON #3: As well as learning to nourish ourselves when outside support is not available, we need to learn to seek nourishment outside ourselves when and where real nourishment is available, instead of attaching ourselves to people and experiences which aren't nourishing. Attempting to drink from an empty well can only leave us feeling thirsty and wanting; we need to turn away from empty wells in order to discover wells which are full.

In learning to nourish ourselves, we must differentiate love and caring from hunger and longing. People who leave us feeling hungry and deprived are not nourishing people; their wells are empty. Their hearts may be stone, and we can't squeeze water from a stone. Those people who know how to love, how to give, how to nourish, do not evoke in us hunger and longing. After we have been in their presence, we feel warm, well-fed and full.

LESSON #4: Capricornian discipline, control and awareness of boundaries can help us to effectively channel Cancerian feelings and meet Cancerian needs. Rather than repress or indulge emotional needs, we can learn to be with our deepest feelings and develop an internal control system which guides rather than suppresses. Like a plant, our Cancerian inner child needs to be both watered and pruned, to be fed and also disciplined, restrained or cut back upon occasion so that he/she may grow healthy and strong. Capricornian limits also enable us to safeguard and constructively express our Cancerian nurturing potential. Only when we can establish our own boundaries and set limits, giving in appropriate ways at viable times, and to people who do not drain us, can we maintain our capacity to give that which really matters.

LESSON #5: Our Cancerian desires for warmth, family and emotional nourishment do not necessarily conflict with our worldly pursuits and ambitions. We can commit ourselves to professional goals which take into consideration our personal feelings and needs. By developing a "family" of professional colleagues with whom we can exchange warmth and experience emotional security, as well as by relating on a caring, feeling level to the public at large, we can not only create emotional fulfillment in our work life, but can also increase our chances of professional success.

Quotations for Cancer/Capricorn Lunar Nodes

Total commitment to family and total commitment to career is possible, but fatiguing. —MURIEL FOX

If you are not cautious, you will start to belong.
—ANONYMOUS

Their love is . . . too tense, or too lax. —LOUISE BOGAN

Learning how to make others trust you is the best protection there is. And it will make you safer than all the armor you can find.
—MERLE SHAIN

Anyone who assumes a position of being responsible for another's care is subject to the corrupting temptations that come with power. Even the most loving care soon is subtly transformed from offering what the dependent asks for to imposing what the donor believes the other person should have.
—SHELDON KOPP

My room is like a bit of June,
Warm and close-curtained fold on fold,
But somewhere, like a homeless child
My heart is crying in the cold.
—SARA TEASDALE

Cancer/Capricorn Concerns:

security, safety and protectiveness • retreat and withdrawal • foundation-building • establishment of boundaries • parenting • support and self-support

Cancer/Capricorn Issues:

child vs. parent • personal life vs. professional • life dependency vs. self-sufficiency • emotional indulgence vs. emotional control • nurturance vs. discipline • involvement vs. detachment • sensitivity vs. insensitivity

Cancer/Capricorn Keywords:

> nurturing discipline • emotional power • strength in vulnerability
> • self-parenting • public warmth • controlled warmth •
> nourishing commitment • stabilized emotion • receptive strength

Leo/Aquarius Lunar Nodes: Lessons

LESSON #1: When we are in contact with our hearts, our egos rest upon a foundation which does not secure ourselves at the expense of other people, but which instead promotes our loving capacities. When we are illuminated by our inner light, we radiate a warmth which includes and embraces the people around us and enables them as well as us to shine.

The more capable we are of resting within the larger energies inside us and around us, experiencing our connectedness to the world at large, the more we can operate from a personal will or ego which is aligned with our collective unconscious and with collective humanity. Our aim need not be to gratify our egos apart from considering the well-being of others, or, on the other hand, to overcome and to lose our egos in self-sacrifice; instead we can open and expand our identities so that we are aware of, aligned with, drawing from and contributing to the larger world.

LESSON #2: Effectively expressing our humanitarianism involves opening our hearts to humanity, not only engaging in progressive activities. We need to live our ideals, developing our capacity to personally model them within our friendships, group affiliations and political or social service activities, rather than attempt unsuccessfully to instigate changes in other people and in society without being willing to open and change ourselves. Means and ends are related; when we impart the loving energy we wish to see in the world around us, we are far more likely to have a significant and constructive impact than when we, from a closed or superior stance, attempt to coerce others to be what we are unable to be ourselves.

LESSON #3: Instead of being isolated in our own world, or on the other hand, committing ourselves to a group and losing ourselves in that larger whole (or using the group just to boost our own egos), we can commit ourselves to a way of being which satisfies both individual and group needs. What are our personal desires? What are the needs and desires of the group as a whole? Where are the intersection points where we as individuals and the group coincide? By seeking to discover and direct our energies toward living at these intersection points, we become capable of experiencing personal fulfillment while being actively involved in and contributing to the group as a whole.

Where might the individuality of Leo and the group consciousness of Aquarius intersect for us? Perhaps we need to discover ways of making our own personal, creative contribution to society, ways of expressing ourselves for the benefit of the greater network, and find possibilities for exercising our leadership capabilities. While meeting our legitimate ego needs for mastery and recognition, we can simultaneously devote ourselves to a goal which benefits others.

Quotations for Leo/Aquarius Lunar Nodes

I arise in the morning torn between a desire to improve or save the world and a desire to enjoy or savor it. —E. B. WHITE

True equality can only mean the right to be uniquely creative.
—MILTON ERICKSON

Finding the center of strength within ourselves is in the long run the best contribution we can make to our fellow man. —ROLLO MAY

After careful meditation
And profound deliberation
On the various pretty projects which have just been shown,
Not a scheme in agitation
For the world's amelioration,
Has a grain of common sense in it, except my own.
—THOMAS LOVE PEACOCK

Emancipate yourself! . . . No one else will, because no one else can.
—HENRY MILLER

I did not belong to the group on Pinckney avenue. For a year I lived with them but left the dinner table early and read in my room when they had parties downstairs. What is wrong with me?, I asked myself, cringing. Why must I hold myself apart? Why can't I enjoy their company? Why am I the black sheep, the albatross, the butterfly with one wing? . . . Now, years later, I look

back in disbelief at the pain of that year in which I felt I was wrong for not adapting, when indeed I WAS wrong, but in choosing the wrong group. I stumbled upon new friends the day I decided to flaunt the bright yellow and red of my healthy wing, rather than shake my stub of a broken wing at nearby predators. And they welcomed me, the other one-winged butterflies . . . I realized then that I could not belong everywhere, and still belong to myself.
—TRACY MARKS, *from* A Passing of Clouds

Leo/Aquarius Concerns:

discovering our interdependence • individuality and creativity • expression of idealism • the loving use of will

Leo/Aquarius Issues:

heart vs. mind • personal vs. universal will • self vs. collective • personal vs. universal love

Leo/Aquarius Keywords:

loving humanitarianism • inspired reform • social confidence • warm friendship • personal truth • creative contribution

Virgo/Pisces Lunar Nodes: Lessons

LESSON #1: One important lesson of the Virgo/Pisces axis pertains to our capacities to infuse the practical facets of our daily tasks and work activities with inspiration and imagination. We need to create a work life in which we provide service which is meaningful to ourselves and others in which we are living our ideals and manifesting our personal vision. We can use our imagination both to perceive previously unrecognized possibilities for growth, fulfillment and service in our daily routines, and to rehearse actions we intend to perform or skills we hope to utilize. We can dedicate ourselves to creating a bridge between our spirituality and our physical reality by looking for ways in which we can express our compassion and idealism concretely in our everyday tasks and interactions.

LESSON #2: Compassion without discrimination leaves us feeling drained and resentful; the critical discrimination of Virgo without Piscean empathy and caring leads to emotional dissatisfaction and often entrapment in meaningless chores. We may need to develop discriminating compassion and sensitivity, to learn how and when and to whom to give (as well as how and when and from whom to receive) so that we may keep our wells from running dry and retain our capacities to love and to serve others.

LESSON #3: Virgoan discrimination involves maintaining and affirming our separateness; Piscean empathy involves experiencing oneness and openness. Integrating Virgo and Pisces, we become able to create a viable balance between being opened and closed, in union and separate. Like flowers, we must close in order to rest and replenish ourselves from within, so that we may reopen in the future. As we become more comfortable with our opening and closing process, we can develop the capacity to experience oneness in ourselves which is fully capable of bearing separateness in relationship, and we can cultivate the separateness in ourselves which enables us to experience openness without losing ourselves in others.

LESSON #4: Caught between our Virgoan perfectionism and Piscean idealism, we may have difficulty embracing the reality of our ragged edges, and we may need to allow ourselves to be perfectly imperfect. When our Piscean compassion and Virgoan self-improvement orientation are turned toward ourselves, we may discover that only through self-acceptance and constructive loving criticism can we and other people transcend limitations.

We may need to heal ourselves first, if we are to develop and retain our abilities to heal others. We may need to develop a holistic approach to healing which involves perceiving the relationship between mind, feelings and body. We can make use of positive thinking and visualization to heal the body, while attending to our body with the loving care which will help purify our energies and clear and inspire our minds.

Quotations for Virgo/Pisces Lunar Nodes

Where love is lacking, work becomes a substitute.
Where work is lacking, love becomes an opiate.
—ALICE LYTTENS

Do not believe . . . that to . . . shut oneself up in a cloister is the way to
perfection. In fleeing from the world you may topple down from heaven
to earth, whereas I, remaining among earthly things, shall be able to lift
my heart securely to heaven.
—COLUCCIO SALUTATI

Instead of putting others in their place, put yourself in their place.
—ANONYMOUS

But to be a woman alive
Requires more than your transcendence,
Requires the integrity of self which will not be lost in another's realm.
—MARY BLACK CROUCH

You can
Contain a large world in a small strict plan.
Your job is to draw out the essence and provide
The word that will endure, comfort, sustain a man.
—MAY SARTON

When I create an image of myself as I wish to be and focus upon it continu-
ally, I empower myself to actualize that vision; the clarity of my intent and
imaginings generate a psychic intensity which helps to manifest the reality I
have projected.

But sometimes the design I have conceived is contrary to the design of my
life; the threads cross at odd angles; the picture is askew; I weave a tapestry
which when completed and displayed clashes with the direction that has sub-
liminally been unfolding inside of me.

I may not know what I most want or need when I begin to weave; I may be
gazing only at patterns known to my conscious mind and based upon previous
knowledge or experience. I cannot imagine vistas I have never seen.

How important it is then to choose those possibilities which resonate with
my innermost core, which are revealed to me by dreams or by intuitive prompt-
ings and accompanied by that rare but unmistakable certainty which with-
stands all questioning. And if those visions manifest and prove faulty, perhaps
that too is part of the pattern and the incomplete drama of one scene will be
resolved in the next scene on another tapestry.
—TRACY MARKS, *from* A Passing of Clouds

Virgo/Pisces Concerns:

the relationship between mind and body • service • introversion
and retreat • perfectionism and idealism • humility, modesty and
inferiority • purity

Virgo/Pisces Issues:

mind vs. body • earth vs. heaven • part vs. whole • separateness vs. oneness • analysis vs. synthesis

Virgo/Pisces Keywords:

discriminating compassion • applied imagination • flowing organization • essential service • relaxed service • grounded spirituality • realistic faith • self-perfection • controlled openness • holistic work • practical idealism • inspired efficiency • loving criticism

PART II

THE OUTER PLANET TRANSITS

Chapter Five

TRANSITS:
THE NEXT STEP IN OUR BECOMING

In order to fully understand the influences of Uranus, Neptune, and Pluto, and to know how to respond to their transits, we need to understand first what transits mean in terms of our own development. We must cultivate a constructive attitude toward transits and toward the planets, so that we may become more capable of making the changes in our lives which they may require.

Our attitudes toward transits, as they aspect our charts, may be negative even when our philosophy of astrology is positive and even when we do, at least intellectually, believe in our own free will. Because outer planet transits, particularly the conjunction, square and opposition, are often painful, our ability to cope with them and use them to our advantage may depend upon how much contact we have with our highest Self or Soul; such contact helps us to develop and maintain a faith strong enough to guide us through particularly difficult periods of our lives. When we are attuned to our higher Self, whether through meditation, prayer, creative expression, or simply living in an open, caring way, we become less identified with our desires and the structures in our lives, and more dependent upon our inner guidance.

As our primary source of security and our primary connection becomes our connection to our inner light, then although we may fear losing the good things in our lives and not fulfilling our conscious aims, we are more able to welcome the transits as messages from the universe, guiding us onward into the next stage in our becoming. The questions we ask then are not so much, "Who am I?" and "What will happen to me?," as if we are fixed entities bound in time by our natal charts and at the mercy of the planets, but rather: What may I become next? How may I actualize and transcend my natal chart? What is the current lesson I have to learn in regard to integrating the energies of the aspecting transits with the planets, signs and houses they are aspecting in my chart? What changes in attitude and action do I need to make in order to most beneficially express this energy? How may I allow the transits to lead me through the next stage of my evolution?

Asking such questions and discovering our own answers requires that we be willing to take responsibility for both our attitudes and actions. As long as we have catastrophic expectations about a particular influence, we are likely to act in a manner which invites catastrophe; as long as we believe that we can only passively respond to the transits, we are likely to attract to us the more discordant energies of the outer planets. If Pluto is conjuncting second house Moon and we continue our previous attachment patterns in regard to spending money and accumulating possessions, we may be forced to relinquish some of those possessions by an unforeseen event such as a robbery in our home. However, if we become aware of and attentive to Plutonian energy, we may then choose to rid ourselves of many of our belongings, eliminating all that does not feel essential. Once we align ourselves with a planetary influence, it becomes our friend and helper.

Teilhard de Chardin once said, "I must continually change in order to remain myself." He tells us that we must accept on a gut level that we are a continuing process rather than fixed entities, that we become who we are by allowing ourselves to keep unfolding and changing. Only through such gut level acceptance can we become capable of letting go of our present and past identity or circumstances when the outer planets require it, welcoming the unknown acting upon us, as frightening as it may at first be. The capacity to relinquish whatever has been important to us in the past without a clear vision of what we will be able to experience or create in the future is difficult to develop, particularly if we have a fixed, earth, or water emphasis in our charts. It means hanging out in the void between two modes of being, face to face with our fear. It means being able to move through that fear, to develop trust. It means also being willing to experience pain and loss, and hopefully to view that experience from a long-range perspective which is concerned more with our over-all growth and well-being than with immediate ease and pleasure. When we resist change and attempt to hold on to our past or present experience, the outer planets are the most threatening, not when we welcome their influence and consciously choose to put their lessons into practice.

The Feeling Dimension of Transits

Welcoming an outer planet transit means being willing to experience its energies internally as it approaches rather than wait for those energies to manifest outwardly in our lives. It means that we must discern subtle changes in our feelings and attitudes and pay attention to them by training our inner faculties, much as an artist trains him/herself to perceive the subtleties in a painting which are not obvious to the average observer. We often forget that the planets are not just outside ourselves, that we carry their energies inside ourselves. Because the ionosphere, which absorbs the electrons transmitted from the planets, resonates at almost the same frequency as the human body, cosmic energies are continually affecting our cells, becoming a part of us. Only when we are willing to experience fully the insecurity, pain or confusion that may be the first expression of an outer planet transit—to open to the cold of the unknown and, by taking it in, to allow it to transform us—can we begin to experience what it is trying to teach us. Then we can determine the best possible course of action. Even the most difficult transits may lead us to a deeper peace and increased wisdom once we experience the initial disorientation.

I emphasize FEELING the transits because many of us, afraid of uncomfortable feelings, jump into our heads and start intellectualizing. We immediately try to figure out what is happening astrologically, or we start giving ourselves negative messages, such as "This is terrible," or "I can't stand it," or "I'm losing control. I'm going to do something awful," or "I'm going to experience this confusion, this problem for the rest of my life." Such negative messages only depress us; they also incline us to run away from the actual experience. Verbalizing is fine, and can eventually help us to create order from disorder and to discover the appropriate changes we need to make in our lives. However, unless we tune into our feeling experience fully before verbalizing and unless we allow the feelings to flow through us and transform us, then we may never know what benefits our outer planet transit is providing. This means that we must not be too quick to interpret our feelings, or to attach them to some particular structure or relationship in our lives and assume that the structure or relationship is the source of our chaos or suffering. Our experience occurs within us, but we may too easily project it outward and believe it to be entirely a result of an external circumstance. We may need to be willing really to FEEL our feelings, to stay with them for a while and allow them in their own time to reveal their lessons.

A personal example: Before my first Saturn return, when Neptune squared Venus while Saturn conjuncted it, I was feeling particularly unhappy in intimate relationships, and hid away for many months writing, occasionally experiencing considerable loneliness. Once I stopped depressing myself with negative messages and allowed myself to feel the emptiness and pain within me, I began to receive images of deserts and cactuses, and to envision myself as a cactus on a desert, able to live comfortably with few sources of nourishment. At this point I began writing about the Cancer/Capricorn opposition, about the difficulty of nourishing others when we ourselves are feeling deprived. In entering my experience fully, I became deeply aware of why my father had never been able to give me what I wanted, how he had become victim to his own Venus/Saturn conjunction in Pisces. I was filled with such compassion for him that I called him, and we had one of our first truly loving conversations. This opening, triggered by both Saturn and Neptune, continued to such an extent that I began, without realizing it, to look for one particular person in my life to whom I could attach these feelings. But when I began to let my feelings of pain and love flow through me rather than attaching them to one person, I avoided the Venus/Neptune trap of romantic fantasy and self-deception, and discovered that such feelings could enrich all my relationships and activities, uplifting every facet of my life, and especially, at that time, infuse my writing with new heights of inspiration.

As we allow ourselves to experience fully what we are feeling under an outer planet transit, to allow our feelings to flow through us, perhaps even releasing them as tears or rage, we may be led to discover a greater peace within ourselves. Then we begin to receive guidance not from our heads but from our hearts or center—guidance that can help us understand and constructively express the transit we are experiencing. Sometimes, we may not receive such guidance for many months, in which case our faith is important, because it enables us to trust that each experience has a purpose, is an important step in our evolution, and that if we don't understand its meaning we may be able to perceive its benefits in the future. We might then ask ourselves, "What can I possibly gain from this experience?" and also, "What part of myself wants this experience—this confusion or tension or turmoil, or the changes in my life that result from it, now and in the future?" We may at first doubt that we actually want some of the experiences we get under the influence of an outer planet, but if we look at ourselves closely, we may find that on some level we do want to make whatever changes we are making. Sometimes we discover later that it was not the immediate upheaval that we wanted, but the future changes which would result from the new modes of being such upheaval makes possible.

Another personal example: Once, under a transit opposing my second house Jupiter and squaring my Mars, my car was destroyed by vandalism. Because of problems with both the insurance company and my mechanic, I collected virtually nothing, which meant I couldn't buy another car, do my daily errands, or even travel to visit friends. When I finally stopped railing against the universe and asked myself what part of myself wanted this experience and what I was gaining from it, I became aware of a whole array of positive consequences—badly needed exercise, new friends I met while walking, organizing my time to do all my errands one day a week, time alone to complete work which needed to be done, etc. Although I'm still not particularly happy with the method the universe chose to bring me these positive consequences, I see that they were important ones, and am more in touch with how I wanted those consequences, and would not have brought them about on my own if my car had not been destroyed.

One of the lessons of the outer planets, in the words of the Rolling Stones, is that, "You can't always get what you want/ But . . . you just might find/ You get what you need." At least, we don't always get what we consciously want or understand, but again, some part of ourselves outside our awareness wants or needs either the experience that happens to us OR its consequences. The more we are attuned to the energy of the transiting planet as it resonates inside us, the more capable we will be of creating events in our lives expressive of its energy, rather than unconsciously drawing events into our lives which force us to readjust ourselves and to deal with that planetary energy. An outer planet transit is particularly difficult to deal with when our ego, our sense of ourselves, has been too limited, has excluded from its awareness and expression the constructive possibilities of this planetary energy. The transit is a message to align our ego with our higher Self, by experiencing and reincorporating that energy into our awareness, and by actively expressing it in the world.

Using Our Transits Constructively

Both our attitudes and behavior or actions are important under an outer planet transit. We must be willing to adjust our attitudes in order to accept our experience; we must also be willing to alter our behavior or actions, to instigate changes in our lives which express the planet's energy and the lessons being revealed to us. If we don't want the universe to burn down our houses or destroy our cars or send our spouses or lovers to bed with other people in order to get us to pay attention to what is happening, we must motivate ourselves to actively live our transit; we must attune ourselves to the energy of the transit as it first approaches, and discover ways to express that energy constructively.

First, we can make space in our lives so that we fully experience the energy, opening ourselves on a feeling level; then we may want to orient ourselves intellectually by attempting to understand how the transiting planet by sign and house, carrying with it also its natal placement, can blend with the planet it is aspecting, influencing not only the house of that planet but also the house it rules. If we are reading astrology texts in order to understand our transits, we must not read merely about the square, if it is a square we are experiencing, but rather read and determine for ourselves the meanings of conjunctions, trines and sextiles between these two planets. We are trying to integrate these two energies, and if we just determine the meaning of squares between them, we may focus upon their negative manifestations and not expand our awareness to perceive their positive expressions. A square can have all the positive meanings of a trine or sextile, PLUS the motivation a 90 degree aspect provides, if we choose to envision the possibilities we wish to create, and to actively create them.

Another personal example: When Neptune first squared my Mercury in Virgo, I started for the first time to make mistakes calculating charts. When I finally tuned in to the Neptunian energy, I realized that it was not the time for me to be doing a lot of detailed work, and I began to use a computer service. Because my creative and spiritual energies were beginning to awaken, I began using role-playing, dialoguing, and visualization techniques in my classes. Neptune was transiting my 12th house at the time, and as I became more attuned to its energies I was also inspired to write my 12th house book, as well as an inspirational fairy tale. Once I was consciously expressing my Neptune/Mercury transit, I had no difficulty coping with Neptune.

Apart from blending the energies of the transiting and natal planet, we need to ground outer planet energies in our daily lives, so that we do not feel overwhelmed and unable to function. We want to avoid experiencing either a deflation of our egos as a result of being overpowered by cosmic energies, or an inflation of our egos, which may occur when we allow these high-powered energies to convince ourselves that we are messengers of God or saviours of humanity. If the planet being aspected is a personal planet, then it provides its own channel; the outer planet must be brought down into our daily lives in accordance with whatever personal planet it is aspecting—that is, if it is Mercury, we process it mentally, communicating that energy; if it is Venus, we allow it to help us redefine our values and enrich our relationships. We can also ground that energy in terms of its lower octave—channelling Pluto through Mars, Neptune through Venus, Uranus through Mercury, according to the natal placement of these planets in our charts. The influx of cosmic energy that occurs with outer planet transits is meant to be integrated into the fabric of our lives, not exist apart from them.

Under the influence of outer planet transits, particularly the conjunction, square and opposition, we may face a number of issues, among them: Is changing our attitudes enough? Must we also instigate major changes in our outer lives? And if so, are the structures and relationships in our lives flexible enough to handle those changes? Are they capable of absorbing a new mode of being without breaking apart? Or must we throw out or cast aside some of those structures and/or relationships, and significantly alter the context in which we live? There are no set answers to these questions; much depends upon our unique circumstances at the time of the transit. It may well be that during a retrograde transit we assess the issues raised by the direct transit, and that during the final direct transit, we make those changes which we believe are necessary.

As Uranus, Neptune and Pluto form powerful aspects to our natal planets, we can benefit most by remaining open to our internal experience without being passive and helplessly allowing them to act upon us. We must also actively express their most positive energies, in combination with our aspected planet, but not act so frantically or prematurely that we do not tune in fully to those energies and allow them to reveal to us the most beneficial course of action. Our response to the outer planet transits should therefore be a response of active openness or active participation. We can respond in both a yin and yang way, receptively and creatively, giving ourselves the space to tune in, to experience our feelings and allow them to flow through us, understanding our experience intellectually, determining positive channels for expressing the transit, tuning in again to our inner guidance, actively expressing the energies of the transit, tuning in again and discovering the next step required of us. In the words of Virginia Satir, we must become "a living mobile," allowing ourselves to be blown by the winds of change and continually rebalancing ourselves, preparing for each wind that follows.

The more deeply we become attuned to our intuitive promptings, the less we are likely to need to use our minds to discover and interpret astrological influences. As we become directly aware of the energies operating within us, we become more capable of responding appropriately and wisely to them. Consider, for example, a woman who decided to take a vacation for the first time in years, to travel in India for six weeks. Without any knowledge of astrology, she booked her plane flight not only at the exact hour of a new moon conjunct her 9th house Mars in Sagittarius, but also the week preceding a transiting Jupiter conjunction to her Mars. Such a person may benefit little from the study of astrology, because she is already in contact with her deeper energies. The choices she makes often reflect awareness of planetary cycles and the lessons she may need to learn from them.

Transformation and Outer Planet Transits

The five outer planets, Jupiter through Pluto, as they journey outside us and resonate within us, are guides which help us to discover and follow our paths. Uranus, Neptune and Pluto in particular influence and restructure our larger personal, interpersonal and transpersonal patterns. Frequently, reading astrology texts, we may associate Uranus with change and freedom, Neptune with inspiration and illumination, and Pluto with transformation and regeneration, failing to realize that all three of these planets are concerned with each of these processes. They differ primarily in the kind of energy they use in order to bring about these experiences.

Because these three transpersonal planets orbit beyond Saturn and were discovered during the past two centuries, after many centuries influenced by mankind's Saturn-bounded consciousness, their impact upon us individually may depend to some extent upon how we have come to terms with Saturn and our Saturn returns. Have we claimed our adulthood? Are we capable of setting limits upon ourselves, of supporting ourselves and maintaining commitments and responsibilities? Are we grounded in reality and willing and able to adapt to the demands of society? The peace we make with Saturn and with the internal and external structures we develop are of considerable importance if we are to become open to Uranus, Neptune and Pluto without being swept away by their potent energies. Of special significance is our capacity to experience and transcend our Saturnian fear, as old boundaries, structures and bases of security are challenged by planets beyond Saturn.

Uranus, Neptune, and Pluto can all help us to become better attuned to our higher Self and the messages it receives from the universe and to experience the inner freedom which results from hearing and following our inner guidance and cooperating with universal energies. Through the influence of these three planets, we can discover new possibilities which enable us to let go of the past and be transformed, and to awaken and learn to use our creative and spiritual resources—in essence, to become what we are capable of becoming, unfolding the highest potentials of our birthcharts.

Interpreting Transits

Many of us are afraid of our approaching transits, particularly the transits of Saturn, Uranus, Neptune, and Pluto conjuncting, squaring or opposing planets in our natal charts. We read interpretations of these transits, often negative in tone, and fear the worst; we wait helplessly for the next transit to "strike," wondering if pieces of ourselves and our lives will have to be reassembled when it is over.

Our knowledge of astrology may indeed increase our fear, particularly if we are resistant to change and cling to our immediate circumstances or our hopes and dreams. But it can also give us the awareness necessary to understand the process of our unfolding in relation to transits, and can motivate us to prepare for that unfolding by actively expressing the constructive dimensions of each forthcoming transit.

In order to derive maximum benefit from the influences of transiting planets, we must not only be willing to open ourselves to change, we must also:

1) become deeply familiar with our natal charts;
2) know how to interpret transits influencing our charts;
3) be able to learn from our past transits;
4) be aware of our future transits;
5) allow ourselves the space to experience and understand transits occurring at the present moment and in the immediate future;
6) utilize each transit, by consciously cooperating with its highest energies and giving it appropriate form in our daily lives.

Let us now turn our attention to some important points, often not covered in astrology texts, which can help us to interpret transits to our charts. Although the following points are relevant to all transits, they refer especially to the transits of Jupiter, Saturn, Uranus, Neptune, and

Pluto, which have a more significant and long-lasting impact upon our lives than those of the inner planets.

Unfolding Our Natal Charts

Many astrologers believe that transits indicate external events and that progressions indicate psychological experience. This attitude presupposes the separation between the inner and outer life, which cannot be considered apart from each other because they are continually influencing each other. Transits, more so than progressions, are indeed often experienced on an external level before they are confronted internally. But if we are deeply attuned to our own psyches, we may experience them within as they are approaching, and may, to some extent, choose the manner in which they will manifest outwardly in our lives. We will experience the transiting planet as a facet of ourselves now demanding our attention, requiring us to acknowledge it and integrate it into our life structure.

Because we are not fixed entities, but rather continuums or processes, our natal energies are always in movement, unfolding in correspondence with the planets as they transit through the solar system. Transiting Saturn cannot be completely differentiated from our natal Saturn; as it aspects planets in our chart, it is carrying along its natal placement by sign, house and aspect, a placement which is actually the foundation from which the transiting sign, house and aspects of Saturn will unfold themselves. If natal Saturn is in our 7th house, then transiting Saturn conjunct our midheaven will bear 7th as well as 10th house connotations. We may at this time be working as a consultant, functioning in one-to-one relationships in our work; we may establish a professional partnership; we may be struggling with the ending of a love relationship we have entered with our boss or with someone important in our public or professional life.

If an outer planet is heavily afflicted in our natal chart, then its transits, perhaps even by trine and sextile, may be difficult for us, forcing us to confront the problems indicated by its natal placement. Jupiter, if forming primarily squares and oppositions natally, may not be the cosmic benefactor we expect, at least not until we resolve its natal dilemmas. Outer planets which form primarily trines and sextiles in our natal charts may be easy to integrate when they form conjunctions, trines and sextiles by transit. But if we have never had to struggle with squares or oppositions to this outer planet, then the transiting squares or oppositions may upset our equilibrium because we have not had prior experience handling the more unsettling manifestations of this planetary energy.

Natal Planets Aspected by Transit

When a transiting planet aspects one of our natal planets, its influence will be related not only to the nature of the natal planet and its sign and house, but also to its natal aspects.

If, for example, transiting Uranus is conjuncting our 8th house Moon in Aries, our experience will be greatly influenced by the aspects formed by our natal Moon. Is our Moon square our fifth house Mars/Venus conjunction? Then we may struggle with issues related to our sexuality, as we attempt to develop intimate relationships which allow us to express ourselves more freely. Or is our natal Moon opposing our second house Mars in Libra? Perhaps then, under this Uranus transit, our focus will be how we can operate more independently of our business partner; we may even decide to end the partnership and start our own business venture.

Houses Ruled by the Aspected Planet

When a transiting planet aspects one of our natal planets, the house or houses ruled by that natal planet, as well as the house in which it is positioned, will be influenced by the transit, particularly if the house doesn't contain any planets. The opportunities provided by the transit, and the conflicts which it activates will have repercussions which may extend to three or more houses of our birthcharts.

Is Neptune, which is natally in our 12th house, now transiting our 3rd house and opposing our 9th house Venus, while the school we are attending is on the verge of losing accreditation? Then the houses which Venus rules in our chart through the signs of Taurus and Libra will also be affected while we are coping with uncertainty about our education.

Activation of Natal Aspects

If a transiting planet aspects one of our planets, it will activate the natal aspect between those two planets as it reveals new opportunities, whether easy or difficult, for integrating those two energies. Two planets in square or opposition natally may operate more harmoniously when one by transit conjuncts, sextiles or trines the natal position of the other. If we have Uranus square Mars natally and struggle with issues of sexual freedom, or flit from activity to activity without accomplishing anything substantial, we may be able to discover ways to resolve those problems when transiting Uranus conjuncts, sextiles or trines our natal Mars. The new possibilities revealed to us will usually be related to the house position of the transiting planet.

Conjunctions by Transit

When a transiting planet conjuncts a natal planet, the expression of that natal planet will be transformed in accordance with the meaning of the transit. Our energy will expand under Jupiter, contract under Saturn, be dramatically stimulated or liberated by Uranus, sensitized by Neptune, or intensified by Pluto. By allowing our natal planets to absorb and channel the energy of the transiting planet, we discover new modes of expressing and new means for fulfilling the needs of that natal planet. In the course of a lifetime, each of our natal planets may incorporate into itself the lessons learned by conjunction with three, four or five outer planets.

If we have Jupiter at 26 Aquarius in the 5th house, then the May/June 2009 Jupiter/Neptune conjunction at 26 Aquarius (repeating nearby in December 2009) will alter the influence of our Jupiter return. Rather than taking up a new aerobic sport, as we did at our last Jupiter return, we may be drawn to a gentler form of physical movement such as t'ai chi ch'uan, or we may become interested in theater, and land a dramatic role in an avante-garde production.

Trines and Sextiles by Transit

Transits which trine or sextile our natal planets may not be consciously experienced. We usually must *choose* to express the aspect being formed in order to discover the flow of energy available to us and the new opportunities it provides. The transiting planet's placement by sign and house will indicate the manner in which we can best release the energy of our natal planet. Transiting Jupiter in our 11th house trine our natal 7th house Sun in Taurus may indicate that through participating in group activities related to our educational or philosophical interests (or otherwise related to our natal placement of Jupiter) we may meet people with whom we can form satisfying close relationships.

Squares and Oppositions by Transit

A transiting planet in square to a natal planet may introduce conflicts related to the expression of the natal planet, forcing us to develop new ways of expressing it in accordance with the transiting planet and its house. Transiting Saturn in our 6th house squaring our 3rd house Venus in Gemini may require us to focus upon our work responsibilities and spend less time interacting with people on the job; we may as a result learn to satisfy our Venus in Gemini social needs by arranging more luncheon dates during our workday or attending courses in the evenings where we can meet and communicate with a variety of people.

A transiting planet in opposition to a natal planet may force us to come to terms with that natal planet in our relationships. Transiting Pluto in our 10th house opposing our 4th house Moon may trigger feelings of being overpowered by our boss and struggles because his/her demands upon our time interfere with our private lives. We may then need to discover ways to fulfill our emotional needs and experience our own personal power both at work and at home. Often, when a transit opposes our natal planet, we may experience another person as blocking us, or may feel obstructed in some way by external circumstances; once we own the transiting planet and its house position as part of ourselves, we can begin to integrate it with the natal planet. In the above situation, we may need to come to terms with our own desire for work which is deeply significant and has a powerful, transformative impact upon other people; we may need to integrate Pluto and the Moon by discovering an effective channel for our own intense feelings and aims.

Inner Planet Conjunctions

Inner planet conjunctions or preponderances by sign or house can have at least the impact of outer planet transits, particularly if they are reinforced by outer planets involved in the conjunction. If, for example, transiting Sun, Mercury, Venus and Mars, as well as Uranus, are all in the late degrees of Scorpio, then we can expect that their house position and the aspects they form to our natal charts will be strongly activated during this period. We can either respond to the Scorpionic release of energy once it manifests, or harness it before it manifests and make far-reaching changes in this area of our lives.

Familiar and Unfamiliar Transits

Transits which are related in meaning to natal planets and aspects may seem very familiar to us because they simply activate our own natal potentials. If we have Neptune in the 9th house and experience transiting Neptune conjuncting our Jupiter, we may discover that the energy of the transit is second nature to us, although it may nevertheless be manifested in a house which, at least natally, is not influenced by Neptune. On the other hand, transits which are clearly unrelated to, or considerably different from, natal placements may feel somewhat alien, although they may awaken us to behaviors and experiences which we did not know were possible. Our Saturn in Taurus will be challenged by transiting Uranus entering our 2nd house, but may then learn that calculated financial risks can in time increase our sense of security; our Venus/Uranus conjunction in Gemini may struggle with transiting Saturn crossing our descendant, but may discover that freedom and excitement in a relationship is possible when we make a commitment and operate within clearly defined limits.

Transits and Progressions

Transits will be particularly powerful when they coincide in time with a related progression. Uranus opposing our 10th house Moon while our progressed Sun is conjuncting it, will have a more significant effect than either transit or progression operating alone; it will clearly direct us to break free of old patterns and create more viable patterns for satisfying our emotional needs and responding to the needs of the public. We may, under such a transit, choose to give up the security of our home in order to pursue our own unique professional aims.

A Transiting Double Whammy

Occasionally, we will experience a transiting double whammy, such as transiting Pluto squaring our natal Saturn while transiting Saturn is squaring our natal Pluto. Such a combined transit is telling us that we must integrate the influences of Saturn and Pluto in terms of both their natal and transiting placements. We might do this by totally involving ourselves in our work or Saturnian commitments or by clearly putting an end to a situation related in meaning to one of the houses influenced by Saturn and Pluto, and by allowing ourselves to fully experience the "death" of one phase of our lives.

Two Transits to One Planet

When two transiting planets are simultaneously aspecting a natal planet, one transit can help resolve the problems created by the other. If Saturn is conjuncting our natal Moon while Neptune is squaring it, we may experience music or meditation dissolving the emotional blockages of Saturn and enabling us to express ourselves in a more flowing manner; likewise, applying ourselves to a project or task which involves our emotions or satisfies some of the needs of our Moon may prevent us from becoming caught in the addictive or oversensitive manifestations of a Neptune/Moon square.

Transits and Aspect Configurations

Transits are particularly important when they are related to aspect configurations in our natal charts or form aspect configurations which do not exist natally. A square to our natal grand trine may activate that grand trine, spurring us to use our physical, intellectual, practical and emotional energies in new ways. A trine to our grand cross or t-square may open new channels of expression which help us to transcend the conflicts of our squares and oppositions. An opposition to the focal planet of our yod or t-square may provoke a crisis which enables us to transform the expression of that planet and operate in a more integrated, directed manner. Transiting aspects to our stellium may spur us to apply the concentrated energy of that stellium to other areas of our chart rather than focus primarily upon the house in which the stellium occurs. (For more detailed information about the influences of transits upon aspect configurations, see *Planetary Aspects,* and *Art of Chart Interpretation*). When transits form a grand trine to a natal trine, a t-square to a natal square or opposition, a yod to a natal inconjunct or sextile, or a stellium to a three-planet conjunction, the configuration formed will function almost like a natal configuration, with the transiting planet functioning as an activating force.

Transits Changing Houses

An outer planet transit leaving one house of our natal charts and entering another may not at first be noticed because it moves so slowly. However, its influence is significant, indicating the beginning of a new phase in our lives in regard to the manifestations of this planet's energy. The lessons of the previous house must now be carried over into the house the transiting planet is entering. Once we have experienced Uranus for seven years in our 1st house, we must now allow our new-found identity to express itself more individualistically through our means of earning or spending money, or otherwise using our physical, emotional or intellectual resources. In this case, we may not fully experience Uranus in our 2nd house until it makes its first aspect to one of our natal planets.

Transits crossing our ascendant or midheaven are usually quite powerful, indicating time periods during which we must begin to externalize energies that have been previously operating internally, or primarily on an emotional or mental level. The subconscious reprocessing of a planet that occurs when it is in our 12th house will flood into our awareness when it crosses our ascendant, and will need to be integrated with our experience of our identity, our physical body and our ways of projecting ourselves in the world. The knowledge we have gained and the belief system we have developed, as well as the new realms of experience we have explored when a transit has been passing through our 9th house, will need to be given form in our public activities or professional lives when the transiting planet crosses our midheaven and enters our 10th house.

Stationary Transits

Next to a progressed planet going stationary, a transiting planet making its station within a degree of conjuncting one of our natal planets is the most powerful influence we can experience, at least five times as powerful as the transit moving at its normal speed. Even Mercury, Venus, or Mars going stationary near one of our planets will affect us significantly. Whatever stationary planet is aspecting us, it is likely to dominate our consciousness until it is at least a degree away from our natal planet; as it hammers its lessons into us, it will compel us to stop and assess how we are using its energies. Such an experience may be very difficult, particularly if our planet forms many squares or oppositions, but the impact of that stationary planet may be strong enough to precipitate needed changes in our lives, related in meaning to the planet and house being aspected. Squares and oppositions, as well as trines and sextiles, formed by stationary planets aspecting natal planets will also affect us more profoundly than normal transits, indicating periods in our lives during which we need to integrate the two planets involved in the aspect. Saturn stationary conjunct our natal Venus may force us to withdraw from all social interactions for awhile, turning toward ourselves to reassess our values, desires and capabilities in terms of relationships. Saturn stationary trine our Venus may have the same influence, but without the feelings of loneliness and self-doubt that may have to be confronted under the conjunction.

Lunations

A New Moon within two degrees of conjuncting a natal planet or angle can indicate a new beginning in terms of that planet or angle, such as a recovery from an illness, if the New Moon conjuncts our ascendant and influences our physical body, or a pay raise if it conjuncts our second house Jupiter. If the planet or angle aspected has many natal squares or oppositions, then entering the new phase of our lives indicated by the New Moon may require us to deal first with the challenges of these squares and oppositions. A New Moon trining, sextiling, squaring, or opposing a natal planet will influence us also, but will be less potent than a conjunction.

Eclipses

Solar and lunar eclipses aspecting our charts may precipitate crises in regard to the planet or angle aspected, particularly if forming conjunctions, squares or oppositions. We may feel as if we have lost conscious control over the natal planet and are at the mercy of our unconscious processes or of unexpected external circumstances which demand our attention. When an eclipse conjuncts, opposes or squares a natal planet, we should allow space in our lives to deal with the irrational or unpredictable events that may occur, and not expect ourselves to express that planet in normal ways. By trine or sextile, eclipses may bring exciting opportunities into our lives, opportunities related in meaning to the planet being aspected; they may also activate our subconscious and awaken our creativity or intuitive insight. An eclipse conjunct our 11th house Mercury may coincide with the dissolution of a group to which we belong, requiring us to discover other ways of meeting our 11th house needs; an eclipse in our 7th house trining Mercury may coincide with the sudden beginning of a new friendship, one which may even, in time, lead to marriage. Eclipses have the influence of Uranus, and an orb of three degrees. We usually experience them for at least five days before and after their occurrence, and again when a transiting planet, particularly Mars, conjuncts the eclipse degree.

Unaspected Planets and Transits

Unaspected planets are difficult to integrate into the structure of our lives, and may operate in an all-or-nothing fashion. If our Mercury is unaspected (by major aspects), we may struggle to make contact with people and may alternate between silently withdrawing into ourselves and speaking compulsively without regard for other people's response. A transiting planet in square or opposition to an unaspected planet may force us to confront the problems of the unaspected planet and search for a solution.

A transiting planet forming a trine or sextile may reveal an easy solution, one which we can apply in the future, even when the transit has passed. When transiting Neptune in our 1st house trines our 9th house Mercury, we may discover the calming effects of meditation, which help our unaspected Mercury to communicate in a more flowing manner.

Transits and Midpoints

Because our natal charts contain dozens of midpoints, and we may lose our perspective by considering too many details, we may overlook midpoints altogether. However, certain midpoints in our charts are likely to be power points, responding to transits almost as if they were actual planets. A list of all our direct midpoints, arranged in zodiacal sequence (as is provided on some computer charts) can easily enable us to observe transits to significant natal midpoints.

What midpoints then should we attend to? First, we should be aware of a planet in our chart which is the direct midpoint of two other planets, such as Sun at 26 Virgo, positioned at the midpoint of Mercury at 23 Leo and Mars at 29 Libra. A transit such as Saturn conjuncting our Sun will activate the channel between Mercury and Mars, and may help us to motivate and discipline ourselves to write our long-delayed thesis or otherwise apply ourselves to some Mercury/Mars project.

Second, we should be aware of the midpoints of each of the aspects of our charts, *particularly* close squares and oppositions. Transits crossing these midpoints will activate the square or opposition, also enabling us to resolve its conflicts. Transiting Jupiter in our 5th house crossing the midpoint of our exact Venus/Pluto square may even lead us to a fulfilling romance, one which is not as obsessive or emotionally exhausting as our previous Venus square Pluto romances may have been.

Third, we can pay attention to transits which occur at the midpoints of planets not linked by aspect in our natal charts. Such transits may enable us to blend the energies of the two natal planets in accordance with the transiting planet. Uranus in the 1st house transiting the midpoint of our natal Mars and Neptune may introduce us unexpectedly to the joys of creative dance or such Neptunian physical activities as t'ai chi ch'uan or ice skating.

Paying attention to our significant midpoints is not a difficult task. We need only periodically check our list of midpoints arranged in zodiacal sequence to discover what near or far midpoints (e.g., in the Mercury/Mars example, 26 Virgo is near and 26 Pisces is far) the outer planets are approaching. Degrees which correspond to several sets of midpoints, such as Moon/Mars *and* Saturn/Uranus *and* Mercury/Venus, will activate all these planets when transited. With so much energy available to us, we might prepare ourselves so that we can use it productively.

Transits Forming Minor Aspects

Few of us have the time or patience to consider minor aspects formed by transits to our natal planets. For the most part, such minor aspects are not as significant as major aspects, although the transiting semi-square and inconjunct may merit our attention when formed by an outer planet, and any minor aspect formed by a stationary planet is going to have an impact upon us. Quintiles, which enable us to synthesize diverse energies in a unique way on a higher than normal plane of consciousness, may also be worth our attention, especially when they activate unaspected or heavily afflicted planets in our charts. Transiting Pluto in the 10th house quintile our afflicted Mars in the 12th may release the energy and motivation we need to step outside our 12th house refuge and to express ourselves actively in public realms, thereby building our confidence in our ability to assert ourselves openly.

We can simplify the process of determining transiting minor aspects by noting on our list of midpoints arranged in zodiacal sequence those degrees which form such obscure aspects as semi-squares and quintiles to our natal planets. Then, we need only consult the degrees of the transiting outer planets to discover which midpoints and which minor aspects are being triggered.

Experiencing an Outer Planet Transit

Now that we have considered many of the influences of transits upon natal planets, how might we experience a transit? When will we most feel its effect? For how long will it influence us? What happens when a transiting planet forms an aspect three times because of its retrograde motion, or even as many as five times when it continually retraces its steps over the same degrees? Let's consider then the entire process of an outer planet transit, from its first approach to the waning period of its last aspect. Because it is virtually impossible to describe here the influences of all the transiting planets according to each aspect that they may form, the description which follows is a general one, pertaining mostly to conjunctions, squares and oppositions of Saturn, Uranus, Neptune and Pluto.

First of all, we are likely to sense the energy of the transiting planet at the periphery of our consciousness by the time it is three degrees before forming a conjunction to a natal planet, or within two degrees of forming a square or opposition. The trine and sextile are usually less conscious, and may not be experienced until the aspect is within one degree of being exact.

If the transit is a conjunction, square or opposition, its energy may at first seem alien to us. Suddenly, we are forced to confront it in ourselves or in the world around us. If we begin to incorporate it into our experience at this time, to express its energy actively in terms of the planet it is aspecting, and to resolve the dilemmas which the square and opposition in particular may provoke, we then can make peace with the transit by the time it becomes exact. We may, particularly in the case of a conjunction, merge with the transiting planet, having fully confronted and assimilated its energy. If we have not come to terms with it, the week of the exact aspect may bring a crisis precipitated by this planet to a peak, and we may be forced to discover at least a temporary means of handling it.

Most transits quickly wane once the exact aspect is formed, although Saturn may linger for a degree beyond the degree being aspected. The issues or opportunities awakened by the transit may then once again return to the periphery of our consciousness and then disappear into the background of our lives, unless the transiting planet turns retrograde and once again approaches the same degree.

The influence of the retrograde period will depend upon how we have dealt with the direct aspect. We may not be conscious of the retrograde energy at all, feeling somewhat blocked in regard to its expression, almost as if we are half-asleep. We may experience the internal rather than the external dimensions of the transiting planet, such as an inner tension and restlessness under Uranus retrograde or psychological blockages and excessive self-control under Saturn retrograde. (See the chapter on transits and retrograde planets in *Planetary Aspects* for more detailed information on the effects of each retrograde planet.) If the issues raised by the direct transit have not been resolved, then we may—and indeed should—be assessing these issues, determining how we might function when the direct aspect forms in the future. Even if we have dealt successfully with the first transit, we may nevertheless need to reassess our experience, aware that the forthcoming direct transit will reveal new lessons and present unforeseen opportunities.

The period following the retrograde transit, particularly if the transiting planet proceeds many degrees beyond the exact aspect, may again be a period during which the issues of the transit are peripheral to us, or at least in suspension. However, once the transiting planet turns direct and begins to approach the natal planet, we will experience its energies quite strongly. Even if we responded well to the first two transits, if we are not now willing or able to attune ourselves to and actively utilize the transiting energy according to its influence in our chart, we may be surprised by the challenges confronting us.

Now is the time during which we may get exactly what we deserve in terms of this aspect. Our reflection, preparation and appropriate action may reap rewards for us or at least enable us to channel the energy we are experiencing; on the other hand, our passivity and lack of understanding, foresight and motivation may result in considerable difficulty coping with this transit, and may introduce unexpected problems in our lives which we do not feel equipped to handle. Unless we attune ourselves to the transit ahead of time, reflect upon it and begin to express it outwardly in terms of the planet, sign and house being aspected, we may learn little from it. Our energy may be tied up in our struggle with the crises now precipitated, crises which we are resisting rather than resolving, or we may, particularly with transiting Jupiter, miss the opportunities for growth that the universe is providing.

Occasionally, a transit of Uranus, Neptune, and Pluto will retrograde again, forming still another retrograde and then direct aspect to our natal planet, perhaps even making its station within a degree of the exact aspect, drumming into us its lessons. Over and over again, then, we will be forced to integrate the energy of that transiting planet with the natal planet. If we merely wait to discover what will happen to us, each of our squares and oppositions will present new crises and each of our trines and sextiles may be missed opportunities. Why then respond like victims at the mercy of transits, when we can incorporate their energies into our lives, learn their lessons and move forward to apply the understanding we have gained to many realms of our existence?

The growth we have experienced under a transit and the wisdom we have culled from the experience may take many years to reveal themselves. Only by cultivating a long-term perspective can we understand how each aspect in a transit cycle is interrelated, and how our experience with one aspect influences the next. What we have incorporated into ourselves under the conjunction between a transiting planet and natal planet can creatively manifest by the time the next sextile between these two planets occurs. Our resourcefulness in using the sextile will help us to confront the square. Our integration of the square can lead to a flowing expression and burst of opportunity at the trine. What we learn from the trine can enable us to synthesize the energies of the opposition and expand our awareness to encompass new possibilities. The cycle continues until we again reach the conjunction (at least with all but the three outer planets) and experience an integration of the two planetary energies. This integration may be partial or total; it may involve the negative expression of the two planets in question or their most positive expression, depending upon how we, in the past and in the present, have developed our understanding and actively applied the energy available to us through our natal planets and through the channels that have opened and activated by transiting aspects.

Preparing for Transits

Transits are the messages of the universe which direct us to unfold the potentials of our birthcharts, discovering and making use of the energies available to us at any given moment. If we wait expectantly for transits to fulfill our desires or dreams, or if we wait anxiously, afraid of the crises they will precipitate, we are not likely to benefit from them. If we experience one transit and do not reflect upon the lessons we have learned, we may not be prepared for the next transit of the planet, because we have not developed our understanding of its energies or applied our insights fully to our daily lives.

We can learn from past transits; we can channel the energies of current transits; we can prepare for transits in the immediate future; we can make wiser decisions in the present moment by remaining aware of the transits which will influence us in the distant future, and what planets, signs and houses they will be activating. We can be directors, as well as actors and observers, of our own cosmic dramas.

Learning from the Past

Transits of Jupiter repeat themselves every 12 years; transits of Saturn, every 29 years. With these outer planets, we can look back to the past and attempt to remember what we experienced when a particular transit last occurred. What happened then? What difficulties did we face? What gains did we make? How did we use the energy of the transit in relation to the house through which it was passing and the planet it was aspecting? What could we have done differently? What can we learn from that experience which will enable us to respond more constructively when this transit occurs again?

Even if we have never had a *particular* Saturn transit or were very young when transiting Saturn last made a specific aspect, we can determine the last few times Saturn aspected that planet by conjunction, sextile, square, trine or opposition, and assess that experience. If Saturn is now forming a waxing square to our Mars, what can we recall of the waning square fourteen years ago? If Saturn is opposing our Jupiter, what was our experience of the previous conjunction, or even of the last trine? With Uranus, Neptune and Pluto, we may not have experienced more than a few aspects each to any one planet, but even those few aspects can reveal to us how we may or may not have integrated the energies of the transiting and natal planet.

Under any transit, a channel of energy linking two planets is being activated. Whatever the aspect, these planets are operating in relation to each other. Our aim is to discover the most beneficial way of integrating these two energies and expressing them in accordance with the signs and houses being aspected. If we look back to their previous conjunction, we can discover how we responded to the blending of these energies in one particular sign and house. Past sextiles and trines can indicate opportunities we may have had (whether or not we took advantage of them) for integrating the expressions of two signs and houses through the channel of the same two planets. Past squares reveal periods of time during which we may have experienced these two planets, and also the two signs and houses which they were influencing, at odds with each other, and may have had to develop an active means for resolving the dilemmas we were facing. Past oppositions indicate times during which we may have projected one of the planets, according to its sign and house, outside of ourselves, experiencing it as an external circumstance in conflict with our own needs and desires, represented by the other planet, sign and house. Under an opposition, we may have felt torn apart by the tension of contradictory pulls, but may have expanded our awareness, eventually owned our projection and discovered ways to synthesize the two energies.

Consider a woman whose natal Mars in Aries in the 2nd house was soon to be opposed by transiting Saturn in early Libra in her 8th house. Natally, Saturn is on her 6th house cusp. She is too young to remember the influence of the last Saturn opposition to her Mars, but she does remember a few of her previous Saturn/Mars transits. When Saturn in Aries conjuncted her Mars, she was working her way through college, using her Mars in Aries physical resources in her job at a women's gymnasium. Both work and school were exhausting, and her income was far from substantial, but she was able to do what her Mars in Aries wanted to do—to support herself, complete her studies and gain work experience which would benefit her in the future. When Saturn in Gemini in her 4th house sextiled her Mars five years later, she was newly married, living and working with her husband on his family's farm. Although they were somewhat isolated, she enjoyed the physical activity and appreciated the stability of their lives. Their long hours of outdoor labor were also financially profitable.

When transiting Saturn in Cancer in her 5th house squared her Mars, she was a resident worker in a home for disadvantaged children. Her work interfered with her leisure time and paid her little, but she felt responsible for the welfare of the children and was committed to helping them. Because she was recovering from a painful divorce, she did not want to focus upon her social life. The first time Saturn squared her Mars, her supervisor was hospitalized, and she took charge of the daily program. During the retrograde transit, she began to feel overcome with frustration because her own financial and emotional needs weren't being met. she quit the job during the final transit, for a similar position which paid more and made fewer demands upon her time.

When Saturn in Leo in her 6th house trined her Mars, her new job, which during the first two years had been disappointing, began to reveal its benefits. Working with handicapped children, helping them to strengthen their bodies and increase their mobility, she began to experience the rewards of her patience. Her income was now stable and substantial enough to meet her needs, and she was developing a close friendship with an older woman in the program, whose unflagging support boosted her self-esteem and motivation.

At the time of my consultation with her, Saturn was entering Libra and opposing her Mars. She was married again, and struggling to cope with the problems created by the impending failure of her husband's business. She was also unemployed, with a six-month-old child, and actively involved in organizing a daycare program for local mothers—a program which she was committed to, but which could not guarantee her and her husband any income for at least a few years. What did she learn from her previous transits which helped her to handle the conflicts she was experiencing?

During the previous few months, this woman had been resenting her husband's poor business judgment and blaming him for the restrictions she was now facing. But self-sufficient by nature, she had always been able to support herself and discover job opportunities related to her interests. Throughout each of her Saturn/Mars transits, she was willing to work long hours and if necessary live within a low income bracket. Assessing her past experiences, she discovered that the part of herself related to her Mars in Aries in the 2nd house actually preferred to earn its own income, and thrived upon the challenges of a demanding job and physical labor. With transiting Saturn in her eighth house, she would not be wise to take undue financial risks as she attempted to start a daycare program; she could instead slowly begin to organize a part-time daycare program while also working at a job which is financially stable. Why should she blame her husband for not being able to support her or finance her new enterprise? She herself had the drive and resourcefulness she needed to succeed eventually with her plans, provided that she listen to transiting Saturn and trust in time, cultivating her patience and willingly confronting and accepting the restrictions she is now facing. By taking responsibility for her own financial state, perhaps looking for daycare work which will provide an income *and* give her experience which can help her in the future, she could establish her own daycare center by the time transiting Saturn entered her 10th house and trined her 2nd house Mars.

Utilizing the Present and Preparing for the Immediate Future

What outer planets are aspecting our charts now? What aspects will they be forming during the next six months? By the time the transit is within three degrees of forming an exact aspect, we may be experiencing it approaching, and can benefit from determining how we might express its energies.

Our aim then is first to understand the energies of the transiting and natal planet in terms of the signs and houses they are influencing, and to discover constructive means for blending their diverse meanings. Whether the aspect formed is a conjunction, sextile, square, trine or opposition, we are going to be attempting to integrate the planets, signs and houses involved.

Consider a 38-year-old man whose natal Mercury at 24 Libra in his 11th house would soon be conjuncted by transiting Pluto.[1] Natally, his Pluto is on his 9th house cusp, sextiling both his 10th house Mars and his 7th house Uranus; it rules his 12th house. His natal Mercury, ruler of his midheaven and descendant, squares his 8th house Jupiter in Cancer and trines his 3rd house Moon in late Aquarius. As Pluto first conjuncts his Mercury, his progressed Moon is conjuncting his Jupiter and his progressed Mars is approaching his Sun/Neptune conjunction, while transiting Uranus is also sextiling it. Transiting Jupiter and Saturn are passing back and forth over his 10th house Mars.

This man was single and had worked for six years as a counselor in an alcoholism treatment program, despite his frustration with the behavior modification techniques used in the program, which did not encourage participants to take responsibility for their own actions. He had numerous ideas in regard to other methods for treating alcoholism, ideas which he frequently expounded upon (Jupiter square Mercury) but had not been able to implement (Sun/Neptune/Mars). In college and graduate school, he earned degrees in sociology and social work. Since transiting Pluto entered his 11th house, he had become increasingly concerned with sociopolitical causes of alcoholism and with the relationship between the economy and social problems. He had recently been considering joining a left-wing political organization. This man had many friends, but was often dissatisfied with the surface level of communication which used to be enjoyable to him; he was frequently bothered by his friends' lack of interest in psychological and social issues. He was also disturbed by his failure to form and maintain stable relationships with women.

Let us turn the clock back and assume that Pluto is now soon to conjunct his natal Mercury. How might he prepare for and respond to

---

1. This example first appeared in the booklet version of this chapter, published in 1981, when Pluto was in Libra.

this transit? He might attempt to deepen his friendships by sharing on a more intimate level. He might withdraw from friendships which cannot be regenerated and begin to form bonds with people with whom he experiences gut-level connections. He might seriously study the psychological, political and social issues which concern him. He might become actively involved in a political group which is in accord with his values and his approach to change.

He might enter psychotherapy, particularly group therapy, in order to explore further his own interpersonal conflicts. Under the influence of Pluto, he would benefit most from an intensive form of therapy, one which facilitates the release of emotion rather than encourages mere verbiage. He might apply himself to developing his communication, writing or group skills, so that he will have more resources to draw upon in his work and his political, social, and personal life.

He might seriously begin to reconsider his goals. With transiting Uranus approaching his ascendant and his progressed Mars approach-

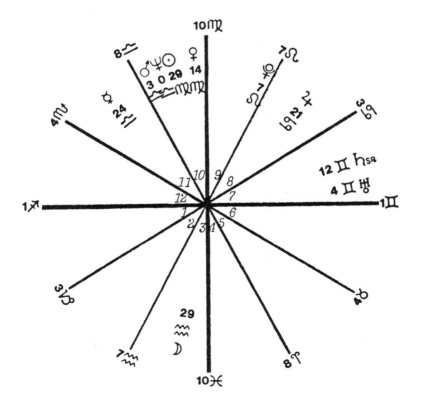

ing a conjunction to his Sun and Neptune, he might reformulate his aims in regard to his work or involvement in society, perhaps preparing to implement his own methods for dealing with alcoholism or discovering a profession through which he can more fully utilize his insights and talents while making a more significant contribution to society.

Considering the Distant Future

Many of us become preoccupied with current transits and rarely consult the ephemeris to discover what will be influencing us more than a year or two into the future. Yet becoming aware of transits which will aspect our natal planets in two or more years may help us make decisions in the present. Becoming aware of transits which will affect us even a decade before they occur may enable us to clarify the direction in which we are moving. Plotting only the house positions of the five outer planets and the major aspects formed by Uranus, Neptune, and Pluto to our natal charts during the next decade, as well as the conjunctions, squares, and oppositions of Saturn and the conjunctions of Jupiter, can reveal to us the areas of our charts which will be emphasized and the important lessons we are likely to be learning. For a complete picture of planetary influences, we might also determine our most significant progressions.

Let's say, for example, that we have an Aries midheaven with Jupiter in the 10th house trining Mars in Sagittarius in the 6th house, and that Saturn is now in Libra in our 4th house. We have recently been laid off from an airlines job which we loved, and have taken a potentially more lucrative but less enjoyable job in real estate. Previously, we could not consider buying our own home because we could not afford it, but we are now about to make a commitment to a condo which will stretch our budget for many years.

Some astrologers might advise us that Saturn in the 4th house is foundation building, and that the timing is right for such a choice. But what if we consider all our planetary selves, not just Saturn, and look ahead a few years into the future? Jupiter will then be in Aries in our 10th house again, and Uranus will conjunct our midheaven and be in 10th house for seven years. Will we not then want more of the freedom to travel which has always been important to us? Might we not lose our interest in real estate, which has only appealed to us since Saturn entered our empty 4th house, and find another airlines job which will allow us to travel more frequently?

Perhaps the pull of Saturn is insistent, and we make the decision to buy our first condo anyway. But if we are aware that we may want to return to a travel-oriented airlines position in the future, we might choose to buy a less costly condo rather than one which will limit our future choices due to hefty mortgage payments.

Consider another example, which involves speculating about the more distant future. A woman with Sun in Leo and Moon in Virgo in the 5th house and a late Capricorn M.C. is starting a doctorate program in child psychology, hoping to complete the program in four years while working part-time. However, she has only recently moved in with her boyfriend, and has just found out that she is pregnant. She does not wish to have an abortion, but she fears that if she has a child now, and makes a commitment to the family life that is also important to her, she will never become the child psychologist she wants to be. Her partner wishes to marry her, and also wants to have several children. But balancing work, a full-time doctorate program, marriage and young children is an impossible task.

Looking ten years ahead, she discovers that three outer planets—Jupiter, Saturn and Pluto—will all be in Capricorn in her 9th house at that time. Indeed, even Mars and the South Node will line up with them in Capricorn. Perhaps knowing this will ease her fears that she will never again have the opportunity or inclination to earn her doctorate and become a child psychologist. She may even realize that having one or more children in the next few years will provide not only considerable happiness but also give her helpful experience in regard to her future work. Indeed, she may not complete her doctorate for ten years or more, but the 9th house transits at that time (and the 10th house transits which would follow) would greatly support that particular purpose.

These examples demonstrate why being aware of the transits in the next few years, and even a decade or more into the future, can help us making viable choices in the present moment. An even wider perspective of twenty years or more may enable us to gain an overview of our lives and clarity in regard to our future direction.

By cultivating a long-range perspective, we view the present as a dynamic moment unfolding from our experiences of the past and presenting opportunities from which we can create our future. In this way, we begin to cooperate with our transits and discover how we can best actualize ourselves. Yet we may not wish to become overly preoccupied with either the past or future, because our primary aim in studying transits may be to more fully live in the now, and to expand our awareness in each dynamic moment of the present.

ASKING THE RIGHT QUESTIONS

Now that we have determined how we might learn from the past, prepare for current transits and consider transits in the distant future, we must begin to apply our knowledge. Of all the transits to our natal charts, the ones most important to us at this moment are probably the ones currently influencing us. Let us then stop and assess each of these transits, not by attempting to interpret them but by discovering how we can cooperate with their energy.

The following pages list a number of questions which we can ask ourselves as we reflect upon our Jupiter, Saturn, Uranus, Neptune, and Pluto transits. Not all of these questions may be relevant to us now, because of the nature of the planets, signs and houses involved in our particular transit, or the aspect being formed. But they can nevertheless orient us toward constructively channelling the energy of the transit and integrating it with the natal planet, sign and house.

We need to consider, as we answer the questions pertaining to us now, the natal position of the transiting planet as well as its transiting position, and the house or houses ruled by our natal planet as well as its natal placement by sign, house and aspect. Even if we fully understand the influence of the transiting planet, we will not be able to determine how to integrate it with the natal planet unless we first are in touch with how we are expressing this planet and how we might express it—all the potentials of its natal position.

Let us begin then by choosing a transit which is influencing us and reflect upon the possible expressions of the planet being aspected. Then, let us turn to the appropriate questionnaire and assess how we might constructively benefit from this transit. We might not be able to respond to each question with a wide variety of answers, nor be able to live all the answers that we do find. But we can at least, in the words of Rainer Maria Rilke,

> be patient toward all that is unsolved in your heart and try to love *the questions themselves* like locked rooms and like books that are written in a very foreign tongue. . . . the point is to live everything. *Live* the questions now. Perhaps you will then gradually, without noticing it, live along some distant day into the answers.

Transiting Jupiter

1. How may I expand beyond old boundaries in regard to this planet and house without overextending myself? How may I reach out to and explore new experiences? What will help me to discover and take advantage of opportunities which arise here?
2. How may I operate more freely in this area of my life? What must I do to give myself the space I need to experience more freedom of action?
3. How may I incorporate travel into my experience of this planet and house? What will help me open myself to new people and places?
4. How may I better enjoy myself in this realm of my life without neglecting my responsibilities? How may I increase my positive energy and enthusiasm? Experience my own abundance?
5. How do I want to enlarge myself here? What may I do "in a big way" without being excessive?
6. What will enable me to operate more confidently as I express this planet and house? How may I grow and expand my own resources?
7. What are my beliefs in regard to expressing this planet and house? How may I open or expand them to encompass new possibilities without becoming impractical?
8. How may I increase my understanding here and assimilate my experiences? What do I seek to learn in this realm of my life? How may I contact my own source of wisdom? How may I better live by and apply my understanding?
9. What have I to give in this area of my life? How may I express my good will and share my wealth of experience? In what ways may I teach, guide or otherwise help others? How may I become more of a leader, manager or benefactor?
10. How may I make my experiences here more meaningful? How may I express and fulfill my life purpose through this realm of my life?
11. What am I seeking here? What might I find? Do I really want to find it? How might I find it? How might I enjoy my quest?
12. What future plans do I have which are related to this planet and house? How may I better consider and prepare for future possibilities in this area of my life?
13. How may I explore new options rather than take the affairs of this planet, sign and house for granted or neglect the needs of the other planets, signs and houses in my chart?

Transiting Saturn

1. How may I organize and consolidate the affairs related to this planet, sign and house? What viable structures can I create here?

2. How may I "tie up loose ends" or otherwise "clean up" this house? How may I bring the issues of the past to a completion? What structures or commitments must I discard here? What must I lose in order to maintain my self-respect and live by my standards? How do I cope with such loss? What future gains can I expect if I face loss or deprivation now?

3. What are my priorities here? How may I narrow my attention to concentrate upon those priorities without limiting myself excessively? What limits are reasonable?

4. What work must be done here? What responsibilities must I attend to? What tasks require me to focus and apply my energy? How may I discipline myself to complete them? How may I function in a practical, reliable and persevering manner?

5. What am I capable of achieving in regard to this planet, sign and house? What do I want to achieve? Is it worth the expenditure of energy and time? How may I find satisfaction in the process of achieving, as well as in the end results?

6. What foundations do I need to build here? How can I make them solid? How can I maintain my patience over a long period of time? What future benefits can I expect from the groundwork I lay now?

7. What obstacles in this area of my life must be confronted and overcome? What concrete realities must I come to terms with? How can I deal successfully with external obstructions and internal blockages?

8. How may I be cautious and realistic here? How may my fear be constructive, keeping me from unwise action rather than paralyzing or enslaving me?

9. How may I strengthen myself and become more self-sufficient in this realm of my life? How may I increase my self-respect and sense of adequacy?

10. What lessons do I need to learn in regard to this planet, sign and house? How can I focus upon what I am learning, gaining and developing rather than upon the difficulties I am facing?

11. How may I exercise the self-control, discipline and responsibility that Saturn demands while also satisfying the needs of other planets in my chart and living a balanced and integrated life?

Transiting Uranus

1. Which behaviors or structures in my life related to this planet and house need to be liberated, reawakened or renovated, and which need to be discarded? Which accord with my "inner law" and which are at odds with it? Are these behaviors or structures capable of being changed? How can I change them? How can I let go of them?

2. What new behaviors, patterns or structures do I want to substitute for the old? What reforms do I want to make? How can I discover and explore alternative expressions of this planet and house? What new, unusual or progressive directions appeal to me? How might I experiment with the new? What risks am I willing to take? Are they worth taking?

3. How may I discover my unique talents here and express my individuality? How may I be different without rebelling for the sake of rebelling? How may I express my originality and inventiveness?

4. In what ways may I operate more independently in terms of this planet and house? What must I do in order to experience more freedom here? How may I operate more freely and independently while remaining aware of my interdependence in regard to the people in my life and humanity as a whole?

5. How may I become more attuned to my intuition in regard to this planet and house? How may I become more aware of universal laws as they manifest here? How may I apply my astrological and psychological understanding to this area of my life?

6. What must I do to satisfy my need for continual stimulation here without creating undue turmoil in my life? How may I allow myself the space to change directions, or to remain open to new possibilities as they reveal themselves?

7. How may I prepare for sudden and unexpected circumstances related to this planet and house—those which I deliberately create or which occur without my conscious choice? How do I cope with the unexpected? How do I live with instability in this area of my life?

8. How may I constructively experience and express my Uranus transit according to the planet and house it influences while also considering the needs of the other planets in my chart? How can I keep from instigating changes which are at odds with all the other parts of myself? How may I utilize Uranus to my best advantage while also functioning in an integrated manner and living by my deepest values, aims and ideals?

Transiting Neptune

1. How may I, if necessary, live with the affairs of this planet, sign and house in suspension? How may I cope with confusion here?

2. How may I make space in this area of my life so that I may clear out the debris of the past and experience inner quiet? How may I demand less of myself as Neptune "reprocesses" my natal planet, enabling it to function more meaningfully in the future? How may I allow myself to drift into experiences of greater fulfillment without drifting off course or neglecting all responsibilities? How may I become more flowing here?

3. How may I keep myself from becoming helpless or dependent in this area of my life? What must I do to become more deeply centered and in touch with my inner light? How can meditation, spiritual study or such sources of divine wisdom as the *I Ching* help me to gain clarity here?

4. How may I be more creative, actively using my imagination and inspiration in relation to this planet, sign and house? What creative arts might I experience and appreciate in the context of this area of life?

5. How may my dreams and fantasies help me to experience more fulfillment here? How may I learn from my fantasies or use my imagination to create positive images related to this planet, sign and house? What must I do to translate my fantasies and dreams into practical form?

6. How may I become more open to my feelings in regard to this planet, sign, and house? How may I cope with my oversensitivity and protect myself from absorbing the negative feelings of others?

7. How may I express my compassion here? What do I have to give, and how may I give of myself here without encouraging dependency or becoming a martyr? What service may I provide for others?

8. How may I keep from deluding myself here or living in a dream world? How may my inner guidance and the perceptions of others keep me in touch with reality? How may I maintain my faith if my illusions are being stripped away and my ideals are being challenged?

9. How may I become attuned to my ideals in regard to this planet, sign and house, and more capable of living by them? How may I express the divine in me?

10. How may I fulfill my need for "higher" experience here and remain open to illumination? How may my expression of this planet, sign

and house become more inspirational and meaningful? How may I experience my oneness with humanity and the universe in regard to this area of my life? How may I allow the healing energies of the universe to infuse me with light and guide me through this period of transition?

Transiting Pluto

1. How may I completely involve myself in the affairs of this planet, sign and house? How may I tap and channel the vast reservoir of energy now available to me through this area of my life?

2. How may I remain in touch with my gut experience here? What must I do to express this planet, sign and house from the core of myself? How may I become aware of what is essential to me here?

3. How may I "die" to the past in this area of my life, and eliminate all that is now inessential? How may I cope with the destruction of the old, if such destruction is necessary? How may I destroy only that which needs destroying, while facilitating the creation of the new?

4. How may I plunge beneath the surface and deepen my experience here? How may I become more perceptive in this area of my life, and use my perceptiveness for my own and other people's benefit? What therapeutic pursuits will enable me to have the depth experience I seek here?

5. How may my desire for intensity here improve my life rather than create undue turmoil? What kind of intensity do I want to experience here? How may I satisfy my need for "a total experience"?

6. How may I constructively release the poisons that may be accumulating in me in regard to this planet, sign and house? How may I transmute my jealousy, greed, rage or unfulfilled desire?

7. How may I regenerate myself in this area of my life? How may I renew or remake myself in accordance with this planet, sign and house? How may I feel more alive?

8. How may I become more resourceful in this area of my life? What resources of my own am I capable of using? How may I effectively work with the resources of others?

9. How may I experience my personal power here, rather than wield power over others or feel powerless? How may I use my power to transform, heal or regenerate others? In what way may I have a constructive and significant impact upon others through expressing my power here?

10. How may I contribute to society through this area of my life? With what reforms or activities of social or political significance might I become involved? How may I use my power and resourcefulness to combat the evils in society and to introduce reforms which are vital and of far-reaching impact?
11. How may I involve the depths of my being in the affairs of this planet, sign and house without neglecting my other planets, signs and houses? How may my experience of Pluto be integrated with all the other areas of my life?

Saturn/Uranus and Saturn/Neptune

When one planet aspects another, we experience the influence of the transiting planet upon the aspected planet, impacting the natal house of the aspected planet *and* the house which that planet rules in our chart.

Usually when an outer planet aspects one of our outer planets, most of us pay less attention to it than we do to an aspect to a personal planet, and may as a result be unaware of the opportunities provided to us. As with any transit, we may benefit most by focusing not on the aspect, but rather the planetary combination—e.g., Saturn/Uranus or Saturn/Neptune.

Understanding the possibilities of a planetary combination is useful to us whether we are considering transit-to-transit aspects (e.g., the Saturn/Uranus oppositions of 2008–2010), transit-to-natal aspects (e.g., Saturn aspecting our Uranus our transiting Uranus aspecting our Saturn), or natal-to-natal aspects (e.g., a Saturn/Uranus square in our natal chart). In each situation, we would want to ask ourselves all the possible meanings of those two planetary energies in relation to each other. We would hopefully then make choices which express their most constructive manifestations.

In the original edition of this book, published in 1985, I discussed at length the then upcoming Saturn/Uranus and Saturn/Neptune conjunctions, and how we might best express these two planetary combinations. Neither of these conjunctions will occur again until 2025; however, Saturn/Neptune oppositions occurred recently in 2006–2007, and a Saturn/Uranus opposition will repeat a number of times between December 2008 and July 2010. As a result, I have chosen to include again a discussion of these two planets in combination, with interpretations and guidance which we also can apply to natal aspects involving these planets.

However, with transits to our natal chart, our experience of this planetary combination and indeed any planetary combination will be influenced by which planet is transiting. For example, under transiting Saturn square natal Uranus, we may lead us to grapple with demands, responsibilities and time pressures which limit our personal freedom, but we may also find concrete forms through which we can express our intuition and individuality. Under transiting Uranus squaring our Saturn, we may discover new opportunities for breaking out of fixed patterns, expressing ourselves in unique ways, and perhaps also making significant changes in our work situation.

Let us consider both the negative and positive potentials of Saturn/Uranus and Saturn/Neptune in combination, so that may prepare for the difficulties they may bring us, and create a vision of possibilities we may wish to actualize.

Saturn/Uranus

The combined influence of Saturn/Uranus or of the Saturn/ Uranus conjunction may at first adversely affect us as follows:

a) We may fear and resist change, clinging to old structures and relationships in spite of continual upsets which call upon us to open up to other possibilities.

b) We may in our frustration with existing structures and commitments blindly break free of all that restrains us, destroying those parts of our lives which are beneficial as well as those which are detrimental.

c) We may experience ourselves oppressively restricting other people's freedom, or attracting situations in which our desires for freedom are blocked by others.

d) We may remain locked within the tension of individuality vs. conformity or freedom vs. commitment, unable to take a stand in either direction or integrate the two polarities.

e) We may in our fear inhibit our expression of our intuition, originality or social idealism.

f) We may become self-willed and power-seeking, and as a result act in a dictatorial and/or inflexible manner in our work, as well as in regard to groups, organizations and causes.

g) We may experience considerable alienation or separation within groups, institutions or society as a whole.

Saturn and Uranus are co-rulers of Aquarius, and as such, truly may be the heralds of the Aquarian Age. Once we are aware of the potentials their energy may bring us on both personal and social levels, we can motivate ourselves to create and manifest any or all of these possibilities:

1) *We can overcome fear.* Attunement to Uranus can help us to transcend the fears which have paralyzed and blocked us, and to open ourselves to unforeseen opportunities which lie behind previously closed doors.

2) *We can liberate and reform old structures.* Now is the time to bring new transformative energy into our work, relationships and other significant commitments. Through our willingness to risk, experiment and change, we can surmount the obstacles in our path and revitalize areas of our lives which are no longer satisfying. We may then discover that the structures in which we have lived are more flexible than we had imagined, and that we are able to function independently within limitations we ourselves have chosen.

3) *We can gain freedom through commitment.* Finding the right person, task, group or profession may actually free our energies so that we are more effective and are more fulfilled by our activities. Once we know our priorities and goals and dedicate ourselves to them, we actualize new potentials within ourselves. Such dedication may liberate us from the "shoulds" we internalized in the past and may enable us to develop our own internal controls as well as self-discipline and self-sufficiency.

4) *We can commit ourselves to our own liberation.* The influence of Saturn upon Uranus can lead us to focus single-mindedly upon awakening our true nature by discovering the laws of our inner being and choosing to function autonomously in a manner which is true to all that we value within ourselves. In the words of Henry Miller, "Emancipate yourself! No one else will. No one else can."

5) *We can develop the internal foundations necessary to cope with a changing world.* As we build our own foundations and become less dependent upon outer structures, we increase our capacity not only to initiate change but also to adjust to the unknown, unexpected and often highly upsetting changes which circumstances may force upon us. In our rapidly changing society, this ability is of prime importance if we are to become directing agents rather than victims at the mercy of forces outside ourselves.

6) *We can master new systems of thought and translate original ideas into practical forms.* As our minds awaken to new possibilities, we can choose to ground those possibilities in reality by giving form to our ideas and ideals. The flashes of insight and invention of Uranus can be translated into concrete forms. Saturn helps us to master and make practical use of computers and technological inventions which characterize the beginning of the Aquarian Age. We can use old systems in new ways and apply new learning to revitalize and expand the potentials of old systems. Applying Saturnian discipline and reality testing to our search for truth can also lead us to develop a firm conceptual base in astrology, new age philosophy, contemporary science and political thought.

7) *We can create and discover the intersection point between the laws of our being and the society in which we live.* Saturn and Uranus together can help us redefine and rediscover our place in society and to express our interdependence in a way which enables us to function independently and yet also in conjunction with the larger whole. Seeking a middle ground between individuality and conformity, we can choose tasks and life structures which celebrate our uniqueness and individuality and also enable us to be included in and involved with society.

8) *We can commit ourselves to social change.* The idealism and humanitarian attitudes of Uranus must be tested and applied in the world if they are to have any real impact upon the structures of society. Our own sense of social responsibility can lead us to work with groups and social institutions in order to bring about lasting change to the political, interpersonal and environmental systems in which we live.

Quotations for Saturn/Uranus

Come to a limit and transcend it; come to a limit and transcend it.
Our only security is curability to change.
—SAM KEEN (*paraphrasing* JOHN LILLY)

Again and again, a voice within commands us to get out of the rut,
to leave bag and baggage, to change cars, change directions.
—HENRY MILLER

The greatest and noblest pleasure which we have in this world is to
discover new truths, and the next is to shake off old prejudices.
—FREDERICK THE GREAT

I challenge the axioms. —BERTRAND RUSSELL

Liberty is obedience to the law which one has laid down for oneself.
—JEAN-JACQUES ROUSSEAU

Freedom means choosing your burden. —HEPZIBAH MENUHIN

Finding the center of strength within ourselves is in the long run the best contribution we can make to our fellow men. —ROLLO MAY

Fear is the static that prevents me from hearing my intuition.
—HUGH PRATHER

A man can be free even within prison walls. The body can be bound with chains, the spirit never. —BERTOLT BRECHT

It is easy in the world to live after the world's opinion; it is easy in solitude to live after your own; but the great man is he who in the midst of the crowd keeps with perfect sweetness the independence of solitude.
—RALPH WALDO EMERSON

I believe in individualism . . . up to the point where the individualist starts to operate at the expense of society. —FRANKLIN ROOSEVELT

Am I my brother's keeper? —GENESIS

No man is an Island, entire of itself. —JOHN DONNE

We are alone, yes, but inside this solitude we are brothers, helping each other to go forward without stumbling. —ELIE WIESEL

He drew a circle that shut me out—
Heretic, rebel, a thing to flout.
But Love and I had the wit to win:
We drew a circle that took him in.
—EDWIN MARKHAM

The highest compact we can make with our fellow is—"Let there be truth between us forever." —RALPH WALDO EMERSON

This is the only true joy in life, the being used by a purpose recognized by yourself as a mighty one . . . instead of complaining that the world will not devote itself to making you happy. —GEORGE BERNARD SHAW

Those who expect to reap the blessings of freedom must, like men, undergo the fatigues of supporting it. —THOMAS JEFFERSON

I place the needs of our society above my own ambitions. —RALPH NADER

And now, Humanity, I turn to you;
I consecrate my service to the world! —VOLTARINE DE CLEYRE

I am in the world
to change the world. —MURIEL RUKEYSER

The reality is that changes are coming. They must come.
You must share in bringing them. —JOHN HERSEY

Saturn/Neptune

The combined influence of transiting Saturn and transiting Neptune likewise has both negative and positive implications. The transiting conjunction, opposition, square—or any blend of these two planets within our charts—may lead us to encounter one or more of the following dilemmas:

a) We may be feeling exhausted, unmotivated, unable to attend to the affairs of the planet, sign and house being aspected.

b) Overburdened and struggling to cope with the responsibilities or normal expressions of this particular energy, we may avoid dealing with the realities before us and easily succumb to fantasies which are too impractical to manifest and/or beyond our capacity to actualize at the present time.

c) We may fluctuate between periods of inspiration and discouragement, sustained effort and avoidance, while experiencing vague anxiety, disillusionment or hopelessness which prevents us from feeling satisfaction in this area of our lives, and also fails to reveal to us either the source of the problem or what we can do to overcome it.

d) We may remain unsuccessful in our attempts to express this planetary energy because we are ambivalent and cannot clearly define our aims, because we have insufficient information to make a firm decision or follow through on our commitments, or because the people upon whom we depend are likewise confused and unable to commit themselves.

e) We may withdraw into ourselves, unable to express outwardly the energies of the planet in question. Alone, we may give in to self-doubt, self-pity, passivity, paranoia or feelings of victimization or indulge more than usual in drink, drugs or sleep.

f) In our relationships we may be oversensitive to rejection and doubt our capacity to give. We may alternate between experiencing Neptunian dependency and passivity and its counterpart of self-sacrifice, and shutting off completely, preferring to be left alone with the muddle occurring in our own psyches.

g) We may yearn for deeper connections with people, for romance or tenderness or soul encounters, but not be willing to invest the energy required of us or to confront in the flesh the harsher realities of human contact. As a result, we may limit our social sphere or cultivate relationships with people who are in some way inaccessible.

h) In work, we may drift aimlessly, mired in unfulfilling tasks, flitting from project to project, desiring to change but neither knowing what we want nor feeling ready to commit ourselves to a new direction.

i) Our material affairs may be in disorder, our bank account leaking uncontrollably, so that we must face giving up expenditures which have been important to us in the past. We may feel deprived, unsure of our capacity to earn or budget money, and helpless in regard to the economic dilemmas of our society.

j) We may feel spiritually, creatively, emotionally or sexually blocked, unable to contact the wellsprings of energy that have sustained us in the past.

k) Finally, we may experience the structures of our lives and the foundations of our identities slowly dissolving, leaving a gnawing emptiness which has not yet revealed the potential latent within it for new structures or foundations, for new activities, relationships or sources of nourishment.

The combined influence of Saturn and Neptune on one or more of our planets, or their influence upon each other by transit, may affect us in any of the above-mentioned ways, but we do not have to remain victim to our confusion, depression or sense of inadequacy. These planets together can provide both the foundation and the inspiration for future satisfactions and accomplishments. But in order to benefit from them, we must be willing to learn from our experience and to allow the subliminal energies within us to awaken and implement constructive change. How then can we respond favorably to Saturn/Neptune influences?

1) *We can remain sensitively aware of our own limitations.* Now is the time to be easy on ourselves, to let up on the pressures we create in regard to the planet, sign and house which Neptune is aspecting. Consciously, we may feel a lack of energy or motivation, but subconsciously our energy is realigning itself, preparing to reveal to us our future direction. We must trust that inner wisdom and make space in our lives for it to consolidate and gradually enter our awareness.

2) *We can allow ourselves to flow into new structures.* The priorities, commitments and structures of the past may no longer be viable for us, but it is not the time either to break loose or wholeheartedly embrace new priorities. Because we do not yet clearly know the next step we must take, we can discover it only by allowing ourselves to drift a little, obeying the voice of our intuition or inspiration, and trusting that it will lead to new sources of meaning. If we relax and follow the promptings of our subconscious, we may neglect people, activities or behaviors of the past, but such neglect can enable us to discover that those facets of our lives are not really nourishing or essential and should be left behind, altered or simply reassessed. The facets of our lives which continue (or begin) to beckon us are likely to be more substantial and rewarding. Only by loosening the structures in which we live can we in time flow into new structures and commitments which will be more enriching than those of the past.

3) *We can reinspire old structures.* If we allow ourselves to remain in touch with the emotional flux within us, without judgment or pressure, we may experience an opening of the heart, a release of creative or spiritual energy which can rekindle our inner light and enliven even the most barren aspects of our lives. Even our most unrealistic fantasies, our bouts of oversensitivity, our muddled responses to the activities and people around us can be doorways to higher realms. Rather than avoid upsetting feelings, we can encourage their release and channel them, nurturing our feelings with quiet evenings of music, meditation or inspirational literature. Such care for our emotional natures can enable us to transcend our feelings of aloneness. The fullness we begin to experience within ourselves can spill over into other dimensions of our lives, injecting new meaning into our work, reawakening the romance of the creative or spiritual communion we may once have had in our relationships. A willingness to experience and confront Saturnian deprivations, fears or anxieties can awaken Neptunian compassion and inspiration; an openness to Neptunian sensitivities can strengthen and solidify our Saturnian commitments.

4) *We can give form to our inspiration.* Although we may be unable to focus upon one project or person for an extended period of time, we can apply ourselves in small spurts of energy to make our creative or spiritual promptings concrete. Neptune may release a flood of previously subconscious feelings which can indeed overwhelm us unless Saturn provides a channel. Now is the time to finish writing that poem we once started, to give form to our sadness by playing our favorite Chopin preludes, to allow our meditations to infiltrate our lives and bring peace to our daily routines rather than exist apart from them.

5) *We can observe, assess, and direct our fantasies.* If we are prone now to fantasize about future activities or relationships, we can learn from our daydreaming by observing our daydreaming process. Our fantasies are a key to what is missing, what is unfulfilled in our lives, and can lead us to new courses of action—ones which may not be as enthralling as those which our imagination can produce, but which can nevertheless be an improvement upon what we can have now. If our imagination wants free rein to explore new possibilities and impossibilities, we need not fear it will threaten our hold upon reality if we maintain an observer stance as we fantasize and afterwards assess the regions to which we have ventured. Desires and needs that we may not be able to satisfy in reality may be acknowledged, experienced, and fulfilled in our fantasies, provided that we clearly recognize them as fantasies and keep them from spilling uncontrollable confusions into our relationships and activities. Eventually, the awareness we gain about our unsatisfied needs and desires can help us consciously to build constructive thought forms—realistic fantasies related to our future goals, fantasies which we can replay in our minds as we begin to manifest them in our lives.

6) *We can clarify our values and ideals and rebuild our faith.* What is really important to us? What values and ideals must we live by to attain peace of mind? How can we best invest our limited energy, time and financial resources in order to improve the quality of our lives? Most likely, under Saturn and Neptune, we are questioning our priorities, perhaps undermining our faith in ourselves, other people or the divine, or even eroding the very foundations of our existence with vague feelings of hopelessness and despair. But such questioning can be a constructive process; it does not have to lead us to reject all sources of meaning in our lives. We may be disillusioned, but such disillusionment can help us to clarify how we have gone astray and to discover those elements of reality we have neglected to incorporate into our faith or value system.

Now is the time to rebuild our inner foundations by restructuring our relationships to ourselves and the cosmos. Saturn and Neptune together can help us to rediscover the middle ground between idealism and practicality, between our capacity to wait and trust and our capacity for committed, directed action.

7) *We can concretely express our spirituality.* Once we have become grounded by facing the limitations within us and around us and have restructured our faith and idealism, we can begin to make our new-found spirituality concrete by translating it into action. Of what value are our ideals if we do not live by them? Of what use are our meditations if we do not open our hearts to the people around us? Instead of despairing over today's political, environmental, economic, and interpersonal crises, we can realize that we are needed. We can ask ourselves how we can be of service to the planet Earth and dedicate ourselves with Neptunian inspiration and Saturnian commitment to manifesting our ideals.

8) *We can redefine our relationship capabilities.* If we are oversensitive now to people around us, ambivalent about our relationships and inclined to withdraw into ourselves, we need to be protective of our sensitivities and not demand much of ourselves with others. Our relationship needs can now be redefined and clarified. Perhaps, if we do not have the energy to form new contacts, we can use what social energy we have to reassess and reawaken the old. If our perceptions of people are foggy, and we delude ourselves about potentials that may not exist, we can at least be aware of our fogginess and refuse to make new commitments until we have clarified what we lack and what we want. The intimacy that we may dream of, which may seem totally unattainable at the present moment, may actually be possible for us once we clearly define what we are seeking and what we are willing and able to give. But how in the context of our lives now, with our sensitivity at a peak and our social energy minimal, can we satisfy some of these yearnings? How can we reinspire the relationships we already have? How can we keep ourselves from despairing over our difficulty in both giving and receiving love? We must answer these questions for ourselves, even if it means discovering that we are associating with the wrong people, even if we must continue to endure the lonely but necessary waiting period which strengthens us and prepares us for more fulfilling relationships in the future.

9) *We can share our confusions, illusions and ambivalences.* If we now feel that we are constantly giving mixed messages, opening ourselves fully one moment and shutting closed the next, we can at least honestly share our experience. Such verbalization may not only invite understanding responses from others; it may help us to develop the art of expressing sensitivity and compassion *while* communicating our limitations and boundaries. The capacity to share our confusions, to give of ourselves and maintain ourselves simultaneously can lead us not only to the higher Neptunian communion we may seek, but also to the solidity and stability of Saturnian relationships which are able to endure and rebuild themselves despite the internal and external fluctuations of our everyday lives.

Images for Saturn/Neptune

foundations of sand • endless labyrinth • barrier reef • clogged drain • frozen pipes • water filter • desert places of the soul • internal fortress • underwater dam • shellfish • weeping willow • slow music • mist-covered mountain • holy mountain • monastery walls • sacred tree • celestial ship • desert oasis • soul construction • foundations of the soul • dream administration • cold water • ice

Quotations for Saturn/Neptune

Once he reached for something golden hanging from a tree
And his hand came down empty. —CAROLE KING

We bruise our feet because no vision is . . .
The pools we plunge in through the ground mist splash
Spurting in stars that vanish as they flash . . .
And if in space we may clearings meet
They serve but to disclose a further fog.
—JOSEPH MACLEOD

Desolate dreams pursue me out of sleep;
Weeping I wake; waking, I weep, I weep. —EDNA ST. VINCENT MILLAY

Your pain is the breaking of the shell that encloses your understanding.
—KAHLIL GIBRAN

You speak of suffering, withdrawal, retreat . . . Face this suffering,
for all the real suffering can save us from unreality. Real pain is
human and opening. —ANAIS NIN

For it is not physical solitude that actually separates one from other men,
not physical isolation but spiritual isolation. It is not the desert island
nor the stony wilderness. It is . . . the desert wastes in the heart
through which one wanders lost and a stranger. . . . If one is out of touch
with oneself, then one cannot touch others.
—ANNE MORROW LINDBERGH

Learning how to make others trust you is the best protection there is.
And it will make you safer than all the armor you can find. —MERLE SHAIN

Your faith, let it be stirred
If only by a dream, a transient word,
A hopelessness you have some hope in still.
—MARION STROBEL

First chill, then stupor, then the letting go. —EMILY DICKINSON

Reality, however, has a sliding door. —RALPH WALDO EMERSON

"This is Serious," said Pooh. "I must have an Escape." —A. A. MILNE

I have discovered that there is a Pattern, larger and more beautiful
than our short vision can weave. —JULIA SEATON

The only limits are, as always, those of vision. —JAMES BROUGHTON

In dreams begins responsibility. —W. B. YEATS

I am indeed . . . a practical dreamer. My dreams are not airy nothings.
I want to covert my dreams into reality. —GANDHI

If there is a faith that can move mountains, it is faith in your own power.
—MARIA EBNER VON ESCHENBACH

If you have built castles in the air, your work need not be lost; there
is where they should be. Now put foundations under them.
—HENRY DAVID THOREAU

Chapter Six

NEPTUNE: HOW TO
SWIM THROUGH COSMIC WATERS

Neptune is an elusive, subtle planet of transformation which dissolves attitudes and behavior patterns of the past as it transits planets in our charts; it also awakens our compassion, receptivity, creativity, spirituality, and idealism. In its natal position, Neptune influences not only the house in which it occurs, but also planets it aspects and our Pisces-related houses. By transit, it extends its influence to other planets and houses, eventually touching all facets of our personality and all realms of our lives with its confusing but also illuminating energies.

Neptunian States of Consciousness

Let's begin understanding Neptune by discovering a number of different realms or related states of consciousness which Neptune represents. In the first state, Neptune overwhelms our awareness of ourselves, so that we are awake but feeling as if we are half-asleep, in a fog with little consciousness of our thoughts and actions. In this state, we "space out" easily, forget things and lose track of time. We may feel as if we are drugged, unable to be fully awake and alert. A second state is also a state of half-sleep, but with a clarity of perception. It is the intersection of two worlds we experience immediately before or after sleep, when our egos are entering into or emerging from Neptune's dream state. We are not aware of ourselves, but our vision is sharp, and we experience images and insights which we may or may not carry over into consciousness. Psychologists call this twilight state before sleep the hypnogogic state, and the twilight state after sleep the hypnopompic state.

A third Neptune state is the fantasy and daydreaming state, in which we again lose awareness of ourselves, although our perceptions are vivid, and our mental imagery may seem at least as real as the world around us. This may be a totally receptive state, in which we do not control the images we are receiving, or it may be directed in part by our conscious minds, as we choose to let certain fantasies unfold and to participate actively in our internal process. A fourth state is the dream state, in which we have no self-awareness or consciousness, and our ego is completely dissolved in astral realms. Although our imagery may be vivid, it is not necessarily carried over into consciousness. Frequently, the themes which occur repeatedly in our dreams are related to the planets aspected by Neptune, whether natally or by transit, and the planets which occur natally and by transit in our 12th house.

A fifth Neptunian state is the meditative state, the deep relaxation also known as the alpha state, in which our awareness, at least in meditation, is focused inward, observing our inner process. Because we are focused, our perception is clear—we identify with the observer within us and yet are able to perceive what is happening inside. A sixth state is the psychic state, in which, although we may not be focused upon our internal experience, we are receptive to it, and receive images and impressions related to other people in our lives or to our own future circumstances. A realm bordering the meditative and psychic states is a seventh state, in which we are in contact with the center of our being and experience what I call "the gap in the midst of silence," the voice of our internal guidance. In this state, we *know* we are being directed by our highest Self; if we have to ask whether we are listening to the right voice or whether we are deluding ourselves (and tuning in instead to our own desires or fears), then we are not likely to be making contact with our center, with the divine source within us.

An eighth state, induced by alcohol or drugs, may seem like many of the other Neptunian realms, but because it is artificially induced, it often releases some of the negative energy in our psyches, pushing upward repressed material from our subconscious before we are capable of assimilating it. Hallucinations are related to this state of Neptunian consciousness, because it interferes with our ability to differentiate fantasy from reality. A ninth state is creative inspiration, similar to meditation because we are also focused; however, we are focused upon a center outside ourselves. Our awareness is crystallized, projecting the Neptunian astral realm outward through the lens of our awareness, translating it into external form. In this state, as well as the meditative state, we may feel as if we are in a trance. Our egos are pulled deeper into our subconscious, only to emerge later with an increased clarity of consciousness.

A tenth Neptunian state is the state of "opening the heart," in which the pains and sensitivities of the past may wash over us, but in which we also experience considerable love and compassion for the people in our lives and humanity as a whole. Neptune is the higher octave of Venus; as Neptune heightens our sensitivity, we become able to transcend our desires and needs and to love from the divine source within each of us.

A final Neptunian state is mystical experience or cosmic consciousness, a blissful state in which we experience inner peace and feel at one with ourselves and the universe. We transcend ourselves; our egos merge with the spirit or Self within us and receive an influx of healing and rejuvenating cosmic energy. A brief sojourn into this state may awaken our spirituality and, for a time, heighten our awareness of the world within and around us. To be able to maintain this cosmic consciousness for more than a few moments or hours is to experience the enlightenment which is the aim of many Eastern religions, such as Zen Buddhism.

These states of consciousness are clearly related to each other. As we become more capable of experiencing and channelling Neptunian energy, we can learn to swim through one of Neptune's realms into another realm, rather than remain stuck frantically splashing the waters in an attempt to free ourselves from confusion, pain or unwelcome fantasies.

Coping with Neptunian Confusion

Let's look at some of these states more closely, beginning with the confused, foggy, low-energy state in which we may feel out of contact with ourselves and others, incapable of making decisions or taking firm action because everything seems amorphous and uncertain. As a result of this confusion, we may be unclear how to express ourselves in the area of life indicated by the houses Neptune is influencing; we may be in a fog as we express the planets it conjuncts, squares or opposes natally or by transit.

We can best deal with confusing Neptune transits when we understand that we are operating on only a small portion of our energy in regard to the aspected planet. Our conscious energy seems to be leaking into our subconscious, while our subconscious energy is simultaneously seeping into our consciousness and dissolving behavior patterns of the past. For a time, we are not likely to be able to operate clearly or productively in the old ways in which we expressed this planet. Neptune is eroding this old expression, withdrawing energy from it and using that energy to prepare subconsciously for a new means of expression. This part of ourselves is actually being bathed in the well of our subconscious, taking a deep rest so that in the future it can spring forth, totally refreshed and bursting with new inspiration.

As in many myths of creation all that existed at first was unnamed, undifferentiated chaos before the beginning of the earth and the birth of humanity, so we are journeying into the primeval chaos in order to give birth to higher dimensions of ourselves. Because of this incubation period, we must not ask much of the planets and houses influenced by Neptune during this transit; we must not pressure ourselves or demand that we function as we did in the past. Rather, we need to trust our subconscious and give it time to prepare for the next stage in our development. We need to cultivate our ability to live with ambivalence and confusion, with important issues in our lives in suspension, with no clear answers available. We need to understand fully that we are in a time of transition, vacationing upon an island in the midst of Neptunian waters, as our energy is being reprocessed to prepare for a future period of greater fulfillment in regard to the expression of the planet, sign and house which Neptune is influencing.

We can, however, begin to grope our way out of the tangled labyrinths of our psyches by getting in touch with the part of ourselves that wants the fog or confusion, the blankness of thought or paralysis of action. On some level, we do not want to think or act or feel in a clear or forthright manner, or to continue to function according to old patterns. Our previous experience of this planet, sign and house is no longer meaningful to us; we prefer to blot it out while we are waiting for new possibilities to unfold into our consciousness.

One factor which may contribute to the internal fog is our psychic oversensitivity, which, under Neptune, may be considerable.[1] Often, we are overwhelmed because we are absorbing the energy of other people. If Neptune is aspecting our Mercury, we may pick up their thoughts; if the Moon, their feelings and needs; if Saturn, their fear; if Mars, their anger or desire. We may have difficulty distinguishing between us and them. For this reason, we may require meditation or relaxation time each day in which we retreat to a quiet space within so that we may revitalize ourselves. Water helps the internal cleansing process—taking a shower or bath, or spending time at an ocean or lake. Soothing music is also recommended.

If Neptune is influencing a physical dimension of our charts, such as our ascendant or ascendant ruler or Mars, we may be suffering from

---

1. A useful book for helping people cope with super-sensitivity is *The Highly Sensitive Person* by Elaine Aron (New York: Broadway Books, 1996).

tiredness or low physical energy, and may only be able to restore ourselves physically by *first* cleansing ourselves of the emotional sludge we have been accumulating in our daily lives. Nurturing and unblocking our bodies is also important. Our minds become clouded when we spend too much time in mental realms due to physical blockages. Massage is especially helpful in releasing the bodily tensions which keep us closed and constricted; once our bodies begin to open, we are more able to relinquish our mental ramblings and rest more fully and contentedly in our larger beingness.

Letting Go with Neptune

Neptune asks us to be willing to take what I call a "journey into blankness" or what is commonly known as the experience of "spacing out." If we do not choose to rest from physical, mental and emotional involvement on a daily basis, Neptune may steal our attention by leading us to become absentminded, to daydream when we need to be paying attention, or to become compulsively addicted to drugs, tobacco, or alcohol. We need to make sure that we give ourselves ample opportunities for disengaging from thought and focused behaviors and allow our minds and feelings to unwind at their own pace. Watching television or movies may be relaxing; however, we may find even more fulfillment in music or other spontaneous creative outlets. Such simple activities as hooking rugs or knitting will not only satisfy Neptune, but will also yield productive results and keep our egos from being critical of our time-wasting inactivity.

Many of us may be tempted to battle against the Neptunian fog, as we fight to gain increased clarity and discover firmer foundations. We may struggle and splash in the waters of our emotional confusion and then panic because we fear we will go down in the whirlpool we are creating. Instead, we may want to lie back and float, allowing ourselves to be soothed and supported by Neptunian waters without attempting to discover how to reach the solid shore. Gradually, we may realize that we can even swim in those waters, enjoying ourselves without trying to reach a particular destination. Doing so, we are likely to venture into the tide that will carry us to land—perhaps to a different shore than the one we were seeking, but indeed the shore which we were meant to find.

Those of us who have always been goal-oriented may be completely disoriented by Neptune's tendency to obscure our goals and our visions of the future and to keep us chained—as well as awakened—to the present moment. We may indeed lose our sense of purpose and direction for awhile. Or we may instead discover a new purpose or direction, one which values the means even more than the ends. Like a river which meanders as it flows toward the sea, diffusing itself into numerous tributaries and streams, we may likewise diffuse and open our attention to new possibilities which reside in the present; at the same time, we may nonetheless continue to progress toward our goals, although we may take considerably more time to achieve them. Under Neptune we can be both goal-directed and flow-oriented.

If Neptune is affecting our minds more than our feelings and we are existing in a mental fog, then we can begin to dispel that fog not by straining our eyes to discern shapes in the distance, but rather by inviting the fog, going deeply into it, perhaps through meditation or directed fantasy. We might even imagine ourselves being a fog, diffuse and formless, spreading ourselves in all directions and permeating all things until the sun burns through us, and we melt away in the clarity of its light. Another way to dispel this fog is simply to watch it surrounding us, to sit quietly and pay attention to our internal process. When and if images emerge, we can begin to align our consciousness with our subconscious by participating in those images, playing with them in our minds, talking with them or transforming them. When we participate and become emotionally involved, the fog no longer overpowers us, pressing down upon us; as we enter and act within it, we begin to spread the mists around and eventually blow them away into the distance.

Sometimes imagining how we might survive in an actual fog can help us understand how to cope with Neptune. We are less likely to be blinded by a fog if we rise above it or stay close to the ground. We are likely to function well in a fog if we rely not only on our vision, but open up to our other senses—hearing, smell, touch—which may give us messages that will guide us.

If the image approach to handling Neptune is not effective for us, and we still remain lost in a maze of circular thinking, confusing ourselves repeatedly with "yes, but's" and unanswerable questions, we can step outside ourselves and watch our process of confusion. Once we separate ourselves from the confuser inside us and become aware of the absurdity of his/her mental machinations, new insights may burst into our consciousness and we may begin to transcend our internal chaos. Sometimes changing, even briefly, our environment or the people we relate to by taking a short trip or becoming involved in a new activity may help to break us out of the "closed circuit" which we have been experiencing. Answers may not exist within the system in which we have been living; perhaps we have been repeatedly shuffling and rearranging the old furniture within the same old room, when what we need to do is to buy new furniture, knock down the walls, or enter another room and explore a different living arrangement. Perhaps we need to change the lens by which we view our reality. At the optometrist's office, we peer through many different lenses until we discover the one which gives us 20/20 vision. No matter how we strain to read the letters through the wrong lens, we fail. Finding the new lens means taking off the old glasses, and risking even more blurred vision before we find an even greater clarity.

Ways of Looking into Neptunian Fog

Neptune can indeed be highly frustrating, immobilizing and even terrifying. Our grasp upon reality may feel shaky. We may feel paralyzed, unable to make any decisions or act in a forthright manner. Neptune may blind us to our real feelings and needs and keep us engaged in internal dramas which seem to lead nowhere and which have little relevance to our actual circumstances. Let us therefore consider a number of additional possibilities which may enlighten us and enable us to transcend or make peace with confusing Neptunian experience:

1) We may be struggling with the wrong problems or asking the wrong questions, and thereby never being able to discover the right answer. Perhaps we do not want what we think we want, but instead want something else which, for one reason or another, we are unable to experience or ascertain. Perhaps we are perceiving our unhappiness as related to job dissatisfaction and feel as if we are running in circles internally as we attempt to plan a new course of action in terms of our career. The real source of dissatisfaction, however, may be due to our lack of contact with our feelings or an absence of emotional connectedness with our partner.

2) We may not be ready to make a change, because pieces are still missing in our development which will be provided in the future. We may not have become yet who we need to become in order to move further in one particular realm of our lives.

3) We may not want to see the way out of our dilemma for a number of reasons. First, seeing a solution might mean feeling compelled to take action we are not yet willing or able to take. Second, our conscious

mind may not now approve of the direction emerging inside of us and may sabotage our attempts to make it happen. For example, we may not be willing to consider leaving our husband because being alone is too threatening; however, when he leaves town for a week on a business trip, we may discover that loneliness has its advantages, and then may be able to consider separation as a viable solution. If we considered separation before coming to terms with aloneness, we might become so overwhelmed with fear that we join our husband on his trip rather than turn to ourselves in his absence.

4) We may not be able to see clearly because seeing can be painful. It might mean acknowledging our unknowing contribution to an untenable situation. It might mean facing the internal emptiness or the lack of love in our marriage. It might destroy our dreams and illusions. Once we see the light, we then know the darkness which we have lived within to be darkness, and we may no longer be able to settle for a life which holds less than what the light reveals to us. However, if a candle flickers for a moment, illumines our dark corner, but then is extinguished, and we do not know how to break free of the darkness or keep the candle burning, the experience of the light may be unbearably painful. Once we become aware of another kind of life, the life we have now may seem barren and meaningless. We may indeed prefer not to see.

5) Another possibility is that we do not want any actual changes in regard to the structures of our lives, but instead want to reawaken our spirit through fantasy. Our dream lover may satisfy us in our dreams, but bring unwished-for heartache in actual reality. The vision of a Caribbean holiday, when we are struggling to pay our January oil bills in a cold apartment, may inspire us more than the actual trip itself, with all its unforeseen costs and obstacles and the unpredictability of winter weather. Once we know we want the fantasy more than the reality, we can cease struggling to make those particular dreams real.

6) Our indecision and paralysis may result from insisting upon absolute certainty and ideal circumstances, both of which are impossible. Neptune is a planet of divine discontent; it provides for us images of perfection and harmony which reality cannot provide. The insistence upon making a commitment only to the ideal job or ideal partner may lead us to make no commitments at all and to spend our lives without experiencing the substantial satisfactions which commitment to imperfect people and imperfect jobs can nonetheless give us.

NEPTUNE WORKSHEET:
COPING WITH CONFUSION

Position of Neptune

SIGN: _____ HOUSE: _____ HOUSE(S) RULED: _____

ASPECTS: _____

HOUSE OF TRANSITING NEPTUNE: _____ ASPECTS BY TRANSIT: _____

TRANSITING ASPECTS TO NEPTUNE: _____

1. Describe the nature of your confusion, how you experience it and what areas of your life it influences. What is the major problem which you seem unable to resolve because of your confusion?

_____

_____

_____

_____

2. Is this the real problem, and if not, what is? What does preoccupation with this problem keep you from facing? What if you weren't confused?

_____

_____

_____

_____

3. How do you keep yourself confused? What messages do you give yourself which keep you confused?

_____

_____

_____

_____

4. What are you avoiding facing? What do you know but won't fully admit to yourself? What do you fear discovering about yourself or others? What is Neptune protecting you from seeing?

_____

_____

_____

5. What would happen if you saw the way out of your dilemma? If you had the answer, what would it be? What would you have to face then?

_____

_____

_____

_____

6. Are you looking for absolute certainty, a level of perfection or magic which doesn't exist, or a solution which requires little risk, effort or responsibility? Are you unable to have a little because you are too attached to having it all? What will it take for you to relinquish your unrealistic expectations?

_____

_____

_____

7. What fantasy/dream is standing in the way of your achieving resolution in this realm of your life? How unrealistic is it? What would you have to face if you let go of it or brought it down to earth?

_____

_____

_____

8. What truly positive, inspirational and fulfilling experiences have you had in this area of your life which have given you meaning which is lacking now? How may you discover or create more of these experiences?

_____

_____

_____

_____

9. What do you think you want? Do you REALLY want what you think you want? What do you REALLY WANT?

_____

_____

_____

_____

10. What is your real dream, and how do you block yourself from experiencing or actualizing it? How can you relinquish the "it's impossible's" and "I can't do it's" and allow yourself actually to experience and explore its real possibilities?

_____

_____

_____

11. What unconscious assumptions are influencing you and blocking you in your area of confusion? How might you uncover them? What do you take for granted which you may need to reassess?

_____

_____

_____

12. What is it about your existing situation that keeps you stuck in it or attached to it? What are you getting out of staying confused or being immobile? Do you really want to make a change or would you rather hold onto the advantages of your present position? How might you maintain some advantages and still move forward?

_____

_____

_____

13. What may need to happen first if you are to achieve some resolution in this area of your life? What might you need to do, or who might you need to become in order to be able to transcend your confusion? What is your first step?

_____

_____

14. What feelings are you not acknowledging or expressing? What unshed tears have evaporated to form clouds of confusion? How might you safely feel and release blocked feelings, in order to recover the clarity you have lost?

_____

_____

_____

15. What is truly essential in your life, and how might you simplify your life in order to live closer to your essential nature? What might you have to let go of in order to "be" with Neptune and to experience greater quality of being rather than quantity of activity?

———————————————————————————

———————————————————————————

———————————————————————————

16. Where is the clarity? What areas of your life are meaningful and fulfilling now? What might you experience if you turned your attention away from the confusion and focused more on areas of clarity and fulfillment?

———————————————————————————

———————————————————————————

———————————————————————————

17. What is on the periphery of your consciousness, trying to emerge in your life? Where do your energies want to go naturally, without conscious interference or the interference of fear and anxiety? What do you intuitively perceive the next development in your growth to be?

———————————————————————————

———————————————————————————

18. How can you shift the context of your life, allowing new energy or experiences to happen or a new perspective to occur, so that you might transcend your confusion or enter a state of being in which it is no longer relevant? What kind of experiences will help you to break free of old limiting structures, and will reinforce the new developments which seek to emerge?

———————————————————————————

———————————————————————————

19. What messages do you need to give yourself in order to transcend your confusion, and increase your clarity, inspiration and trust?

———————————————————————————

———————————————————————————

———————————————————————————

When we are confused by Neptune, we may want to ask ourselves how we are choosing to keep ourselves confused, and why. What are we not seeing? What are we avoiding facing? What have we known all along, but have been unwilling to admit to ourselves? How are we deluding ourselves? If we could see the way out, what would we see? If we had the answers, what would they be? What are we really feeling and desiring? What do we really want? What do we fear, and how does our fear keep us from perceiving and following our path? Completing the worksheet in this chapter may help us get in touch with how and why we are creating confusion for ourselves and in what way, when the timing is right, we can transcend it.

Sometimes the solution to our tangled dilemmas may be a simple motto: Go where the clarity is. The issue in which we are enmeshed may be unresolvable at the present time. The more we focus upon it, the more entangled we become. But other realms of our lives may offer promise and fulfillment—indeed may even lead us to a state of being in which we are capable of resolving the original problem. Perhaps we have been unable to find a new job because we are unwilling to compromise by accepting what is available. Finally, we set the issue aside and pay attention instead to our social life, which is thriving. At a party, in a relaxed frame of mind, we meet a successful businessman who is impressed with our social skills and wants to hire us for his company—for a position more viable for us than anything we've uncovered before. We let the issue alone and followed our natural inclinations; as a result, we become more open, and invite in exactly the energy which we need.

Occasionally, however, we cannot set aside our issues for a time. Reality makes demands upon us. Our boss will not wait for Neptune to finish transiting our Sun for us to decide about an impending project. Application deadlines are two weeks away, and we must choose now whether to aim for graduate school for next fall. In such a situation, our best course of action is to make choices with full awareness that we are in transition and that our decisions may have to be temporary, short-range, and open to re-evaluation. Consider a man who was offered a high-paying new position across the country the summer before his twin daughters, both cheerleaders, were entering their senior year in high school, and only a few months after purchasing and renovating his "dream home." Neptune was transiting his Capricorn Moon, on his nadir and ruling his 10th house. Should he sell his home and compel his wife and daughters to begin a new life in an unfamiliar city? Knowing there were many unforeseen variables and that he needed exploration time, he left his daughters with friends, sublet his house, and moved with his wife to a temporary apartment in the new location. There, he discovered that his promising new job was not at all to his liking. Yet how much more difficult his circumstances would have been if he had completely given up his previous life and subjected his family to considerable upheaval for the sake of a questionable opportunity.

Listening to Inner Guidance

Neptune rarely helps us cope with external reality and concrete issues; it is more concerned with awakening our inner self and our sources of inspiration. One of the positive benefits of the confusion we may experience is that it may motivate us to contact the center of our being and to discover the capabilities of our intuition and inner guidance. Because we may be easily lost in the twisted mazes inside us, we may need to journey deeper and deeper into ourselves to reach our center. As in a fog which thins out as it nears the ground, the closer we get to the center of ourselves or foundation of our being, the more clarity of vision we will experience. An attempt to center, through meditation or creative activity, can help us to disperse the fog and listen to our inner guidance. However, our inner voice may at times be silent, or it may advise us simply to wait and flow with the moment rather than to force the situation at hand to resolve itself. If this voice does not speak, we can at least listen to the silence at the center of our being, beneath the clamor of our many internal voices. Any attempt to unite consciousness and unconsciousness by tuning in to our center will facilitate a Neptune transit because it will keep us from making hasty or unwise decisions or from deceiving ourselves or feeling overcome by negative images, thoughts and emotions. Consulting the *I Ching* and tarot, and listening to our intuition as we interpret them rather than relying entirely upon an author or translator's explanations can also help us to become attuned to our inner voice and to learn to trust its guidance.

Knowing how to differentiate the voice at the center of ourselves from the multitude of peripheral voices representing each of our planetary personalities takes time and practice. If we hear it and do not obey it, it will be more difficult to discern the next time we seek to listen. If we do not treat it reverently and respect it even when it contradicts the promptings of our rational minds, it will become increasingly more inaccessible. We are able to hear and trust this inner voice only when we are willing to give it precedence over the chatter of all our other inner voices. We become clearly attuned to it each time we hear it and follow it. When our inner guide speaks to us, we feel calm and at peace; our energy is quiet and clear. Knowing what it feels like or sounds like,[2] we become able to determine when the guidance we are receiving is the guidance of our fear or desire or other manifestations of our ego rather than the guidance of our Self.

One important lesson we may learn under a Neptune transit as a result of our deepening attunement is the difference between essence and form. Our attachments to the forms and structures in our lives may cause suffering until we learn to let go of them. If we are focused on loving and being loved by a particular person or obtaining a specific job, we may experience ongoing dissatisfaction. However, if we become in touch with our desire to open our hearts and commit ourselves to loving in and of itself, we may attract to us a different and more appropriate partner; if we can define for ourselves the essential qualities we seek to express in our working life, we may discover job possibilities we had not considered before which truly meet our needs.

Often in relationship workshops, I facilitate an exercise which involves creating shapes out of paper which represent ourselves, and assembling those shapes in relationship to another person's shapes in order to create a combined entity. Some people alter their paper constructions as they attempt to adapt to their partner's constructions; others do not. Those who refold or even cut or rip their forms in order to create a perfect union may be operating from one of two different perspectives—identification with the paper itself or identification with the particular forms they have created. Those who are identified with the paper can substantially alter their form without experiencing loss of identity; those who are identified with the form have less freedom, and experience every alteration as a compromise and as a threat to self. One of the lessons of this exercise, and of a Neptune transit, is that of discovering and committing ourselves to our essence, relinquishing forms, structures, identifications and attachments which prevent us from becoming who we truly are.

Neptune and Creative Expression

Who we truly are may be far less rigid and controlled than we have known ourselves to be. Awakening to who we truly are may involve regaining contact with our inner child, and the spontaneity, playfulness and creativity which this part of ourselves possesses. Creative expression related to

2. I experience it not as a voice or image, or even as words, but as a puff of air emerging after a slight contraction from that gap in the midst of silence. Other people's experience may differ. Some people do indeed hear a voice; others actually see the path they are to follow.

Neptune, such as music, dance, photography and poetry, is also an effective means of centering and channeling the energies of a Neptune transit, as well as of experiencing the more celestial realms of Neptune. As we focus our "astral experience" outside ourselves through expressing ourselves creatively, we will benefit most by allowing Neptune to reveal the exact form our creativity requires, rather than trying to force ourselves to conform to some predetermined pattern.

Neptunian creativity results from being in contact with our feelings and willing to flow with our inspiration. Perfection is irrelevant. Instead, we exist totally in the present, unconscious of ourselves and unfettered by rules and regulations which block our spontaneity or the expression of our individuality. We are open, receptive, trusting, and willing to play with whatever emerges without judgment, without destroying possibilities before they have had a chance to develop or to lead to even more exciting and original modes of expression. We are willing to experiment and to tolerate chaos. Later, after we have given free rein to our imagination, we may allow Saturn, and perhaps Mercury and Pluto, to perfect the form which we have created, but to allow them to restrict us at the beginning is to prevent ourselves from ever discovering our creative potential.

The nature of our centering technique or creative expression can best be determined by Neptune aspects and house placements, natally and by transit. An aspect to Mars may lead us to creative dance or t'ai chi chu'an; Venus, to music or art; Mercury, meditation or imaginative writing. In the 11th house, Neptune may call us to experience these activities through creative or spiritual groups; in the 9th house, through study, through consulting the *I Ching* or through travel; in the 6th house, through incorporating our creative or spiritual expression into our workday and becoming involved in psychic or spiritual healing.

A Neptune transit is also the perfect time to appreciate creative expression—to read literature (especially poetry and fantasy), watch films, and particularly, to listen to music. Music not only helps us allow our feelings to stream through us and release their tension; it may also awaken our imagination and spirituality, inspiring us to express actively the light and love we feel inside.

Working with Dreams and Fantasies

Apart from creative and spiritual outlets, a Neptune transit is also an excellent opportunity to work with our dreams and fantasies. Often, our dreams will be related to the planet or house being aspected, as well as our 12th house planets.[3] We can train ourselves to remember our dreams by programming ourselves before we sleep and replaying them by writing them down as soon as we wake, so that their fragments do not slip out of our consciousness before we can grasp them. We can also use a variety of techniques to explore their meanings, such as:

1) free associating from the dream images or scenes;
2) dialoguing with symbols or people in our dreams;
3) identifying with a dream image or person and telling our internal observer what we, as the dream content, represent and what guidance we have to impart;
4) consciously continuing the dream during our waking hours. Although dream interpretation books may be helpful to us, our own interpretations are likely to be more meaningful. Nevertheless, our dreams reflect our subconscious process rather than our rational minds, and can be a source of wisdom and guidance only if we are willing to experience them fully—to feel the feelings they generate, to play with their images, to enter creatively into their scenario rather than intellectualize their meaning.

Under the influence of a Neptune transit, we may need to allow ourselves to daydream each day, rather than struggle always to maintain consciousness. By observing our daydreams, we can discover what is missing in our lives or what our next direction might be, since our daydreaming tends to compensate for what is lacking in our reality. If Neptune is configurated with our Venus, or our 5th or 7th houses, we may be especially prone to romantic fantasies about a particular person, and may need to contact and express the love and inspiration within us more fully so that we don't project it unduly onto that person and prepare ourselves for pain and disillusionment. Since our fantasy life may be particularly active under a Neptune transit, we might also create an imaginary person or experience to daydream about, so that we do not confuse our actual relationships and experiences by infiltrating them with too much fantasy. One of the lessons of Neptune has to do with separating fantasy from reality, while also using our imagination to enrich our reality. If we choose to use our fantasy consciously in a way that does not interfere with our daily lives, and also check out our perceptions with the people whom we trust, then Neptune is not likely to confuse our relationships and activities.

---

3. My book, *Your Secret Self: Illuminating the Mysteries of the Twelfth House*, focuses entirely upon the twelfth house and dream interpretation.

Neptune is the planet of the metaphorical mind, of nonlinear thinking, of our capacity to enrich our experience and enhance our creativity by perceiving analogies and exploring the potentials of our creative imagery. Even if we are not normally attuned to internal images, Neptune transits may dissolve the limitations of our rational minds and enable us to observe and even direct the phantasmagoria within us. Reading fairy tales, fantasies and poetry, listening to music, or free associating as we write in our journals may stimulate our imaginations and generate a wealth of meaningful imagery. Involvement in Jungian therapy, psychosynthesis, or such techniques as Silva Mind Control may help us to harness the energy of Neptune and to use our imagination to our own advantage, rather than feel overwhelmed as it infiltrates our consciousness.

Receptive Imagery and Active Imagination

We can, under the influence of Neptune, pay attention to the imagery naturally occurring within our psyches, frequently referred to as receptive imagery; we can also use techniques of active imagination or directed fantasy to control or direct our mental images. If we choose to attune ourselves to our receptive imagery, we must first allow ourselves to become completely relaxed, free from the internal chatter which interferes with our inner vision. If our eyes are closed and our minds at rest and still no images appear, we might imagine ourselves descending in an elevator to the depths of our beings, and then observe what is before us as the elevator doors open. As images float before our eyes, we must not attempt to interpret or verbalize them. Only by first observing and experiencing them fully and remaining aware of the feelings they generate within us can we fully benefit from such internal exploration. If we wish, we may choose to take a more active role, consciously involving all our senses in our experience, moving around internally and viewing the images or scenes from different angles, consciously transforming them, dialoguing with them and asking them what they are and what they can teach us, or entering the scene and interacting with the images which abound there. Or we might, as we enter the state of receptive imagery, ask our subconscious to provide images which help us to discover the solution to some problem in our lives.

Most visualization techniques involve a combination of both receptive and directed imagery. We might choose the situation we wish to envision, a situation which may be related to Neptune's influence in our chart; once our inner eye perceives it, we might then allow the situation to unfold of its own accord. Many schools of psychology, such as psychosynthesis, which use techniques of active imagination suggest beginning our sojourn inward by imagining any of the following:

1) walking along a beach, observing the ebb and flow of the tide and the ripples it makes in the sand;
2) being a lake or ocean churning with waves and then gradually becoming still;
3) swimming underwater and encountering the animal, plant and mineral life which resides there;
4) walking through a sunlit meadow;
5) climbing a tall mountain and reaching the summit;
6) being a tree, experiencing the light and dark, the wind, the weather and the passage of time;
7) being a mirror turned inward within our subconscious, reflecting ourselves;
8) entering a hut in the woods and encountering a wise man or woman, asking them the questions which trouble us and listening to the answers;
9) entering a hut in the woods and encountering our subpersonalities or personas—perhaps the crybaby within us or the fairy princess or the street bum—and asking them who they are, what they want, what they need, and what they have to teach us.

We might also facilitate our process of psychological integration by focusing our attention upon such universal images as a flower or a diamond, or envisioning a mandala which is particularly meaningful to us.

Apart from universal images, our own personal images, those which appear frequently in our dreams or fantasies or in our speech and writing, may merit further exploration. We might even envision the images related to the Sabian Symbols of key planets in our charts, or create images for each of our planetary positions by sign and house, playing with them in our minds and allowing them to unfold their meanings. Our Venus in Sagittarius in the 2nd house might be a hope chest; Saturn in Pisces in the 5th, ice melting in a playground; Jupiter in Virgo in the 4th, an explorer plotting coordinates on a map as he searches for his homeland; Mars in Leo in the 10th, a rooster crowing from atop a barn roof; Pluto in Virgo in the 12th, an archaeologist analyzing artifacts found beneath the soil; Neptune in Libra in the 2nd, two people displaying the sign, "Dreams for Sale"; Jupiter in Sagittarius in the 9th, an escalator to heaven; Venus in Scorpio in the 3rd, a passion flower blooming on a neighbor's yard.

The chapter on creative and meditative astrological techniques in *Planetary Aspects* provides images for planets which may be a starting point for developing personal archetypes. The list of images for "Neptune (and Pisces) Through the Houses" which follows can aid us in attuning ourselves to the essential meaning of our natal and transiting Neptune. Our personal archetypes of images can even be blended, as shown in the following section entitled "Astrology and Imagery" (see page 188), to help us uncover the meanings of our natal aspects.

In addition to such exploratory techniques as using imagery and directed fantasy, we might take practical advantage of a Neptunian influence by visualizing changes we hope to make in the future. Because our imaginations may be active and powerful, we may be capable of influencing our future behaviors by preparing first through fantasies and meditations. Perhaps Neptune is aspecting our 5th house Mars; although we may not have the energy to maintain our daily tennis schedule, we might instead perfect our technique by fantasizing each movement we might hope to make on the court. If we are struggling to overcome an illness, particularly if Neptune is influencing our 1st or 6th houses, we can facilitate the healing process by visualizing a white light around the afflicted part of the body. If Neptune is overwhelming us with anxieties and fears, we might use techniques of systematic desensitization, first meditating or otherwise relaxing our bodies muscle by muscle, and then, while feeling at peace, envisioning ourselves coping successfully with fearful circumstances and affirming ourselves with positive statements which help dissolve our anxiety and build our self-esteem.

Whatever planets and houses Neptune is influencing in our chart, we can imagine ourselves functioning happily, clearly and competently in these areas of our lives, involving as much as possible our bodies, minds and emotions in our fantasies so that our experience is complete and powerful enough to transform our reality. As we create these practical fantasies, we might turn inward to make sure that we really want whatever experience we are imagining, because if we rehearse it frequently enough, it is likely to become reality. Such practical visualization techniques are most successful when we do them repeatedly, when we affirm our capacity to actualize them, when we have faith in the outcome, when we focus only on the positive, and when we concentrate our energy upon the visualization rather than scatter it by informing other people about our experience, our progress and our goals.

NEPTUNE THROUGH THE HOUSES

Basic Neptune Images

fog	fairy princess	sea gull
cloud	fairy godmother	lamb
camouflage	angel	sheep
mirage	elf	dolphin
smoke screen	unicorn	chameleon
silhouette	prince	guerrilla
mirror	alchemist	sniper
prism	magic wand	vagabond
masquerade	crystal ball	martyr
soap bubble	grail	dancer
rose-colored glasses	candle	seashore
trance	wizard	sailboat
labyrinth	monk	harp
ferris wheel	guru	melody
merry-go-round	saint	surfboard
beacon	muse	parachute
harp	bartender	kite

FIRST HOUSE:

a one-way mirror • an approaching cloud • a smoke screen • a fairy godmother • an inspiring Muse • a chameleon changing colors • a mystery person at a masquerade • an angel playing a harp • an enchantress weaving a spell • a magician playing tricks

SECOND HOUSE:

an unemployed angel • a poet's treasure chest • a surfer's soggy checkbook • an alchemist's gold • a unicorn in a department store • an entrepreneurial lamb • shopping center enveloped by fog • guerrilla warfare over a wallet • social worker at a vocational center • a savings of hopes and dreams

THIRD HOUSE:

fog on city streets • crystal ball at a science fair • dolphins in communication • socialist newspaper • hypnotist on t.v. • sightseeing tour of

the clouds • labyrinth of city streets • a wine tasting course •
an alcoholic in driving school • the neighborhood space center

FOURTH HOUSE:

castles in the air • an island monastery • a seaside villa • a waterbed
• an aquarium of fish • a field of marijuana • the dream of a father/
motherland • bartender at a restaurant • sailor at home port •
a poet's tenement • a nurse at a daycare center • a houseboat

FIFTH HOUSE:

a children's puppet show • fog on lover's lane • a monk on lover's lane
• merry-go-round at a carnival • house of mirrors at a funhouse •
children blowing soap bubbles • loveboat • drunken sailor at a bar
• a lost child • a game of make-believe • a dollhouse • waterskiing show
• a child actress

SIXTH HOUSE:

factory by the sea • animal rescue squad • alchemist in a laboratory •
temporary job center • elves' workroom • pet fish • a holistic health
center • crystal ball in a doctor's office • photography studio • a maze
of offices • labyrinth of paperwork • dolphin at a desk

SEVENTH HOUSE:

a duet of angels • two mirrors face to face • waterskiers in tandem •
wedding on cloud nine • a pair of chameleons • candlelit dinner for
two • a foggy wedding day • a drunken marriage proposal • two clouds
converging • couple on a merry-go-round • sacrificial lambs •
soulmates in communion

EIGHTH HOUSE:

angels atop a volcano • monk in a whorehouse • occult center guru •
cloud of judgment • mystic rites • chemist mixing dangerous liquids •
an elegy or poetic funeral rite • fog over an abyss • heavenly initiation
rites • mist over autumn foliage • cosmic orgasm • drug dealer in the
underworld

NINTH HOUSE:

magic carpet to Katmandu • refugee in a foreign country • escalator to the Holy Grail • princess in ivory tower • a sacred diploma • a college dropout • fog over tomorrowland • globe-trotting chameleon • pilgrimage to India • meditation class • the university of intoxication • a purpose-seeking porpoise

TENTH HOUSE:

the heights of intoxication • a celestial ship • penthouse by the sea • angel on the cover of *Time* • shy prima donna • crystal ball on a pedestal • dolphins leaping out of the sea • headland veiled by fog • mist over a mountain lake • beacon in the sky • a fisher king or fisher queen • labyrinthine skyscrapers

ELEVENTH HOUSE:

a circle of light • a flock of sheep • knights at the round table • Alcoholics Anonymous • a celestial choir • space cadets • convention of fairy godmothers • a spiritual brotherhood • a "save the whales" campaign • the socialist party • a meditation group • social service agency in the clouds

TWELFTH HOUSE:

soul in exile • guardian angel • cosmic pool • unicorn in captivity • waters of the soul • hidden spring • cloudy seas • forbidden magic • soul music • closet mystic • backstage dancer • internal tidal wave • private mission • internal beacon

Astrology & Imagery

The following is an excerpt from an unfinished manuscript, *Your Planetary Archetypes,* which presents: 1) images for every planet in every sign and house; 2) techniques for creating planetary images; 3) examples demonstrating how integrating two images together, both inharmoniously and harmoniously, can help us discover the underlying meaning and potential of aspects in our natal charts.

The first image which came to mind as I meditated upon my retrograde Jupiter at 29 Aquarius at the end of my 2nd house (also ruling my 12th house and ascendant) was a large air-filled balloon or blimp bearing the words, "Develop your intuition. Study astrology. $10 per hour." Since the only major aspect my Jupiter forms is a square to Mars at 0 Sagittarius, positioned in my 12th house and ruling my 4th house, I meditated also upon Mars and received the image of a submarine ascending toward the surface of the ocean after underwater combat. Blending these images to better understand the square, I then envisioned the submarine bursting upward through the surface of the water, shooting at the balloon/blimp and attempting to deflate it.

This image was followed by a sudden flash of insight related to childhood memories of my mother repeatedly criticizing me for being fat (blimp-like), while simultaneously filling the cookie jar with my favorite cookies. I began to realize how those criticisms increased rather than decreased my compulsive overeating and also led me to splurge my entire allowance each week buying books which inspired my desire to become a writer. Because my physical self was rejected, I attempted early to compensate for a weak self-image by developing my understanding and focusing upon my spiritual and creative development. Now, years later, I am no longer overweight, but the compulsive patterns of book-buying continue, as if I am still trying to fill myself up and prove to myself my own worth.

Once aware of early patterns related to my Mars/Jupiter square, I then decided to create a harmonious image for Mars and Jupiter operating together, an image which might enable me to discover the positive potential of the square. Working first with my earlier images, I envisioned a submarine ascending from underwater combat, shooting upward into the air to announce its victory over the enemies of the deep; meanwhile, an air-filled balloon flying above advertises, "Make friends with your subconscious. Let Sagittarius Rising help you discover your inner wealth." Immediately then, I perceived my Jupiter as a psychology professor, not lecturing abstractly upon principles of psychology, but rather helping students to explore their subconscious process and to confront the internal "demons" which threaten their self-esteem and their awareness of their own capabilities.

These images helped me to realize how my current direction in astrology (from working with 12th house planets to exploring the psychodynamics of the t-square to dialoguing with planets and ex-

pressing myself more personally in my writing to attuning myself to the internal experience of the outer planets to using imagery to explore the underlying meanings of planets and aspects) is a direction which will help me not only to integrate my Mars/Jupiter square, but also my full Moon opposition, and to express my North Node in Pisces instead of retreating into my South Node conjunction to three Virgo planets. As I envision my Martian submarine emerging from its underwater victory, I realize that I am becoming more willing to face the "demons" which have been buried in my subconscious, more courageous in expressing my 12th house Mars actively in both my personal and professional life, and more able to recognize and transmute the aggressive instincts which, when unacknowledged and unexpressed, become distorted and self-destructive and lead to compulsive behavior. I understand more fully how my Jupiter, which has been a problem in the past, can be an advantage to me once it confronts, assimilates and expresses that buried Martian energy, discovering the wealth of wisdom that resides even in the darkest corners of the subconscious, and imparting it to others through teaching, counselling, writing and publishing.

❦

Swimming with Neptune's Currents

Such directed fantasy techniques can help us benefit from a Neptune transit, but a desire to direct or control our lives is not particularly Neptunian. Under the influence of Neptune, we may begin to experience what the Chinese refer to as *wu-wei*—the wisdom of non-action, of swimming with the current, of aligning ourselves with the *tao* or the Way of nature and all life. Such non-action does not mean refraining from taking any action at all or allowing ourselves to become inert and unmotivated. Rather, it means that we need not force a situation or battle resistances, that we can instead flow with each circumstance, adapting ourselves to it, trusting our feelings and acting without strain.

Although we may feel passive, apathetic and unfulfilled about expressing a planet Neptune is transiting as we have expressed it in the past, we are likely to feel quite inspired and energized when we discover new ways of expressing that planet. Only by giving ourselves space to drift, to flow or meander, without judging ourselves for not behaving as we used to behave, can we discover these new attitudes, behaviors, activities or experiences. What we drift into, not what we consciously choose under Neptune may be what we most need to incorporate into our lives. Influenced by a Neptune/Mars transit, we may no longer have the energy for jogging, and may discover instead, moving rhythmically to music as we wash dishes, that we really want to become involved in creative dance. Under a Neptune/Venus transit, we may not have the energy or desire to maintain certain past relationships, but we may find ourselves naturally talking to people we wouldn't have talked to before, unconsciously beginning to develop relationships which may become important to us in the future. Unless we allow ourselves to drift in terms of this aspected planet and house and pay attention to what is emerging, we may not discover what Neptune has to teach us.

Basically, any difficult Neptune aspect to a planet is a message that the energy of that planet must now be expressed in a flowing, feeling, inspirational and meaningful manner. It cannot be forced. It must, like water flowing down a mountain, find its own pathway. Only by following our inspiration can we flow into the new structures or new relationships which await us. We should, however, be careful as we surrender to the tides of Neptune that we do not flow too far or too fast toward the wrong shore. We can maintain some conscious control over the nature of our drifting; by remaining in touch with our center and becoming more attuned to our inner guidance, we can prevent ourselves from being pulled by external circumstances into situations which might be destructive to us. Our aim is not to surrender to each whim or impulse or to outside influences, but rather to surrender to the *tao* or life force as experienced from the center of ourselves, and to follow our inner guidance. In the words of the *I Ching,* hexagram two, the Receptive:

> The person in question is not in an independent position, but is acting as an assistant. It is not his task to try to lead—but to let himself be led . . . The superior man lets himself be guided; he does not go ahead blindly, but learns from the situation what is demanded of him and then follows his intimation.[4]

We can develop our attunement to the life force within us by allowing ourselves to experience our closeness to nature, which is also the source of metaphor and can awaken our creativity. Under a Neptunian

---

4. This and all subsequent passages from the *I Ching* are from *The I Ching or Book of Changes,* translated by Richard Wilhelm, Princeton University Press, 1967.

influence, trees, mountains and meadows may seem to speak to us; but we are likely to feel most at peace, in contact with our feelings and aware of the divine within and around us, by spending time near the water. Rivers, lakes and oceans can guide us to our internal source of inspiration and can help us release feelings accumulated from the past until we at last become still.

The Experience of Neptune

The following excerpts from my unpublished manuscript, A *Passing of Clouds,* were written when my progressed Moon was in Pisces in my third house, and when transiting Neptune was in my twelfth house, trining my heavily afflicted fourth house natal Moon. My natal Neptune is in the tenth house, in opposition to the Moon, square to Uranus, sextile to Pluto and semi-sextile to twelfth house Mars.

#202

Unemployed, experiencing months of leisure for the first time, I hold the reins of my life loosely in my hand and trot through the countryside. I am not concerned with reaching a destination, only with being where I am now, turning onto random paths here and there without direction. This is the phase of trusting the horse. Perhaps when night approaches, I will want to grasp the reins tightly and take control, but now I am enjoying letting go.

Yet as soon as I become aware of all the hours lost in my rambling, I become anxious and dissatisfied. I tell myself that eventually I will return to the main path and journey in a predetermined direction, but the further I stray from the trail, the more difficulty I may have finding it. The more freedom I give my horse, the less willing he may be to obey my commands again.

When this year ends, I will have nothing to show for these wasted months, these aimless wanderings, but memories of the wind blowing in my face and the rustling of the leaves.

This is enough to justify these months of leisure.

#291

My difficulty in clearly defining my direction in life is not that it is as yet unformed, but rather that it is intangible, incapable of being translated from one symbol system to another. I cannot see it or feel it or verbal-

ize it, and yet I know when I am following the right path and when, mistakenly, I have strayed from the trail.

If I attempt to put it into words, I shudder, as if committing a sacrilege. The ungraspable is reduced to the level of the commonplace. The indecipherable, once deciphered, is destroyed. My conscious mind, like a bird clutching its prey, gains control of my understanding and clings to its own literal interpretation, diverting my unconscious mind from following its natural rhythm.

The vagueness, the indeterminacy of the vision I follow is for me a key to its validity. The truly original, the truly meaningful, the truly essential in my experience cannot be categorized or defined. My real growth, I know, is happening offstage.

ॐ

Dealing with Heightened Sensitivity, Escapism, and Dependency

As we flow with the currents of Neptune, we are likely to discover that our feelings are also flowing freely, especially our tears. Neptune heightens our sensitivity; under its influence, we become more compassionate, but also more vulnerable. Neptune is dissolving our boundaries, releasing the pain we may have carried within us, and awakening our capacity to love. In the words of the *I Ching,* hexagram 59, Dispersion:

> Through hardness and selfishness the heart grows rigid, and this rigidity leads to separation from all others . . . When the warm breezes of spring come, the rigidity is dissolved, and the elements that have been dispersed in ice floes are reunited. When a man's vital energy is dammed up within him, gentleness serves to break up and dissolve the blockage.

It is therefore important under a Neptune transit, particularly a transit to a personal planet, that we allow our feelings to flow, that we fully experience them, even the pain, because it will enable us to open more fully to others. Often the clouds of confusion are unshed tears which have condensed and fogged our minds. Now that the wounds of the past are reopened, and we experience the suffering we have sought to avoid, we can heal and begin to love again. Through experiencing and expressing our hurts and vulnerabilities, we awaken our compassion and become more receptive and responsive to the pain around us. However, we may encounter problems when we too easily attach the love and compassion within us to one person and become lost in romantic fantasies or heartache. The love of Neptune is not meant to be focused upon one particular person, but rather to be dispersed, spread around, to uplift all our relationships and activities. Neptune teaches us that love is not just a feeling toward someone special, but rather a way of life.

Another danger of a Neptune transit is that we will be overwhelmed with anxieties, fears and self-doubts and feel that we are drowning in a whirlpool of uncontrollable emotions; we may even become depressed and listless by repeatedly giving ourselves negative messages. Usually, we can deal with these unpleasant side effects by experiencing our feelings fully in our bodies and releasing them without translating them into words which exaggerate and increase their power over us. We can also take the opposite approach and disentangle ourselves from them; by observing how we allow them to permeate our consciousness, we may discover that they exist apart from us and do not have to destructively influence our self-esteem or interfere with our functioning in the world. Under the influence of a Neptune transit (particularly in aspect to our Sun, Mars or Saturn), if we feel paranoid and helpless in our awareness of being victimized by something outside of ourselves, we might attempt to determine if we are projecting our own will or anger or hatred or negativity outward because we are unwilling to acknowledge it in ourselves. The paranoid attitude usually results from being unable to acknowledge and express our own anger. By owning our real feelings, however negative they may be, and allowing them to stream through us, we can release them and be freed of their influence.

One reason for the negativity we may experience under Neptune is that in opening us to other dimensions of being, Neptune also inclines us to perceive the limitations and pettiness of our everyday lives. We feel a divine discontent; we yearn to transcend the realms we have known and to experience and actualize the ideal. Our normal mundane activities no longer suffice; we need to do an internal inventory of peak experiences or transcendent moments we have known, as well as those we dream of knowing, and to choose to allow these to occur more frequently. A summer sailing jaunt on a lake, a romantic candlelit dinner, an inspiring concert—introducing such activities into our lives frequently may help us to remain in contact with Neptune's inspirational energies and thereby retain a frame of mind which enables us to remain uplifted even in narrow and uninspiring circumstances.

Still another danger of Neptune is the possibility of our seeking to escape from all that is unpleasant in our lives, running from one difficult experience to another, with the illusion that through each new experience we can avoid the problems of the past. For a while, our patterns of escapism may work for us, enabling us to discover new sources of meaning. But after repeatedly settling into new situations and discovering that they are not as we hoped, we may become bitter with disillusionment. Although under Neptune we may gradually leave the past behind and explore new possibilities, we may also learn that to escape repeatedly from our conflicts and to avoid confronting and responsibly "finishing up" previous commitments is to invite more confusion, self-doubt and guilt than we may wish to experience.

Sometimes, our escapist activities may guide us along our chosen path. Reading a fantasy novel instead of completing a homework assignment, we may come across a passage which opens doors in our awareness and leads us to resolve a problem with which we have been struggling. Avoiding a business meeting which does not interest us, we take a walk in the park and meet a woman with whom we experience a soul connection, and who becomes a much-loved guide in our development. Allowing some room for escape is essential if we are to experience Neptune's blessings; however, we may have to assess continually the degree and extent to which avoiding responsibilities really serves us.

One other danger of Neptune is that we may become overly passive and helpless, and cling to some means of support—with the square, perhaps become addicted to drugs or alcohol; with the opposition, become overly dependent upon another person. Here again, the *I Ching* gives us guidance; hexagram 30, the Clinging, advises us indeed to cling, but to cling to what is right, to cling to the light which shines in each of us:

> What is dark clings to what is light and so enhances the brightness of the latter. Everything . . . is dependent on something to which it clings, in order that it may continue to shine . . . Human life on earth is conditioned and unfree, and when man recognizes his limitation and makes himself dependent upon the harmonious and beneficent forces of the cosmos, he achieves success . . . In order that his psychic nature be transfigured . . . it must cling to the forces of spiritual life.

Neptune urges us not to be independent, but rather to be dependent—dependent upon the inner guidance we receive by becoming attuned to the highest dimensions of ourselves and of the universe.

Rather than cling to others, we may, under the influence of Neptune, form relationships in which others cling to us. The compassion we feel may lead us toward people who are in need of our love and support. Eager to give, we may not be aware of how we are creating dependency; believing our motives to be altruistic, we may become bitter when those people to whom we have sacrificed ourselves do not improve themselves or are not capable of appreciating us and returning what we have given. We may at first unconsciously glory in our selflessness, and then, quite consciously withdraw, feeling used and victimized.

One of the lessons of Neptune is that giving strengthens others and ourselves; it does not weaken and embitter. Giving is not taking responsibility for others, but helping them to take responsibility for themselves. Love is not an unrestricted flow of compassion and kindness, but includes within itself the capacity to say no, to challenge, to turn away if necessary, to refuse to support behaviors in others which are detrimental to our welfare and theirs, while all the while accepting and treasuring their essence and encouraging them to express their own divine nature.

Neptunian Issues in Relationships

One manifestation of the compassion and love which may be awakened under a Neptune transit, particularly to Venus or the Moon, is the desire to form spiritual bonds with other people, to meet soul-to-soul and to experience a oneness of spirit. Because of this longing to merge on the highest levels, we may easily delude ourselves that we have found our soul mate or may rationalize our dependency upon others or their dependency upon us, believing that we are achieving a cosmic togetherness when indeed we are attempting to return to the security of the womb. The spiritual connections, the I–Thou communions we may seek are certainly possible under the influence of Neptune and may inspire and uplift us long after the transit has passed. But such connections are likely to occur only when we are honest with ourselves and each other, and when we bring to the bonds that we are forming selves capable of bearing separateness, capable of turning inward and generating the illumination we seek without needing other people to do it for us. Such connections are likely to occur and to endure when instead of looking to another person to provide what only God can provide, we find and nurture our own spiritual source; we then become capable of celebrating the beauty of another but not requiring the other to be a paragon of virtue.

When Neptune is influencing our 7th house, Venus, descendant, or ruler, we are especially prone to delude ourselves about those we love and about who we are in relationship. Some of us may choose inaccessible partners, while yearning for closeness, unable to acknowledge that at this phase of our lives we are too vulnerable or fearful of a complete relationship. Some of us may fall in love with an image of our partner, unwilling to face the reality before us because we are in love with love and prefer our fantasy to reality.

In the *Psychology of Romantic Love,* Nathaniel Branden differentiates between relationships based upon shared blindness and those based on shared sight. Blind relationships operate on the principle of "don't spoil my dream and I won't spoil yours." Once our partner's shortcomings are fully confronted, our love disappears. Relationships based upon shared sight, however, involve being willing to face the other person as he/she truly is, with all his or her imperfections, and still be able to keep the seeds of love and romance alive. Neptune can create the phenomenon of individual or shared blindness; however, if we are committed to moving through the false security of our illusions and to accepting a relationship that is not and cannot be ideal, we can experience the love based upon shared sight.

Kahlil Gibran once wrote, "Love is not about gazing into each other's eyes; it is about, together, gazing out at the world." One of the requirements for a viable Neptunian relationship may be that the bond we form not exist for itself alone, but for a purpose beyond itself. Our relationships may need to be co-creative—created and dedicated to the actualization of values and ideals which we share with our partner. Such values and ideals may take the form of a spiritual commitment, a professional venture, attitudes regarding childrearing or a sociopolitical cause which we and our partner share in common. Whatever our common vision may be, it needs to be strong enough to sustain us through those inevitable periods of emotional dissatisfaction.

Knowing and actualizing our ideals with and without a partner involves defining and committing ourselves to a clear sense of priorities. Such awareness and commitment may enable us to express the true meaning of the word "sacrifice," which is frequently associated with Neptune. Too often we may become victims of a lower form of sacrifice which involves compromising or playing martyr. We may sacrifice our integrity because we are unable to assert or affirm ourselves and stand our own ground apart from another person or because we do not know or commit ourselves to our truest values. The word sacrifice actually means "making sacred." When Abraham chose to sacrifice his son to God, he made that choice not because he failed to love his son, but because he loved God even more. Being willing to relinquish a secondary love for the sake of a primary love may be painful, but its pain becomes bearable when we are able to affirm that primary value which we indeed are choosing. By committing himself to God, Abraham, in the end, gained God and was spared his son. By sacrificing our lower values for our highest values, we often open new doorways and discover that we are, in the long run, gaining far more than we are losing.

Service to the World

Neptune teaches about loving and giving, both in regard to ourselves and others; it also helps us expand our love and inspiration to embrace our work or involvement in society. Particularly in association with the 1st, 6th, 10th, 11th, and 12th houses, Neptune urges us to ground our spiritual promptings by being of service to the world, to do what is meaningful both to others and ourselves, to respond to and fulfill important needs, and to uplift and inspire. We may be confused about the nature of our service or mission under Neptune's influence; we may become infused with idealism but unable to translate that idealism into practical form. Neptune, as the cosmic deceiver, can lead us to delude ourselves that to serve is to become a saviour of humanity, to abolish poverty and eliminate pain. Because we can do none of these things, we may give up our idealism or refuse to discover ways in which we can serve that do not glorify our egos. Neptune teaches us that service may be a kind word to a customer as we bag groceries or an arm held out to an old lady crossing a busy street. We may, under Neptune's influence, seek to do more—to choose a vocation in which we help the suffering or oppressed or inspire those struggling for meaning in life. But as we dedicate ourselves to our ideals and grapple with our inability to fulfill them completely, Neptune strips away our illusions, refusing to allow us to become spiritual egotists.

To what extent are we devoted to our mission, and to what extent are we attempting to compensate for our own lack of self-esteem? To what extent are we serving only to be valued, respected or loved? We each have the divine within us and are capable of expressing it, but we cannot expect to be Christs. Neptune teaches us that by stripping away our illusions, by maintaining our humility, by willingly experiencing and revealing our own inadequacies and vulnerabilities and remaining sensitive to those of others, we become even more capable of loving and serving than by attempting to be saviors.

Neptune and the Experience of Oneness

Neptune is the planet of faith and cosmic experience. Under its influence, we may long to transcend ourselves, to surrender our egos to the cosmos, to let go of our pettiness, our narrowness, our fear. Because of our spiritual yearnings and receptivity, Neptune may indeed heighten our consciousness, introduce us to celestial realms we never knew existed and allow us to experience our oneness with humanity and with the universe. Only through such experience of oneness, only through contacting the center within ourselves through which the highest cosmic energies flow, can we develop the faith necessary to cope with the pain of being dissolved by Neptune, of allowing our cherished illusions to be stripped away, of keeping our hearts open even when they are threatening to break. Neptune brings us insecurity and confusion, suffering and sacrifice, but it also, through revealing to us our own smallness and insignificance, leads us to reach out to God, to ask for help from the universe, and to discover that, by opening ourselves to that which is higher than we are, we are raised, bathed in cosmic waters and capable of experiencing our own divine nature. Neptune illuminates, and through illumination deepens our faith that we are each an essential part of a divine plan, and that we are capable of fulfilling that plan and enduring the suffering and insecurities in our lives, if only by allowing ourselves to remain attuned to our own sources of inspiration.

We are all one, although we are separate. We are all blessed, although we are cursed. We are all beings of vast potential, with a little bit of God inside each of us, although we are also weak and fragile, capable of regressing into infantile helplessness and humiliating inadequacy. These are the ambiguities of Neptune, the lessons that extend beyond logic, that confuse us only when we are unable to transcend ourselves and experience ourselves and the world from our still, small center of faith.

How then, can we experience Neptune? How can we handle the confusions and sensitivities of our Neptune transits? We can give ourselves quiet time to tune into our center and clear ourselves of each day's debris; we can allow our feelings to flow; we can enter and trust our confusion, knowing it to be a means of transition to a greater clarity; we can soothe ourselves with music, literature and art; we can become creators ourselves, giving form to our inspiration; we can learn from our dreams and fantasies; we can check out our perceptions with others and with our own sources of inner guidance to avoid deluding ourselves; we can maintain our faith as our illusions dissolve; we can open our hearts and respond compassionately to others without encouraging dependency; we can share our vulnerabilities and insecurities; we can experience our humility; we can allow ourselves to be of service, grounding ourselves by living our spiritual promptings on a daily basis; we can dedicate ourselves to our ideals, translating those ideals into practical form without glorifying our egos; we can experience our oneness with humanity and with the universe; we can open ourselves to cosmic energies; we can become illuminated; we can deepen our faith; we can cling not to our desires or any means of external support, but to our own inner light which inspires us, which sustains us, which enables us to experience and value our own divine nature and to embrace, with infinite tenderness, the divine in others.

Chapter Seven

PLUTO: FROM DARKNESS INTO LIGHT

Pluto, like Neptune, is linked to the Moon in terms of its relationship to our subconscious processes. The more rooted we are in the instincts, feelings, and needs of our Moon, the more likely we are to be able to effectively handle intense Plutonian energies. Rootedness and grounded-ness are essential if we are to make constructive use of Plutonian energy rather than be overcome by it. Like a tree which stretches its branches high and wide and develops a root system which extends as far and as deep as its branches stretch, so we must make contact with our Plutonian natures if we are to keep from becoming lost in Neptunian confusion, helpless in Neptunian vulnerability, and deluded by Neptunian idealism and fantasy. While Neptune guides us upward into ethereal and spiritual realms, Pluto forces us to venture downward into the basement of our beings to confront the shadows lurking there and to discover the power source without which Neptune is impotent. The Neptune/Pluto sextile of the mid-to-late twentieth century may be a message to us that the difficult times we face personally and collectively may indeed require the integrated expression of these two planets in cooperation.

Pluto, whether natally or by transit, usually leads us to experience an intense release of energy, which most often occurs on the emotional and physical or sexual level, but which may also occur intellectually or spiritually. The level of the release depends upon the planet Pluto is aspecting and the houses which Pluto influences—the house in which it occurs natally, the house or houses it rules natally, and the house through which it is transiting. Pluto is, after all, the higher octave of Mars, which is clearly related to the release of physical energy. Often, the Plutonian experience of energy release from the core of the subconscious feels like an eruption of poisons from some unknown source within our selves, much like the eruption of a geyser or of a boil or pimple which is a natural cleansing reaction of our bodies. At first, we may be aware only of the poisons released by Pluto—frustrated passion, twisted fury, all-consuming jealousy or greed which may threaten to overwhelm us. However, as we become more in touch with the core of our being and more willing to allow Pluto's energy to flow through us, we may recognize that we are being cleansed and freed of all that is useless in our lives. We become more capable of contacting what is really essential within ourselves.

Handling Intensity, Finding an Outlet, Experiencing Power

One of the lessons which Pluto teaches us is how to live in a state of extreme intensity. "To be alive is to be burning," Norman O. Brown once wrote; the burning that he refers to is certainly one of the most basic experiences of Pluto, for although it is a water planet, Pluto is also a fire planet because of its relationship to Mars. The fire of Pluto is psychological, primal fire; we could quite appropriately refer to Pluto as burning water or boiling fire or the fire underwater, and we could describe this blending of fire and water as a kind of internal steam, which if not released may lead us to explode in powerful ways. The alchemists used heat to transform metals and regarded the transformation of the human psyche as taking place through a process of psychological heat applied to the waters of the body and emotions. This heat can feel like internal hell if not channelled properly, but it is one of the primary means our psyches have of burning away the waters of the past and converting the energy released from that process into a new state of being.

Learning how to live with that intense heat of feeling and desire is important when Pluto is strongly placed in our charts or aspecting us powerfully by transit or triggered by progression. But the internal experience alone, apart from any external outlet, is usually not enough for us to handle effectively the vast energy inside of us or to transform the outer dimensions of our lives in the way that Pluto requires. A second lesson of Pluto has to do with the necessity of finding an appropriate and constructive channel, so that we are not fully consumed by its burning energy and can harmlessly release the poisons that are erupting within us. A neutral channel, for no particular purpose other than release, such as jogging or yoga or bouts of primal screaming, can be helpful to us. But rather than merely release the poisons erupting within us, we also have the choice of transmuting them by using the vast reservoir of energy now available to us for an important purpose, especially a purpose of social significance.

Under the influence of Pluto, we are likely to operate in extreme, sometimes obsessive ways. Our approach to life may become all-or-nothing. We are also likely to feel overcome by a powerful need for total involvement in some experience, a need to surrender or lose ourselves in something or someone. We desire to merge so that we and the other person, object or pursuit to which we are surrendering become one. Obsessions usually occur when we do not consciously choose a channel for the intense amount of energy boiling within our subconscious; instead, it chooses us. If we are going to be driven or obsessed under the influence of Pluto, then one of our aims might be to CHOOSE our obsession, to choose the end to which we are driven, so that we release energy in a constructive way and for a constructive purpose.

What we get out of any experience is quite obviously related to what we put into it; because we have so much energy available during an experience of Pluto, we are capable of funneling a tremendous amount of power into a person, project or aim of any kind. The particular outlet, again, is dependent upon the houses Pluto influences natally, by transit and by progression, and the planet or planets it is aspecting. As we prepare for a Pluto transit, we can already begin, emotionally and intellectually, to discover a channel related to the planets and houses influenced by Pluto; we may then amaze ourselves at how capable we are of accomplishing in this particular area of our lives.

Yet a conscious choice of an outlet for Plutonian energy may be ineffective if we are not attuned to the energies of Pluto stirring within us, directing us toward actions and experiences which enliven us. Sometimes we may need to surrender to obsessions or compulsions in order to contact the energy we have given away to one small part of ourselves or to a person or influence outside ourselves before we can become more centrally identified with that energy and able to use it constructively.

A third lesson of Pluto is related to the experience of power. The energy awakened by Pluto can lead us to contact the dynamic core of primal energy within us, and as a result, to experience fully our own personal power as individuals. Only when we are willing to experience it fully, in effect to allow ourselves to become large enough to contain that energy or power, is it likely to reveal to us the best channel for its release.

What is this personal power which Pluto, at its best, can awaken within us? A number of definitions may be useful for understanding its manifestations and the kinds of internal development we may wish to promote under a Pluto transit. Personal power may include:

a)   the ability to contact the dynamic core of energy within ourselves, to be fully with ourselves and able to experience that core energy;

b) trust in our core, and the willingness to be true to it, to maintain our self-respect by following its dictates;

c) the power of self-determination, the experience of "I CAN" which enables us to make our own decisions, control and channel our energy, to wield some control over our lives;

d) the power to meet our needs, to take care of ourselves and provide for ourselves what we can't gain from outside, as well as to learn how to gain what we need from the outer world;

e) the power to risk, to be able to be with our vulnerability or our fear without allowing it to limit us or prevent us from going after what we most need and want;

f) the power to endure, to know that we can cope with any feelings, bear any loss, and handle crises in our lives without giving up or completely breaking down;

g) the power to be significant, not only to ourselves but also to other people or society as a whole, aware that we can make a difference or have an impact, particularly as a positive or transforming influence;

h) cooperative or co-creative power, the power to form mutually satisfying relationships based upon a WIN/WIN attitude rather than a WIN/LOSE attitude.

Such power, as described above, is not necessarily visible on the surface as assertive or forceful energy. Personal power is often quiet and self-contained, indicative of a sense of presence resulting from rootedness in one's own being. Having personal power does not necessarily imply that we function in roles of power as defined by society. We can, for example, work under the authority of a boss or supervisor and yet: a) maintain our power by knowing that if we choose, we can undergo the risks of leaving the situation when it becomes untenable or unduly threatens our integrity; b) express ourselves as fully as possible within the limits of the situation and use whatever capabilities we have to better it; c) freely choose our attitude toward the situation itself, even when we are constricted in regard to our actions. We have the power to accept or not accept, to conceptualize or reframe circumstances in our lives in order to give them meaning, to discover possibilities for integrity, self-esteem and growth in even the most dire circumstances.[1] The greater our personal power, the more capable we are of encouraging others to empower themselves, and

1. See *Man's Search for Meaning* by Viktor Frankl, which describes his experiences in a WWII concentration camp and the philosophy of life he began to develop there.

the more we can opt for mutual empowerment without being threatened or afraid that the other person's gain is our loss. In his book *Power and Innocence,* Rollo May refers to nutrient power, the power to be for ourselves and for the welfare of another person simultaneously, maintaining ourselves while also promoting the development of the other. Martin Buber also refers to the conjoint energies of love and power when he suggests, "We cannot avoid using power. So let us . . . love powerfully."

The house in which Pluto is positioned and the house which Pluto rules in our charts are keys to areas of life through which we may most fully experience and own our personal power. Pluto's transit through a house may also introduce us to experiences of gaining power in still another realm of life, often after we have come to terms with our powerlessness or misuses of power in regard to the experiences of that house. During the experience of Pluto, we often feel a need to assert power over others, or we feel overpowered by something or someone outside ourselves. Both experiences are related to our not being fully able to experience and own our personal power or to channel it constructively.

Plutonian Struggles: Powerlessness and Projection

One of the negative manifestations of Pluto is the urge to dominate, which may also be experienced as the urge to manipulate, destroy or devour. This urge may seem to take us over when we feel powerless in regard to all that is happening inside us; our ego is too small and too rigid to invite the influx of energy we are experiencing, and so we feel overwhelmed, at the mercy of the internal demons of our passions and desires. Because we don't feel in possession of ourselves, we may try to possess others or objects outside ourselves; because we fear the loss of ego control that we are experiencing, we may try to control others. We attempt to force them to conform to our needs or satisfy our desires as a means of re-establishing the power of our egos. The urge to assert power over others is not really an expression of power at all, but rather a way of responding to an innate sense of helplessness.

This powerlessness, rather than the urge of power, may be our predominant experience with Pluto, particularly when we are unable fully to experience, own and channel the energy that is being activated within us. Usually, we feel powerless when we feel overwhelmed by something outside ourselves, when we have given our power away to a person, group, experience or activity and feel small and inadequate in the face of it. We may feel powerless in the realms ruled by Pluto in our charts when:

a) we experience other people in charge here, dominating us, possessing what we want or preventing us from attaining it;

b) we are confronting seemingly insurmountable obstacles or limitations;

c) we are blocked by such internal obstacles as our fear of the unknown, fear of humiliation, fear of pain, fear of losing significant relationships or attachments, or disbelief in our own capacities;

d) we are being influenced by false or inappropriate assumptions, attitudes or perceptions of reality, or by habit patterns which keep us from seeing clearly and acting effectively, or when we don't have the awareness or understanding we need;

e) we are out of touch with our physical and emotional energy or blocked by unconscious motives and resistances which are preventing us from developing our motivation and will.

One form of powerlessness frequently experienced under a Pluto influence is obsession. A part of our psyche attaches itself to something outside ourselves and dominates the other parts of us, so that we may feel possessed or at the mercy of our attachment. Obsessions and other experiences of feeling powerless or giving away power may result from projecting the energy and power awakening within us because we are frightened by it, overwhelmed by it, and cannot enlarge our sense of Self enough to experience and encompass it fully.

This tendency to project, characteristic of Pluto oppositions, may manifest in a number of ways. First, we may, instead of projecting our power outside of ourselves, project it upon one part of our psyches; perhaps, under a Pluto/Mercury transit, we may feel overpowered by our mental activity as we become obsessed with certain thoughts and worries. Second, we may project our power onto specific people, particularly when we have Pluto natally in a relationship house, especially the 7th, but also the 3rd, 5th, 6th, 8th, and 11th, or when it adversely aspects our Venus or Libra planets or opposes other planets in our charts.

What happens with this kind of projection is that we may experience ourselves as being dominated by the person in question, as we experienced our parents dominating us when we were children. Myths and folk tales about giants reflect this fear of domination, this tendency to feel small and helpless as we confront someone who appears to be more powerful than ourselves. Rather than actually feeling dominated by a person, we may act out this projection by becoming obsessed with someone or with our relationship with someone who has become very important to us, often because what he or she gives us has become essential to us in some way. If we have a 5th house Pluto, we may become obsessive about our children; an 8th house Pluto, our lover; an 11th house Pluto, a friend; a 4th house Pluto, some member of our family; a 7th house Pluto, our spouse or mate. We may then experience matters pertaining to these relationships as profoundly affecting our survival and our basic sense of identity and self-esteem.

A third type of projection common with Pluto, especially an 11th house Pluto, is the projection of our power onto a group of people, such as an organization to which we may belong and which seems to control our every action, or onto groups in general which may awaken feelings of powerlessness or alienation within us, or onto society as a whole. We may feel threatened in group situations unless we are in a position of control, because we want our presence to have an impact upon the group; and yet, because we are unwilling or unable to play the social games required of us, we experience the group as having an upsetting impact upon us.

A 10th house Pluto, and the current transit of Pluto in Capricorn, may influence us to project our power upon authorities such as our boss, political leaders, and the government in general. We may, for example, feel exploited and reduced to helplessness by the economic and/or war-related politicies of the U. S. government. However a 10th house Pluto, and the collective influence of Pluto in Capricorn, suggest dramatic unmasking of our leaders, and their fall from power.

A frequent means of projection, common to astrologers and astrology students who do not realize that the planetary energies exist *within* us, not merely *outside* us, is the projection of power onto the planets or the universe or God, so that we feel like small, helpless beings in the face of cosmic energies which are controlling us. Such a projection may be common with 8th, 9th, or 12th house Plutos; it may lead us to speak of free will without really experiencing our own freedom of attitude and action, because we are so aware of cosmic forces influencing every moment of our lives.

Wherever we project our power, we may become obsessively attached to that particular person, object, pursuit or belief system, because it helps us to remain in contact with the primal core of ourselves. Only through our experience with that projection may we feel fully energized, in contact with ourselves, and alive. The worksheet on personal power on the following pages is an aid to discovering how we disown and misuse power, and it is also an aid for attuning us to our potentials for self-empowerment.

PERSONAL POWER WORKSHEET:
PLUTO IN THE ASTROLOGICAL CHART

HOUSE POSITION _____ HOUSE(S) RULED: _____

OTHER HOUSE(S) CONTAINING SCORPIO: _____

PLUTO ASPECTS: _____ 8TH HOUSE PLANETS: _____

SCORPIO PLANETS: _____ ASPECTS OF TRANSITING PLUTO:_____

TRANSITING ASPECTS TO NATAL PLUTO:_____

Choose one issue in your life or area of life in which you struggle with Plutonian issues of power and powerlessness.

POWERLESSNESS:

1. How do you experience yourself as powerless in this area of your life? What desires or compulsions overpower you? To whom and HOW do you give your power away?

_____

_____

_____

_____

2. What do you get out of giving your power away or remaining powerless? What needs are being met through remaining powerless here?

_____

_____

_____

3. How can you meet those needs apart from remaining powerless or mired in ineffective or destructive behaviors?

_____

_____

_____

4. What messages do you give yourself which keep you powerless?

_____

_____

_____

PERSONAL POWER WORKSHEET: *cont.*

5. What other messages might you give yourself which would be more empowering? What attitudes might you cultivate?

_____

_____

_____

_____

POWER IN RELATIONSHIP:

6. In what ways do you misuse power in relationship, by manipulating or aggressively (or indirectly) using your power against others?

_____

_____

_____

_____

7. What need are you trying to fulfill by doing so?

_____

_____

_____

_____

8. How might you more constructively meet that need? What other ways are available to you?

_____

_____

_____

_____

9. How do you use your power FOR others?

_____

_____

_____

_____

PERSONAL POWER WORKSHEET: *cont.*

10. How else might you use your power FOR others—cooperatively or co-creatively? How might you help others to empower themselves?

_____

_____

_____

_____

PERSONAL POWER:

11. How have you experienced personal power in this area of your life?

_____

_____

_____

_____

12. How would you describe your internal experience of personal power, and the effect it has had on your life?

_____

_____

_____

_____

13. How would you like to experience your power here?

_____

_____

_____

_____

14. What keeps you from experiencing your power? What internal obstacles and external obstacles block you? What do you fear you might lose or might have to experience?

_____

_____

_____

_____

15. How would your life change for the better if you were to experience more personal power here? What constructive possibilities do you envision?

_____

_____

_____

_____

16. What would it take for you to empower yourself more here? What would you have to confront, give up, risk, or do?

_____

_____

_____

_____

17. How might you begin to overcome these obstacles? What attitudes and actions might help you to empower yourself?

_____

_____

_____

_____

18. How might you utilize the resources of others or of your environment to empower rather than weaken yourself?

_____

_____

_____

_____

19. What small step can you take during the next week or month to experience your personal power and/or cooperative power in this area of your life?

_____

_____

_____

_____

Many of us choose to remain powerless, especially in the areas associated with Pluto in our charts (and in regard to planets in square or semi-square to Pluto), because powerlessness is familiar and may seem to be less risky and more rewarding than our fearful visions of owning our power. We may, in our powerlessness, feel justified in feeling sorry for ourselves, gaining sympathy from others, or glorifying ourselves for behaving as virtuous martyrs. We may be lazy, or fear the responsibility and accountability of owning and directly expressing our power. We may choose to boost our self-image with fantasies of our potential rather than risk losing or pruning those fantasies in order to ground and actualize them in the world. We may fear threatening or losing significant people in our lives, hurting others, or otherwise undergoing changes and ventures into the unknown.

Without possessing a center in ourselves, we may hesitate to relinquish the people or activities that have become centers to us, and which have promoted our dependency. We may be overly influenced by our negative ideas about power, or by attachment to attitudes and values which uphold the virtues of the loving, unassertive, responsive feminine or the feminine which exists and gains significance only in relation to men. We may lack role models for becoming loving, empowered men or women. Finally, we may indeed be out of touch with our bodies, ungrounded, and as yet unable to effectively handle and channel the energies of desire, anger and sexuality which, when transmuted, clearly become our source of constructive, generative power.

Some of us, when we are unable fully to experience and accept the energy and power being released within us, when we are unable to surrender to the process of our own transformation by journeying so deeply into ourselves that we contact our core and are revitalized by it, may alternate between feeling powerless and wanting to overpower something or someone outside ourselves. This usually happens when a person or event in our lives threatens our most basic sense of identity or security; we may feel totally humiliated, stepped upon, exploited, and may respond with such intense fury that we are driven to revenge. We feel that we have been annihilated, and we want to annihilate in turn. If this is our experience, then one of our Plutonian lessons has to do with letting go of the part of our identity which feels annihilated; it responds with such rage because it was too big, too important in the first place; it is a shaky, distorted or enlarged part of our ego which needs to be reincorporated into a more viable sense of Self. Some facet of our self-respect, perhaps related to our ambition in society or our desires in relationships, has developed upon the wrong foundation, and now must be given up. The fury that we are experiencing is the fury of that part of ourselves resisting its own death. When we continually focus it upon the person whom we consider to be responsible for our humiliation, we lose touch with the actual death and rebirth experience happening inside us.

Pluto and Death/Rebirth

Pluto is the planet of death, and the death that it brings is more often psychological death than physical death—death to past identities, patterns, behaviors and attitudes which no longer serve us. People with Pluto on an angle, conjunct the Sun or Moon, or in the 1st or 8th house may need to go through powerful experiences of psychological death many times in the course of their lifetimes. Close squares to Pluto may also require such experiences. Most of us undergo psychological deaths of one kind or another in the areas of life Pluto influences in our natal charts; we are likely to go through such transformations particularly when Pluto conjuncts, squares and opposes natal planets, demanding that we give up some past expression of the planet, sign and house being aspected.

Probably the best analogy for the psychological death experience is that of a black hole in space, in which matter becomes so dense that it collapses into itself and vanishes. The gravity of such collapsing stars becoming black holes is so powerful that it draws everything around it into the emptiness of the collapsed center. I stumbled upon this analogy of the black hole in 1972, when I was beginning my study of astrology but not cognizant enough of transits to know that Pluto was stationary on my Sun at the time. This particular month, I was deeply absorbed in writing a series of poems entitled "The Black Sun Poems" which described my struggle with feelings of emptiness and powerlessness, as well as the psychological experience of collapsing or even dying. Attempting to cope with this difficult emotional state, I also spontaneously began to create a collage of black circles with missing centers whirling on a white background. During 1972, astronomers discovered a black hole and publicized information about this unusual phenomenon. I was struck by the connections in meaning between the black hole and my internal experience, as well as my creative expression.

My own experience of Pluto conjuncting half the planets in my chart plus the South Node and Midheaven in the course of ten years, as well as the experiences of other people I have known who have been through intense Pluto transits, have led me to believe that Pluto can, at times, lead us to the void at the center of our beings and force us to confront our fear of annihilation. If we have not been living in harmony with the universe, if we are overly attached to parts of ourselves or our lives which hinder rather than promote our own development, we may feel as if we are falling into a black, endless abyss; we may live in terror of being wiped out, becoming nothing, losing all we know of ourselves. During the two-year period of Pluto's transit over my Sun, I repeatedly threw the same *I Ching* hexagram, the Abysmal, which clearly expresses this dimension of Pluto. The Abysmal, water over water, represents the abyss, a situation of repeated danger. Richard Wilhelm wrote of this hexagram, "The soul locked up within the body, the principle of light enclosed in the dark." Like water, we must not "shrink from any dangerous spot or any plunge," or lose our own essential nature. "In danger all that counts is really carrying out all that has to be done—thoroughness—and going forward, in order not to perish through tarrying in the danger."

Pluto is especially difficult to deal with when our sense of identity is narrow and shaky. In the words of Dylan Thomas, we "rage, rage against the dying of the light." Such a fight may end in virtually giving up, feeling passive, beaten, destroyed. But we live through it, and in living through it discover that we were not wiped out at all, but rather that a part of our past selves, a part which is no longer useful to us, has been annihilated so that we can begin to rebuild our identity on the more solid foundation of our larger Selves and establish a more viable relationship with the universe. We may not discover the extent to which we have benefited from a Pluto transit until many years later, when we will be thankful for those traumatic experiences which allowed us to be reborn.

Because our society has no living cosmologies or myths related to the actual experience of death, or which incorporate death into the larger framework of the soul's evolution throughout many lifetimes, and because few rituals or initiation rites exist which allow us to experience the death of various phases of our lives, this experience of psychological death, lived through alone without any collective support, may be devastating. We may have no awareness at all of what we are gaining. Face to face with the unknown, experienced as some vast threatening darkness, we may actually believe that we are at the end of our existence, unaware that we are also arriving at a new beginning.

The Journey into the Void

This experience of psychological death is hardest to deal with when we resist it, when we are so overcome with terror that we run away emotionally from what is happening within us, and do not go deeply enough into ourselves to allow a release and transformation of energy to occur. In my lectures on depth astrology I have spoken about the great void that exists in space and in the atom—a void or space so vast that the matter that composes planets and the matter that composes atoms is infinitesimally small in comparison; if the matter in the atoms within our bodies were compacted, it would be no more than the size of a speck of dust. All else would be void. This void inside us and around us is not really empty space but rather oscillating patterns of energy, what the Chinese refer to as *ch'i,* the dynamic energy of life from which all matter comes into being. As Chuang Tsu said, "When one knows that the great void is full of *ch'i,* there is no such thing as nothingness." In space, particles come into being in the void and vanish into it; according to the cosmologies of many cultures, the world and all living beings are born from this void. The void, the darkness, the nothingness around us and inside us is actually what gestalt therapists call a fertile void, a source of energy, the source of all being and becoming.

One of the most important things we can do under a Pluto transit, particularly a transit to our Sun or Moon, is to enter that void, that darkness within ourselves. We can actually journey fully into its center, not with any self-destructive aims, but with the aim of absorbing the darkness and finding the deeper center within ourselves which resides there. Such a journey is terrifying; it is indeed a descent into an inferno. But it is also an ascent, because when we fully identify with that darkness and experience ourselves as nothing, when we embrace, rather than battle, the emptiness we feel, we experience a powerful release of energy which can regenerate us and enable us to transform whatever twisted emotions have been polluting us. Such a descent may occur without our conscious choice, and it may be so frightening that we need the help of a therapist or spiritual master so that we do not become stuck in the energy-draining outer realms of the darkness, but are able to penetrate to its core and move through it. Under a Pluto transit, we might benefit especially from intensive, releasing forms of therapy and spiritual development—primal therapy, re-birthing, gestalt therapy, bioenergetics and yoga, although we should be wary of engaging in a powerfully cathartic approach without adequate supervision and support. A passive therapy or spiritual path such as meditation may have little effect upon us; Pluto, by its nature, demands the total involvement of body and emotions and the release of physical and emotional energy.

When Pluto conjuncted my Sun (while semi-squaring my Pluto) in 1972, I discovered on numerous occasions how allowing ourselves to experience our powerlessness can lead to discovering our power. Once, in a primal/gestalt group, the experience of my own terror led me into and through the void; when I released that terror aloud in the group, bellowing "I'm afraid" for several minutes, my normally meek voice transformed into a strong gut-level resonance, and my body shook for hours afterwards with the energy that was surging through me. On another occasion, pouring out the anguish of an ended love affair in "The Black Sun Poems," I wrote the lines, "Strike me. I cannot light myself. Strike me. I will not light myself. I am a matchstick and my head is black, my body bent, my power—spent." Yet in writing from the misery of my own powerlessness, I awakened a level of creativity which not only revitalized me at that time, but which also led me to write eight books in the following six years.

If at any points in our lives we experience the psychological death and powerlessness of Pluto, we may want to keep in mind that we can benefit by: 1) going to the center of our experience, rather than recoiling in terror at the periphery; 2) finding a supportive, therapeutic environment or helper to accompany us through the descent; 3) discovering a powerful physical or creative channel. For many of us, only when we have descended fully into the abyss of ourselves and have experienced and accepted the suffering that may reside there, can we begin the ascent—an ascent which may not begin to occur until after our Pluto transit has ended, but which may last for the rest of our lives. Usually, when we are descending, the possibility of ascent seems inconceivable. Yet the experience of psychological descent and ascent clearly parallels the theories about death and rebirth in many spiritual teachings. As Stanislav and Christina Grof wrote:

> The soul has to face a strange paradox; in order to be able to continue its journey, it has to accept that it will stay in hell forever . . . It is only when this situation is fully accepted that one has experienced hell, and the journey can continue. After a deep confrontation with the evil forces and the "dark night of the soul" comes the glorious turning point . . . The soul emerges into the radiance of the Divine Light and experiences spiritual rebirth.[2]

2. Stanislav and Christina Grof, *Beyond Death: The Gates of Consciousness* (London: Thames & Hudson, 1980).

The experience of psychological death, like the experience of physical death, is therefore not an end at all, but rather one stage in an ongoing process of becoming and evolving. It is a rebirth, a means of casting away the useless portions of the past, so that the new can emerge. Modern physicists are discovering that black holes vanish only to appear again in the void as white holes, new stars, new galaxies. They die only to be reborn. In the Greek myth of Demeter and Persephone, Demeter descends into hell in order to bring her daughter Persephone back to life. Because Persephone eats a pomegranate seed while in the realm of Hades, she must descend into the underworld for six months every year—die during the months of fall and winter, so that spring can come and life can be continually renewed. This death/rebirth theme is fundamental to the mystery religions; it is also fundamental to various rites of initiation in which an individual undergoes tremendous suffering, often has to fight for survival, and then, leaving a past identity and role in society behind, is born into a new name and new role.

In terms of physical death, there are numerous accounts of patients who have been declared dead and were revived, returning to describe the celestial planes they visited—spacious, light-filled, joyous realms existing beyond death. Many dying patients, overcome with visions during their last hours, have surrendered peacefully to death, knowing it to be not an end, but rather a birth into a new dimension, one stage of transition in the soul's journey through time and space.

The more contact we have with our own higher Self or spirit, the more we identify with it rather than our ego or the various planetary manifestations of our ego which make up our chart, the more we fully experience that we are more than our normal, daily consciousness of ourselves, the more we open ourselves to the energies of the universe and welcome the unknown, allowing ourselves to be transformed by it, and the more we become capable of trusting our own process of becoming and trusting in a divine plan which is guiding our evolution—the more capable we will be of handling and benefiting from a Pluto transit. The experience of annihilation, which may or may not occur, is traumatic, but does not have to be devastating if we are conscious of what is happening to us and trust in its eventual outcome. Just as the *Tibetan Book of the Dead* instructs our souls how to consciously undertake our own physical process of dying, it is possible for us also to consciously undertake our own psychological dyings, but only if we are at least partially identified with our soul or higher Self, and not totally invested in our earthly attachments, desires and feelings. Through this identification with our soul, we will experience Pluto less as an annihilation of ourselves and more as a moving toward release, awakening or rebirth.

As I reflect upon my own cycle of seven Pluto conjunctions to five planets, Midheaven and South Node, as well as squares and oppositions occurring at the same time, I indeed believe that I experienced a long process of rebirthing. At the end of my last Pluto conjunction, preparing the first version of this chapter on Pluto, I asked the *I Ching* what attitude I should now take toward bringing this Pluto cycle of my life to a close while writing about the lessons of Pluto. The hexagram I threw, most appropriately, was After Completion—water over fire or fire under water—again an apt description of Pluto. "When water in a kettle hangs over fire, the two elements stand in relation and thus generate energy—the production of steam," the *I Ching* (Richard Wilhelm edition) told me. "But the resulting tension demands caution. If the water boils over, the fire is extinguished and its energy is lost. If the heat is too great, the water evaporates into air." The *I Ching* advised that even rebirth, the completion of a Pluto cycle, must not be considered a final end; the fire and water activated by Pluto demand caution, careful balancing, care. We may be reborn under Pluto, but such rebirth is a continual process; it means that we enter a new cycle of experience with more energy and power at our disposal, and must exercise repeated caution in our use of this energy and in the expression of this power.

Plutonian Concerns: Merging, Social Transformation, Elimination

We have considered various experiences and lessons related to the power and death/rebirth issues of Pluto, but have not explored many of the other manifestations of Plutonian energy. One of the experiences which usually occurs under a strong Pluto transit, particularly one affecting our Sun, Moon, Venus or Mars, or our 1st, 5th, 7th, or 8th houses, is an overwhelming desire to merge, to unite with something or someone beyond ourselves. This longing is often experienced as sexual desire; we may become obsessed with our own sexuality and feel consumed by our own fire. We may become obsessed also with the particular person or people we desire, and our sexual experiences with them are likely to be some of the most powerful, releasing and blissfully transcendent experiences we have ever known. However, increased sexual desire, not only in the sense of energy release but also related to merging, is only one of the dimensions of Pluto, and it may become destructively obsessive when we have no creative or spiritual outlets that allow us to raise or sublimate that energy. Through creative expression or such releasing spiritual disciplines as yoga, we may become capable of transmuting our passion and desires, and we may discover that our longing to surrender or merge is to some extent a longing to reunite with the universe, to enter the cosmic womb. Our desire is to become one with all that is outside ourselves and to lose our limited consciousness of our own ego.

Through such surrender and the opening to cosmic energies we may experience through whatever outlet we choose for releasing our Plutonian energies, and through experiencing fully the void within us, we lose our narrow sense of ourselves and gain a wider awareness of Self. This process allows our ego to restructure itself to become able to encompass the experience of our higher Self or Soul. It is possible also that through total involvement in some activity or goal, by surrendering ourselves to some cause in which we believe, by taking an active part in the reform and regeneration of society, that we can, under a Pluto transit or through expression of our natal Plutos, experience this cosmic merging.

Pluto, as an outer planet, is concerned not only with primal dimensions of our own psyches, but also with the collective—with society and social transformation. In terms of our individual charts, if we have not established a satisfying role in society which allows us to make a contribution which we believe is meaningful and which others also regard to be meaningful, we are likely to feel alienated, in relation both to our own psyches and to the world in which we live. Such alienation can twist us and lead us to destroy rather than regenerate. If a Pluto transit influences us in this way, unleashing powerful forces of destruction, then we can at least constructively channel those forces of destruction by devoting ourselves to destroying what needs destroying—tearing down a slum, fighting cancer, exposing political evils. But to destroy for the sake of destroying is not a lesson of Pluto; the fury released by Pluto, which we may experience as the urge to destroy, is a passion, an energy which can better be used to rebuild, renew, reawaken. When experiencing the urge to destroy, as we may experience it in the houses Pluto influences natally and by transit and in terms of the planets it is aspecting, it is important for us to ask ourselves what new modes of being are we creating, and to channel our energy at least as much into the creation of the new as into the destruction of the old.

One of my personal mottos, which is really a genuine guideline for dealing with Pluto, is "go where the energy is." "Go where the energy is" does not imply following each momentary impulse and desire, but rather, through contacting the energy at the core of our being, to allow it to direct us to the most appropriate activities and behaviors, one which will help us to release that energy for a constructive purpose. Pluto is, after all, the planet that indicates our gut-level, core energy—the energy which is even more instinctual and powerful than the energy of the Moon and Mars, and certainly more difficult to experience and fully harness. The house in which Pluto is positioned in our natal charts, and to some extent the house which it rules, may indicate where we give our power away, but it also indicates how we can most productively contact, experience and channel the energy available to us. If Pluto is associated with our 10th or 11th houses, we may have an overwhelming desire to make an important contribution to society. But even if Pluto is positioned in or rules other houses in our charts, we can and need to establish our connection to society by using our energy, our resources, our power here for some purpose which extends beyond ourselves. We need to channel our Plutonian energy into some purpose which is regenerating, healing or otherwise a means of transforming the darkness around and within us into light.

There are two other lessons of Pluto which we need to consider if we are fully to actualize the potential of our natal Plutos and also respond favorably to Pluto transits and progressions—particularly the long period, usually as many as ten years, during which Pluto may be stationary by progression in our charts. One lesson is the lesson of elimination. As we allow ourselves to experience the energy release and transformation taking place within us, we become more in touch with our inner core and less satisfied with the surface realm of our life. We now directly perceive the essence or are striving to perceive it; we want to live from that essence. This means that we experience the urge to eliminate from our identity, from our lifestyle and experience, all that is inessential. For that reason, we may be somewhat ruthless under Pluto, choosing to free ourselves from the attitudes, behaviors, people, possessions or structures which do not resonate with the core within us. If we are not fully in touch with our core energies, we may experience facets of our lives being taken from us—structures or beliefs or people or possessions destroyed without our conscious consent. However, the more we are in contact with our inner depths, the more we will consciously choose to rid ourselves of this excess baggage, so that our external lives reflect and resonate with our internal experience. Pluto urges us to penetrate beneath the surface of our experience, to eliminate all that is unnecessary, and to discover all that is vital, alive, invigorating and regenerating to ourselves and others. The surfaces that need penetrating, the parts of ourselves or areas of our lives that need eliminating, will usually be related to the houses, the natal and transiting Pluto influences and the planets which natal and transiting Pluto aspects in our charts.

Pluto's Healing Power

One other lesson of Pluto, and likewise a lesson of Scorpio, which is so clearly an expression of Plutonian energy, is that Pluto gives us the capacity to heal, not merely physically, but also psychologically. The psychological healing of Pluto is directly related to the energy we release as we contact, confront and transmute the darkness within ourselves. Many Scorpios and people with powerful Plutos in their charts who have been transformed by their own darkness have a healing presence. They have dealt so much with their own demons that they can actually neutralize the power of the demons within us—the fury, desire, greed or jealousy which we regard as evil or unfortunate and give power to by our very rejection of it. As a Libra with a 12th house Mars, often hesitant to face my own dark side, I have felt healed through close friendships with Scorpios and Plutonian types, people who continually struggle with their own jealousies, fears, angers, hatreds and desires for power over others. They have learned to regard their own dark side as an integral part of their humanness and as a strength.

What is the healing power of these Plutonians who are struggling to transcend their own urges to judge, condemn and destroy? Perhaps it is their ability to say, when we have falteringly revealed what we believe to be some monstrous feeling within ourselves, "Oh, that. I understand. I live with it constantly, every day." By so easily accepting what we regard to be our own evil nature, they release us from the struggle we have had with it and free our energy for a more worthwhile purpose. We may feel as if we have had some social disease which has been cured by their words or even their mere presence. The Beauty and the Beast legend is an expression of this healing power of Plutonian acceptance and acknowledgement, which requires loving and accepting the beast within. Ursula Le Guin's award-winning fantasy, A *Wizard of Earthsea* likewise teaches Plutonian (as well as 12th house) lessons in its portrayal of a wizard learning to confront and absorb his own shadow.

As Pluto releases energy within us, it releases first what we would consider to be negative energy—angers, frustrated desires, hatreds, jealousies—all the poisons that have clogged our center and have become twisted and distorted because they have accumulated inside without the light of conscious awareness and acceptance. Dealing with those dark forces is a coming face to face with our inner demons—we may feel possessed, out of control, or we may lose confidence in ourselves. But what happens when we fully experience those dark forces, when we allow them to become incorporated into our identity and consciously integrate them into our awareness by confronting them and accepting them as human? The energy that is released with those feelings is transmuted; it is available now for other purposes. We are able to draw upon more of our own resources, to uplift ourselves, to motivate ourselves, to accomplish more than we thought possible. We have more energy available to channel into fulfilling our goals. We also become, through experiencing that energy, more in touch with ourselves; we are in contact with our core, able to draw upon and listen to the center of our being, to experience our own personal power. A final result is that we become capable of helping others handle their own demons; we are able to penetrate beneath the surface of their experience, to perceive what is happening inside them and guide them through their own processes of transformation. We can now heal and regenerate others as we have healed and regenerated ourselves.

Plutonian Relationships

Those of us who have Pluto in or ruling the seventh house, or in close aspect to Venus, have Plutonian lessons which clearly relate to contacting our personal power through relationships. When Pluto is a "relationship planet" in our charts, we are likely to seek as a partner someone who is intense, perceptive, deep, and strong-willed, someone whose energy awakens our own experience of aliveness. Such a Plutonian person, however, may also be dominating, demanding, judgmental, jealous and/or destructive; our Plutonian relationships, negatively, can degenerate into relationships of mutual manipulation, power struggles, psychological warfare, or obsessive, all-consuming symbiotic attachments. We or our partners may overemphasize the sexual or monetary facets of our connection, or may become so overly invested in each other that the survival of the relationship becomes equated with our own survival. Unable to meet our own needs, we may demand that our partner compensate for our incapacities. Unable to experience and affirm our aliveness on our own, we may be compulsively drawn to a person who awakens intense realms of emotion and sexuality. We may mistakenly regard such intensity to be an indicator of love or of "the right relationship." We may indeed expect a love relationship to involve dramatic shifts of hatred and desire, and to embroil us in an atmosphere of constant crises or turmoil.

But a Plutonian relationship need not be destructive to our own or our partner's welfare. Ideally, a relationship in which the Plutonian or Scorpionic energy predominates is often intense and transforming and does guide us deeply into ourselves. But in such a relationship, we use our psychological perceptiveness in order to promote our own growth and our partner's growth, not as a means of overpowering the other. A constructive Plutonian relationship is a relationship of shared power, mutual power, in which we are secure enough in ourselves to be able to encourage each other's empowerment, and capable of adapting an "I WIN YOU WIN" attitude rather than "I WIN YOU LOSE" or "YOU WIN I LOSE." Partners engaged in a viable Plutonian relationship often experience deep and significant changes in their way of relating, changes which may completely alter the form of their relationship, and give them a sense of continually recreating the bonds between them. Positively, a Plutonian relationship is invigorating, alive and passionate, and yet the aliveness awakened in interactions together is not channelled exclusively into preoccupation with each other, but is also directed individually or mutually into productive expression in the world.

We who have Pluto as a relationship planet (associated with our seventh house or Venus) need to utilize our Plutonian energy in other relationships besides our primary partnership. We need intense emotional involvement with several people with whom we can explore psychological depths. We need to apply our psychological insight in many of our one-to-one interactions. We also need to constructively satisfy our urge for power and control by developing important relationships in which we have the capacity to impact others, to influence them profoundly, in ways which we and they value.

We have, in the course of this chapter, covered most of the meanings of Pluto in terms of psychological experience and have considered the lessons it teaches us. In summary then, what can we do when Pluto is powerful in our charts, forming difficult aspects natally or by transit to our planets?

1) We can renew our contact with our spirit or higher Self, so that we can more easily allow ourselves to experience fully the process of psychological death and rebirth without completely losing our sense of identity or our ability to function in the world;

2) We can make space within our lives and within ourselves so that we can willingly experience the energy being released within us;

3) We can turn to some intensive form of therapy or a powerful spiritual discipline to help us through the experience;

4) We can study philosophies of religion, such as Tantric Buddhism, and mythologies concerned with death and rebirth, allowing them to guide us symbolically through our own death and rebirth experience;

5) We can discover constructive releases for our energy—physical outlets which help us to eliminate accumulated poisons, and more importantly, pursuits which totally involve us, physically, emotionally and intellectually, so that we not only release and transmute energy, but also fulfill some worthwhile purpose and perhaps make a meaningful contribution to society;

6) We can actively involve ourselves in social reform, not only destroying what needs to be destroyed, but also discovering what needs to be created;

7) We can eliminate from our lives attitudes, behaviors or experiences which are no longer essential, and substitute those which are vital;

8) We can deepen our ties with Scorpionic or Plutonic people who have dealt successfully with their own darkness, and can help us to deal with ours;

9) Finally, as we begin to emerge from the darkness we may have experienced, and discover within ourselves the light of dawn, we can become healers, helping others who struggle with disease or with the demons of the psyche. We can allow our presence to be a light to them, a healing and sustaining force as their descent leads them through their own transformation, their own regeneration, their own awakening.

As T. S. Eliot wrote in *Four Quartets,*

In order to possess what you do not possess
You must go by the way of dispossession.
In order to arrive at what you are not
You must go through the way in which you are not.
. . . We must be still and still moving
Into another intensity
For a further union, a deeper communion
Through the dark cold and the empty desolation
. . . In the end is my beginning.

Letter to a Scorpio

The following excerpts are from a letter I wrote in April, 1980 to a Scorpio friend, a man with Sun conjunct Mercury in close square to Pluto, and six other Leo/Scorpio squares bridging his 2nd and 5th houses. I share this letter, as personal as it is, only because I believe it may speak to those of you struggling with the darkest sides of Pluto, and may help you to come to terms with, transmute and channel the energy which resides in the darkness.

You ask why you must struggle with the darkness—with the vast abyss of fury and passion and desolation within you; why it sometimes takes you over, overcomes you, leads you to destroy all that you love. I see that the darkness within you, the black hole in space at the center of your being is your gift as much as your curse . . . the gateway to the powerful, transformative, healing energy within you . . . to the white holes of awakening within you. . . . The darkness is a path, a channel of energy, the void from the atoms within us which can be unlocked, released, to reaffirm rather than deny our beauty, our light. Not high ungrounded light, not Hare Krishna chanting divorced from life, not floating away into space, not the spirituality that claims to love all humanity but is incapable of fully opening the heart to a tree or a woman or a child. The light that counts is the light that embraces darkness, that absorbs it and is not destroyed but rather intensified by the energy the darkness provides. . . . Fight the darkness with light, they say. Yes, light. But light that can meet the darkness, as dawn meets the night, not shimmer like a thin veil over it. Light that absorbs the darkness, contains the darkness. Light that can break, bleed, and then, regaining its wholeness, travel forward like a laser beam, condensed, unified, directed, affirming.

We can do t'ai chi; we can meditate; we can spread high high vibes. But are we really transmuting the darkness, or escaping from it? Are we really going down, contacting the energy at the core, the pain and emptiness and fury and passion, and working with that, uplifting that? I no longer believe in moving upward, chanting mantras, wrapping auras of light around each other as we step in the dog dung on the sidewalk, as we cast our eyes away from the muck within ourselves. We must each journey through the pain and not above it. Through the fury and not away from it. There is the source of our energy; only there is the energy necessary to counter the horrors in and around us. We must claim them as our own, use them, unlock the nuclear energy within ourselves, unleash bombs that do not kill but open us to others. . . .

Forty years ago the Nazis unleashed their demons upon humanity. Now, the death camps are gone, but Nazism continues, around us, within us. The Nazism of our psyches is our refusal to go into, transform the darkness inside. We do not go far enough; we get close to the core and run from it in terror; we project it outside of ourselves and must destroy others in order to break free of our own demons. In doing so, we give those demons more power; we allow them to dominate us, to destroy rather than awaken us. . . .

Yes, I, like you, wrestle with demons, feel twisted by forces beyond my control. But slowly, I am learning to recognize that underneath that twisting is an affirmation of life. Each pang, each cruel slash of the knife, each writhing scream is the healthy, beautiful sensitive part of ourselves crying out for expression, refusing to be stomped upon, destroyed, denied by the atrocities around us. It is only twisted because it has not been allowed its full expression, because it has not found a space in the world where it can experience and express the full range of its beauty.

I too have darkness within me. But I am learning not to fight it anymore, not to rage against it. Instead, I plunge into its center—I plunge into that void, I grasp those dancing wave/particles inside me, I become them, I begin to use them to affirm, to open, to awaken, to love. That is the secret. You ask where the animal and spiritual meet. That is where the animal and spiritual meet. With our fury, we will build bridges toward each other rather than burn bridges. With our pain, we will play music. With our terror, we will plunge into the abyss of our isolation and find in the desolation there a full capacity to love. . . .

You are driven, you say, at the mercy of your pain, your anger, your passion. . . . If you want to go on recreating your past identity, proclaiming to yourself, to me, to the world, that you are a person who must destroy what you love, shatter it, glean the cinders from the devastation and move on, that is your choice. But it is not a choice I will participate in; it is not a choice you have to make. There are other choices. If you must destroy something, must wreak revenge upon something, then smash the evil in the world that needs smashing, join a wrecking crew and tear down a slum, set a torch to the ruins of a worthless car. But don't destroy me; don't destroy the beauty that is you. Go ahead, rail, scream, fill the night with your fury. But let it be a celebration not a devastation. Let it be an affirmation of your capacity to live, of your capacity to love. Bleed the colors of anger and frustration, pain and isolation, but let those colors become the colors of a radiant dawn.

PART III

ASTROLOGY &
SELF-DEVELOPMENT

Chapter Eight

PRINCIPLES OF DEPTH ASTROLOGY

*We are all framed of flaps and patches and of so shapeless and
diverse a texture that every piece and every moment playeth its part.*
—MONTAIGNE

*Do I contradict myself? Very well, then, I contradict myself. . .
I am large. I contain multitudes.*
—WALT WHITMAN

*He who attends to his greater Self becomes a great man;
he who attends to his smaller self becomes a small man.*
—MENCIUS

*The centre that I cannot find
Is known to my unconscious Mind;
I have no reason to despair
Because I am already there.*
—W. H. AUDEN

We astrology students and practitioners are continually faced with
questions in regard to the purpose, validity and uses of our art.
Of what value is the study of astrology? Doesn't knowing the influences of the present and future lead to feeling helpless, or acting in accordance with self-fulfilling prophecies? How does astrology account
for free will? How can we use astrology in order to empower ourselves
and others, rather than remaining helpless in the face of circumstances
seemingly beyond our control? The questions we are asked may indeed
lead us further in our own internal quest to understand the aims and
uses of astrology, and to develop a philosophy and approach to interpretation which is constructive and empowering.

Let us take a moment then and really ask ourselves some important questions about our astrological study and practice. Why are we
studying astrology? Why are *you* reading this chapter? What are you

looking for? Are you interested in astrology simply because it works? Because it provides a structured system of thought which helps you to feel more secure in the world in which you operate? Because you feel unsure of your ability to cope with your life and want to know what to expect from the future? Because your own sense of identity is shaky, and astrology helps you to define rather than experience directly who you are? Is it a system which can help you maintain your rationalizations, continue in old behaviors, both good and bad, and resist change? Do you, in your use of astrology, become more dependent upon interpretations you have read or heard for planets, signs, houses and aspects, or do you become attuned to your own inner guidance, more capable of giving to others and experiencing your own connectedness to the universe?

It is important for each of us to face honestly why we are interested in astrology and how we are using it, because our own motivation and approach has a direct impact upon how the planets affect us and how helpful we can be to the people around us. How can we help others to contact the center within themselves, make peace with their conflicting energies, learn to cooperate with rather than combat universal energies, become more self-directing (in terms of allowing themselves to be directed by their own higher Self), if we ourselves feel that we are victims of the planets, unable to respond constructively to the energies affecting us at any given moment?

Astrology and Our Life Purpose

Increasing our knowledge of astrology is an important aim in itself, but not without consideration for an even more important aim—that of improving the *quality* of our lives and the lives of the people around us. Astrology is meaningful only to the extent that it furthers our own development and enables us to live more peacefully with ourselves and our environment. Astrology serves this purpose when it helps us to unify and integrate our conflicting parts so that we can turn our attention to important tasks outside ourselves. I am not a believer in knowledge for knowledge's sake, art for art's sake, science for science's sake, or astrology for astrology's sake because all of these approaches to life are concerned with a variety of transient goals rather than one overriding, unifying goal or purpose.

Life today has become incredibly specialized and fragmented. Since faith in God and most of the cosmologies associated with God have begun to dissolve, we seem to have lost touch not only with a unifying center outside ourselves, but also with a unifying center within ourselves, and have substituted a myriad of unrelated goals or interests or impulses in order to fill the vacuum. We may look to our work, our lover, our family, our studies to provide meaning which we cannot provide for ourselves. In terms of our charts, we may be allowing one planet to dominate and then the other, so that we skirt around like dodgem cars, veering first in one direction and then another, colliding with other people who like us are also directionless and struggling to find some source of meaning in their lives. We may not know how to contact or maintain contact with the center within ourselves, the inner light, the well from which we can draw upon the healing energies of the universe. Our planetary voices may constantly be arguing, refusing to listen to each other, resembling voices in a barroom brawl rather than cooperating like a planetary symphony, a symphony which depends upon a conductor, a central and unified Self in order to create inner harmony.

It is important for each of us to ask: What is the purpose of our lives, individually and collectively? Toward what ends should our attitudes and actions be directed? Is our use of astrology really in accord with our purpose? Are we using it to improve the quality of our lives and that of others? Are we really furthering our own development if we are merely filling ourselves up with data rather than assimilating and applying the data we have already collected? Are we promoting our growth if we allow ourselves to believe that we can't hold down a job because Uranus squares our 6th house Mars? Are we helping others if we are infusing our friends and our clients with fear over upcoming Saturn transits rather than encouraging them to begin to respond to and express those forthcoming transits constructively?

Astrology has been at odds with science for centuries, ever since science began to oust religion from its throne and abolish all that it deemed superstition. But astrology is following the same path as traditional science when it does not consider toward what end it is being directed and how it is being used. We all know from reading the newspapers what happens when ultimate ends are not considered and people do not face the consequences of their actions—when industries are motivated by profit and ignore the environmental implications of their acts, when governments attempt to assert their power rather than recognize their interdependence and cooperate, when individuals become criminals, driven by their frustrated desires, unwilling or unable to respect the needs of others. Consider Einstein, who had a yod to Uranus in the 3rd house, and allowed himself for too long to neglect 9th house questions, as he pursued physics for physics' sake rather than humanity's sake, and only began to consider ultimate questions when he informed FDR of the wartime potential of nuclear energy.

I am urging each of you studying astrology not to continue accumulating knowledge without looking closely at the meaningfulness of that knowledge, at how you are using it in terms of your own life, and in interpreting your own chart and the charts of other people. I am urging you not to lose yourselves in the details of a chart, reading it as if it were a jigsaw puzzle composed of separate pieces, as if your main aim in interpretation is to prove how right you can be or how easily you can reduce the complexities of a person or of future possibilities into a neat system. To reduce the complexities is to avoid experiencing the chaos in and around you—the chaos which, when fully experienced, can enlighten you and transform you into a more integrated whole. I am urging you not to focus your attention upon such questions as: *What does Saturn square my Mercury mean?* or *What will happen when Pluto opposes my Sun?* but rather upon such questions as:

What is the highest potential for the combined energies of these planets operating together? How can I best unfold this potential in my life? What attitudes and actions expressive of these two planets in aspect will benefit me and other people? How can I keep myself open to the experience of a transit, and learn from it as it approaches and apply what I have learned as it becomes exact? How can I integrate the experience of each transit with the expression of all my other planets, so that it does not dominate my consciousness and pull me away from center, but rather awakens the center more fully? How can natal planets and aspects, and each transit and progression I experience, improve the quality of my life, my relationships, my participation in society, my connectedness with the universe?

We may not be able to answer many of these questions. But unless we ask the right questions, unless we continually remain aware of how we are using astrology and how we could be using it, unless we are willing to commit ourselves to understanding, experiencing and expressing the highest potential of our planets, signs, houses and aspects, we are not likely to be able to discover or to live the right answers.

Dialoguing with Our Astrological Subpersonalities

An important principle of depth astrology is that our planets are actually personalities within us, not merely parts or qualities of ourselves, but entities in their own right, with lives of their own. In psychosynthesis, a spiritually oriented psychotherapy developed by Roberto Assagioli, we do directed fantasies and dialogues with subpersonalities within us which are similar to our planetary selves. We may discover that we have a fairy godmother inside, a crybaby, a workaholic, a wrestler, a cheerleader, a social butterfly, a rebel. Most of these subpersonalities may actually correspond to our planets. Our first house Uranus may be our rebel, Venus in Leo in the 5th house our cheerleader, Saturn in Virgo in the 6th our workaholic, Mars in Taurus in the 7th our wrestler. Moon in Pisces in the 4th our crybaby, Venus in Gemini in the 11th our social butterfly.

Frequently, we are in touch with one or two of our subpersonalities or planets at a time—first we may experience our 7th house Mars and provoke an argument because we are angry, then we experience our 4th house Pisces Moon and withdraw, feeling hurt, and then we perhaps may activate our 11th house Venus in Gemini and plunge into a whirlwind of social activities so that we can forget our anger and vulnerability. We may express one planet for a moment, an hour, a day or even longer, without consulting or expressing other planets until they too are activated.

Perhaps our 4th house Sun in Virgo is being aspected by Saturn, and its subpersonality is currently dominating our lives. For months, we may be concerned with our responsibilities to our family, obsessed with organizing our domestic affairs. Then Saturn opposes our 10th house Mars in Pisces, and we are overwhelmed by the work we have neglected in our job. In the manner of an opposition, we may seesaw into our Mars and identify with our Mars subpersonality, turning our attention to our professional affairs, now totally neglecting our home and family. Mars may dominate our lives for several months, before we switch gears again and allow our 4th house Sun in Virgo once more to devote itself to our personal lives. We create numerous problems for ourselves and throw our lives out of balance when we allow any of our planetary personalities to dominate our awareness for too long and block our the desires and needs of other planets which must also be fulfilled if we are to make peace with ourselves.

It may be necessary, at least in the case of oppositions, to do some seesawing; but if in the course of alternating between and among our various planetary selves, we allow one to dominate and forget entirely about all of the others, we may behave in the manner of split personalities and create a state of constant chaos in our lives. In the above example, we may, while focused upon our family, neglect our work to such an extent that we almost lose our job, and then, in order to regain professional security, block all awareness of our family's needs out of our consciousness. We work every day and night until we discover that our husband is preparing to leave us, and our children are failing in school while expressing their neglect by spending all their time on the street. If we were, while involved in a work phase, capable of allowing our 4th house Sun even a minimal amount of expression, and if we were, while involved in a domestic phase, capable of allowing our 10th house Mars to assert itself and apply itself at least to the most essential facets of our job, we might not create as much disorder as we would when one planetary personality runs off with us and does not allow any of the others to emerge.

In order to express and integrate all our planetary selves, we must first be aware of how each one operates in our lives—what it needs, what it wants, how it manifests, how it can best be fulfilled. We need to be able to observe ourselves in action, attuned both to our internal state and to our behaviors which reflect different planetary selves. In order to identify and become acquainted with our subpersonalities, we first need to cultivate the attitudes of acceptance and compassion, attitudes which are helped by understanding our past and how different facets of ourselves, which may not serve us now, were developed as a means of coping with our environment. Getting to know our subpersonalities and learning to appreciate rather than judge ones which have been troublesome in our adult lives takes time and attention.

Subpersonalities-by-Sign[1]

The following list indicates a number of subpersonalities-by-sign which we may experience in ourselves. Although we may at first glimpse seem to possess many related to our predominant signs, we will usually discover that only a few are central features of our personality. Many of us may, for example, possess "a hungry child" or "a pleaser," but the specific form this subpersonality takes and its particular wants, needs, aims and behavior patterns will be unique to each of us.

---

1. Copyright 1982 by Tracy Marks. Reprinted from *The Square Aspect* by Tracy Marks, published by Sagittarius Rising Publishing Company.

ARIES

fighter	leader	narcissist
excitement addict	adventurer	speed demon
doer	athlete	risk-taker
confronter	competitor	"Me First"
spoiled brat	rabble-rouser	initiator
pioneer	spontaneous child	Miss True Confessions
crusader	aggressor	revealer
macho		

TAURUS

Earth Mother	sensualist	conformist
cultivator	artist	"Grabbie"
materialist	laid-back	holder
lazy bum	egotist	immovable rock
puppy dog	producer	entrepreneur
locomotive	money-maker	good guy
bulldozer	Miss Complacent	glutton
manager	self-indulger	big spender
hoarder	epicurean	

GEMINI

fast talker	scientist	friendly neighbor
"Gabbie"	inquirer	switchboard
the wit	the fly-by-night	centipede
the gossip	schemer	salesman
dabbler	messenger	librarian
social butterfly	the live wire	know-it-all
Miss Trivia	juggler	talk show host
logician	the fidget	manipulator

CANCER

hungry child	psychic	softie
turtle	hysteric	Little Miss Muffet
good mother	crybaby	sponge
octopus	martyr	"Poor Little Me"
protector	clinger	Mother Hubbard
housewife	hoarder	munchkin
supporter	brooder	nurturer
ostrich	mother hen	comforter

LEO

star	commander	glowworm
playful child	lover of life	braggart
hero	creator	prizewinner
handsome prince	egotist	lamplighter
Romeo	the show-off	Cowardly Lion
Don Juan	heart of gold	romantic
shining light	dictator	Queen Bee
king	Miss Bubbly	Center Stage
actor	playboy	Mr. Confidence
entertainer	jock	

VIRGO

analyst	puritan	invisible man
organizer	nun	keeper of morals
accountant	Miss Humility	dissector
skeptic	helper	fussbudget
secretary	worrier	nurse
petty tyrant	health fanatic	friendly servant
workaholic	busy bee	good deed doer
Miss Priss	timid one	spotless
perfectionist	menial	

LIBRA

pleaser	cooperator	middle-of-the-
princess of peace	sweetness & light	roader
fairy princess	mediator	impartial judge
angel	aesthete	seesaw
happy hostess	evaluator	tag-along
gracious guest	Charlie Brown	Miss Poise
smiley	flirt	beauty queen
accommodating	charmer	woman-behind-
child	flatterer	the-man
pretender	gentle dove	negotiator

SCORPIO

investigator	wallower	silent one
underground	power addict	hide-away
explorer	extremist	detective
jealous bitch	destroyer	manipulator
tester	rebuilder	taker
sex maniac	dictator	wolf
intensity addict	"heavy"	scorpion
truth-seeker	judge	psychologist
grudge-bearer	stoic	healer
powerhouse	volcano	pressure cooker

SAGITTARIUS

seeker	guru	know-it-all
professor	bookworm	dogmatist
eternal student	slob	generalist
moralist	procrastinator	ethics professor
friend-to-all	overdoer	wise old man
free spirit	overextender	philanthropist
explorer	wanderer	sportsman
missionary	optimist	guide
philosopher	Mr. Generosity	hang loose

CAPRICORN

administrator	Big Daddy	pillar of strength
businessman	Mr. Responsibility	mountain climber
stoic	Atlas	rugged individualist
withholder	loner	status seeker
workaholic	authority	Macchiavelli
deadbeat	boss	Mr. President
realist	miser	Sad Sack
denier	misanthrope	tough lady
conformist	pessimist	provider
fearful	Mr. Security	Mr. Committed

AQUARIUS

humanitarian	weirdo	individualist
nonconformist	groupie	scientist
bohemian	free soul	mad genius
truth seeker	uncommitted	saviour of humanity
friend-to-all	uninvolved	anarchist
reformer	dissenter	mad hatter
liberal	sparky	misfit
rebel	heretic	outsider
inventor	group leader	Mr. Politics

PISCES

mystic	spineless	sensitive listener
bum	Miss Humble	daydreamer
idealist	joiner	Miss Vulnerability
space cadet	Cinderella	tearful
all-giving	visionary	angel of mercy
chameleon	lost soul	escapist
poet	parasite	sponge
psychic	avoider	Miss Helpless
martyr	victim	elusive one
drifter	elf	rescuer
chosen one	Miss Empathy	cynic
musician	brooder	"Poor Little Me"

Amazingly enough, we are likely to discover that as soon as we recognize and acknowledge a part of ourselves, and give it permission to be, it transforms and begins to reveal its positive potential. When we stop judging the needy child of our Cancer Moon, she stops crying and whining and begins to reveal her nurturing sensitivity to others as well as her capacity to nourish us with warm feelings; when we stop judging our lazy, unfocused Piscean Mars, he begins to relax and guides us into creative, inspiring activities.

As we begin to observe the subpersonalities within us as they appear and disappear from our consciousness, we begin to know when we are in contact with only one or two, and when our awareness is wide enough to encompass most of them at any one time. As our consciousness expands, we become more capable of awareness of all facets of ourselves, of shifting from one planet to another and consulting each of them when making a decision. As we develop a lifestyle which incorporates each of our planets, we become less identified with our planetary personalities and more in contact with the center within us that provides the power and illumination which can enable us to transmute even the most difficult aspects in our charts.

In *Planetary Aspects,* I introduced some of my own planetary selves and allowed them to dialogue with each other and begin to learn how to cooperate. The technique of dialoguing with our planets, talking to each one or allowing them to talk to each other is a powerful technique derived from gestalt therapy and psychosynthesis subpersonality work, which can allow us to make direct contact with parts of ourselves and bring them into alignment. Consider the following:

> *"Give me a hug," says Moon in Aries, when Neptune is lost in her favorite fantasy novel. "I want some tomatoes," she tells Sun in Libra (in the 9th house), who is trying to decide what to do about this chapter's expanding length. Moon then turns to Uranus (in the 7th house), who is preparing for a client. "Let me tell you what I did today!"*
>
> *"You leech! You crybaby! You minx!" shrieks Uranus. "You mollycoddled nincompoop! You whimpering bootlicker! You snivelling bloodsucker! You snot-nosed whippersnapper! You blubbering, puling, mewling dunderhead!!!!!" Uranus zaps Moon in Aries again and again with her electronic tommy gun, amazed at Moon's ability to rise anew from even the most staggering blows.[2]*

2. From *Planetary Aspects: From Conflict to Cooperation* © Tracy Marks 1979, 1987.

Creating a dialogue between our planets, as in the preceding dialogue involving Sun and Neptune in Libra involved in a t-square with an exact Moon in Aries/Uranus in Cancer square, can not only reveal hitherto unrecognized dimensions of our own internal dramas, but can also, through direct experience and expression of our personal archetypes, catalyze their own transformation.

Astrology and Transformative Process

Another principle of depth astrology is the idea that we are not a static entity, defined and limited by the specific planetary placements of our charts, but rather we are patterns of energy in constant motion, processes, interrelationships of innumerable possibilities of becoming. Modem physics has taught us that everything in the universe consists of wave/particles of energy, that matter is merely energy vibrating at a low frequency, that within our bodies our atoms vibrate at approximately 10^{15} cycles per second, nuclei at 10^{22}, molecules at 10^9, cells at 10^3. We believe that we are solid, virtually fixed over time because our bodies, as we are aware of them, are dense and our physical manifestations change slowly. We carry within our consciousness a series of interrelated memories, and we operate through set structures and relationships which we use to define and solidify our sense of identity.

Most of the time, our consciousness is so limited to an infinitesimal part of ourselves that we do not realize that our bodies, which consist of approximately 10^{27} electron-proton pairs, form literally trillions of nuclei which form trillions of atoms which form trillions of—actually 10^{14} or 100 trillion—cells. Each subsystem within us has laws and a consciousness of its own that determines and regulates its developments. Each sub-system interchanges energy and transforms itself through its relationship to all other sub-systems and through the energy it exchanges with systems outside the body. So often, we forget that we are more than our consciousness of ourselves; we cling to what we have defined as our identities, as determined by our past, and resist the change and development that may well be planned in exquisite detail by the innumerable parts of ourselves outside our awareness.

Modern physics and Eastern religion, particularly as expressed through such wise texts as the *I Ching*, teach us that change is the only reality, that we are continually being recreated anew, that we are a *becoming* rather than a *being*. In terms of our charts, we may define ourselves by our planetary positions and not realize how, by contacting the light at our own center, we can become more than our planets, we can awaken previously unexpressed dimensions of each planet, transmute squares and oppositions, and open the channels created by midpoints and minor aspects and activated by transits and progressions. Our birthcharts are not maps of who we are but rather mandalas indicating potentials for energy transformation, suggesting the dynamic potentials we were born with and which we can unfold in cooperation with the energy continually available to us from the universe.

It is difficult for us to view ourselves as an everchanging process because we structure our lives so that we seem to operate in set patterns, and because we speak in a language that is virtually dead, replete with nouns which represent static entities, weak in verbs which more clearly indicate the actual reality within us and around us. Our consciousness of ourselves and other people is influenced by our use of the verb TO BE; we say, "I AM, YOU ARE" as if we are photographs fixed in time rather than an ongoing motion picture with past, present and future integrally related and unfolding from each other. We cling to a definition, an identity in order to feel secure amidst the fluctuations around us and the flux of our own emotional experience, but by doing so we continually define our present according to our past and limit our future possibilities.

According to modern physics, nothing is certain; everything that exists TENDS to exist; all is probability, not unshakable reality. We may declare that we are Sun in Libra or Sun in Pisces or that Venus is in Scorpio square Mars in Leo, but actually a more accurate description would be that we OFTEN manifest as our Sun sign in Libra or in Pisces, that we TEND to experience dramatic, intense conflicts in love in accordance with such planetary combinations as our Mars/Venus square. There is a full range of expression in each position and aspect in our chart, yet we often limit ourselves to expressing only a small portion of the range available to us and rarely draw upon the channels of energy created by all our aspects, midpoints or other energy networks to extend beyond the range of even these facets of our charts.

In order to experience ourselves as a process, in order to allow ourselves to become continually what we are meant to become, we must not attach ourselves too powerfully to past patterns or to definitions, astrological or otherwise, of our identity. To be open to transformation and flow with the energy of the universe, to be able to constructively use and transmute the patterns in our chart, to allow transits and progressions to awaken us to the possibilities that we are capable of actualizing, we must be willing to embrace uncertainty and experience the pain and confusion of changing, to trust in a divine plan that is teaching us the lessons we are meant to learn, whether or not they are the lessons we consciously seek. We must open ourselves to the universe, listen to its voice through the stillness at our own center, and respond to it with the affirmation: "*I surrender, I open, I allow myself to be transformed, I subordinate my own small will to the Universal Will, I accept the next stage in my becoming.*"

Transcending Our Natal Charts

An important principle of depth astrology, which is really an extension of all its other principles, is that we can transcend our charts. We carry our natal charts within us all our lives, but as we develop a center within ourselves, learn to trust our inner guidance and become more attuned to universal energies, we are less at the mercy of the stresses indicated by our planetary positions. Perhaps we have Uranus opposition Venus natally; we may resist being tied down by a loved one, and as a result form relationships with people who fear to make a commitment, people who give us the freedom we seek by refusing to be fully available or by leaving us after only a brief period of time. Throughout our lives we may resist the limitations which occur in a committed relationship, but our fear of these limitations does not have to prevent us from forming meaningful commitments. In time, we may become more aware of the kind of freedom important to us, more able to define what we are able and unable to tolerate in a relationship, more capable of expressing our needs to others and forming relationships which allow us to satisfy the more important of these needs. We may begin to experience and draw from the light at the center of our being, therefore becoming a source of illumination to ourselves as well as others. Through this process we may experience such fulfillment in who we are that we are less at the mercy of what we may have considered in the past to be important needs. Our Uranus opposition Venus may at times remain a source of conflict—an occasional yearning to break free and explore new relationships, to have more territory we can call our own—but its stresses may no longer dominate our consciousness.

The analogy of a marionette theater is useful in describing the natal chart. As we expand our awareness, as we become more capable of rising above our charts and directing our energy rather than being driven by our lower nature, as we become more familiar with the expressions of each of our planets and aspects and develop a lifestyle which incorporates all our conflicting needs, we become the puppeteer rather than the puppets in our own cosmic drama. We are no longer tangled in our own strings, but rather situated above the stage, directing the show.

We may, at this point, ask if our aim is to actually take control over our planets, to be the puppeteer or conductor of our planetary symphony, or if our aim is to surrender ourselves to God, the universal Will, the divine plan or whatever we choose to call the highest forces in the universe. These two approaches, of directing and surrendering, may at first seem contradictory. However, when we understand that this divine force operates at the center of the universe and helps us to develop a central Self that integrates all our divisive selves, the contradictions dissolve. If we are to become the directors of our cosmic dramas, then our task is to make sure that the Self that is directing is not our ego, not our lower needs and desires, not one or two of our planets, but rather a Self that transcends those planets, a center of consciousness which incorporates and yet extends beyond our planetary selves. Developing and becoming attuned to that higher center is, of course, a lifetime (and perhaps many lifetimes) process.

Later in this chapter, we will briefly consider how we can contact and develop that center. But first, let us consider some of the ways we can, consciously or unconsciously, begin to transcend the lowest dimensions of our charts and unfold our highest potential. First, we are constantly being given new opportunities for self-development by transits and progressions which awaken new channels of energy in our natal charts and introduce us to alternative ways of feeling, thinking and acting. Throughout the year, the inner planets are forming every conceivable aspect to our natal planets. Every 27–30 years, our progressed Moon allows us to experience internally all of the signs and come to terms emotionally with each of the planets it aspects. Saturn too completes its cycle around the chart every 29 years, and urges us to concretely apply each of our planets, to bring our current phase of each planet's expression to completion so that we will be ready to experience the next phase.

In the course of a lifetime, the trans-Saturnian planets aspect all our natal planets; although they may not complete an entire series of aspects to any one planet as they journey through a quarter or more of our charts, they introduce each of our planetary selves to three different modes of transformation—the shattering but liberating tumults of Uranus, the dissolving but also transcending mists of Neptune, the annihilating but renewing power of Pluto. Our solar return charts too are guides to our becoming—revealing yearly possibilities for unfolding our potential, for integrating planets, signs and houses which may be at odds in our natal charts. Years during which planets in natal square or opposition are in conjunction, trine or sextile in our solar returns are years during which we can most easily discover alternative means for expressing and integrating these energies. When, for example, transiting Saturn trines our natal Moon or solar return Saturn trines either our solar return or natal Moon, we may learn how to blend these energies advantageously. We may discover how to commit ourselves to an important task or person, to stabilize rather than repress our feelings, to experience the satisfactions of behaving maturely and responsibly in many phases of our lives. If we remain aware of how we are integrating these two planets, then we can apply the lessons we have learned the next time we allow ourselves to be depressed or oppressed by our natal Saturn/Moon square or opposition.

Second, our relationships provide us with opportunities for becoming. When we are close to other people, particularly when we are sexually involved with them or sharing the same living quarters or otherwise interacting with them in powerful ways, an energy exchange occurs. We influence them; they influence us. Their presence leads us to behave in ways which may surprise us because they are activating latent parts of ourselves or opening new channels of expression. Comparing charts, we may discover that our highly afflicted Venus, oversensitive and prone to self-deception when at the mercy of its Neptune opposition, or frequently demanding and restless in love when expressing the lowest dimensions of its Jupiter square, responds differently to people whose planets trine or sextile it. We may even enter into a satisfying marriage with someone whose Mars sextiles our Venus and whose Saturn trines it, someone whose Martian sexuality and vitality stimulates us without encouraging us to engage in unrealistic fantasies or expectations, and whose Saturn awakens in us a sane and mature love, feelings of loyalty and the desire and capacity to form solid and enduring ties. We may, on the other hand, discover that our articulate and consistently rational Mercury in Virgo now experiences difficulty organizing and communicating its thoughts with this same partner whose Mercury in Pisces closely opposes it. Our struggle for clarification and better communication may in time lead not only to deeper understanding with our loved one, but also to a more intuitive, imaginative and wholistic thinking process, and to the capacity to speak in a more feeling way and to allow our latent creativity and spirituality to surface.

The important people in our lives not only activate different facets of our charts; they also enable us to develop qualities and modes of being that may not be indicated by our natal charts alone. We may, of course, lean on their trines and sextiles to our afflicted planets and depend upon them to ease our conflict; then, when and if these people depart from our lives, we may be suddenly confronted with those conflicts and disturbed that we have not made progress in resolving them. But we can also learn from their influence upon us, become aware of how we express our afflicted planets in their presence, so that if in time they disappear from our lives, we can apply what we have learned and consciously continue to express our planets in favorable ways. It will not be easy, but if we've really learned from the experience, it will certainly be possible.

Ways to Cultivate Our Natal Chart Potentials

Apart from transits and progressions and the influence of relationships, we can transcend the limitations of our natal charts by understanding and consciously expressing the highest potentials of our planets, signs, houses and aspects.

First, we can study and focus upon the most positive meanings of each of our planetary placements. Surely, Moon in Capricorn has virtues despite its detriment in this sign, as does Venus in Virgo, Saturn in the 12th house, Mars in the 7th. Most astrology texts emphasize the difficulties of such placements as these, but every position has its strength as well as its weakness. What then are the strengths of each of our planetary positions? We can't consciously express them unless we know what they are.

Second, we can apply ourselves to understanding and using our unafflicted planets and their trines and sextiles. These harmonious aspects usually need to be consciously activated; the more we channel energy into them, the more we free our squares and oppositions from the excess tension that may prevent us from resolving their conflicts.

Third, we can use the ruler of a house that contains heavily afflicted planets. If the ruler is less afflicted, expression it in terms of the house it rules may ease the stress we experience in this particular area of our life and unlock the potential of its afflicted planets.

Fourth, we may begin to synthesize our squares and oppositions, turning our attention first to those which are most exact, and attempting to discover ways in which their planets, signs and houses may be integrated. *Planetary Aspects* demonstrates how each house and sign opposition may be synthesized, how they may cooperate and work to each other's advantage rather than operate in conflict. In terms of planets, we can begin to understand how two planets in opposition might cooperate by interpreting the meaning of a conjunction between those two planets; we can interpret a square as if it were a trine. How can we begin to know the potential of our Pluto/Mercury square if we study astrology texts that tell us only of the problems we will encounter if we have this aspect? Why not begin to understand the possibilities of this aspect by reading about, or better yet determining for ourselves, how Mercury and Pluto might function as a trine? By looking back to periods in our lives during which transiting or progressed Mercury trined our Pluto or transiting Pluto trined our Mercury, we can discover how, during those periods, we may have begun to integrate those energies. Two planets in square have the potential to exist not merely in harmony, as in trine, but in *dynamic* harmony because of the motivation provided by the square. Two planets in opposition have the potential not only to blend their energies in the manner of a conjunction, but also to cooperate in a focused manner, with the awareness provided by the opposition.

The relationship between planets in their signs and houses may indeed be even more significant than specific planetary placements themselves. As we have learned from modern physics, the nature of reality is basically a network of oscillating patterns of energy, and nothing is solid, certain, fixed in time or space, or existing by itself without relationship to everything else. Aspects, and to some extent midpoints which link planets, signs and houses that might not otherwise be related, indicate energy channels within us, channels which may or may not operate to our benefit depending upon how we respond to them and use them. An important principle of depth astrology is that each aspect may be transmuted. A square may TEND to create conflicts between two parts of ourselves; an opposition may TEND to indicate that we project some of our qualities onto other people. However, we need to remember that a dynamic energy is linking two planets, not merely a particular aspect, and this energy carries within itself the possibilities for its own transformation.

Consider, for example, Saturn/Neptune aspects discussed in chapter five. Of course, we can focus upon the problems related to these two planets in relationship to each other and moan because we are confused about our work and unable to focus, or are anxious and insecure, unable to contact our own sources of inspiration or creativity. But if we are influenced by a Saturn/Neptune aspect, we can remain sensitively aware of our limitations; we can allow ourselves to flow into new structures; we can reinspire old structures; we can give form to our inspiration; we can clarify our values and ideals and rebuild our faith; we can concretely express our spirituality. All our aspects and planetary combinations (even two planets not linked by any major or minor aspects natally, but related by transiting aspects or transits over natal midpoints) can be integrated and transmuted if we understand how they may be combined and then apply that understanding in our lives.

A fifth technique for constructively working with our natal charts is to consciously use natal planets which conjunct midpoints of two other natal planets, particularly of planets in square or opposition, as a means for synthesizing the expressions of these two planets. The midpoints of squares, forming two semisquares, and the midpoints of oppositions, forming a t-square configuration, can provide an effective release for the tension of the square or opposition. Even planetary midpoints linking planets that are not in aspect natally can help us to awaken and express dimensions of ourselves indicated by these two planets. In my own chart. Mercury, at the midpoint of Neptune and Pluto has taught me that writing can activate the Neptune/Pluto sextile and allow me to become a channel for universal energies. Giving my Arian Moon the freedom to personally express herself in my writing has enabled me to draw upon emotional energy and inspiration which I never believed I possessed because my Moon on the nadir, as well as my midheaven, are the midpoints of both Sun/Neptune and Mars/Pluto—both combinations of planets otherwise unlinked by aspects.

A sixth technique to use with our natal charts is that of studying and then consciously expressing our minor aspects—particularly quintiles and biquintiles which expand our consciousness and enable us to discover unique and creative ways of blending two of our planetary selves. Minor aspects are particularly significant in charts with many squares or oppositions, because the tensions of these conflicts easily awaken whatever channels of energy are available in the chart. In charts that contain few close or exact aspects, minor aspects which are close in orb may actually be quite dynamic. Because we have little specific knowledge of the meaning of these particular aspects, we can best take advantage of them not by trying to figure out exactly how a sesquiquadrate or a semisextile operates, but rather by looking at the two planets linked by these aspects and asking ourselves how we can constructively blend their energies.

A seventh technique for use with charts weak in a particular element or quadruplicity is to begin to develop that element or quadruplicity by using the signs representative of it in the houses where they occur, and also by attempting to develop that facet of ourselves through our use of the planets most related to it in meaning. Saturn, for example, can teach us about earth, the Moon and Neptune about water. Mars about cardinal energy.

An eighth technique is to actively express the North Node of our Moon, and the planet which rules the sign of the node and indicates how we can best attune ourselves to and express our life task. Living our North Node is rarely easy; we may wish to study it carefully, understanding every possible expression of its sign and house combination and of its planetary ruler as placed in our chart. We can then consciously attempt to apply our understanding, even when drawn like a magnet into the secure past patterns of our South Node. Our South Node must be used too—its energy is more accessible than the energy of any of our planets—but we must use it not for its own sake, but rather in order to fulfill the purpose of the North Node.

In addition to awakening our North Node and integrating our nodal axis, we might also pay particular attention to nourishing ourselves through the acceptance and expression of our Moon. Any attempt to satisfy the higher needs of the Self without first owning and fulfilling the basic instinctual needs of the Moon may lead to self-deception and the deception of others. The needs of the personality must be respected first before they can be transcended. To be in touch with our own nature as well as with our environment, to flow with the cycles of the planets as experienced through our own feelings and instincts, to trust in the cosmic tides and allow them to carry us to the safe shores of our highest Self is to unfold the potentials of our natal Moon. We can liberate our natal Moon from all of the judgments we may place upon our instinctual nature, and experience love for that part of ourselves. Then we can let the Moon express itself and reveal to us how we can best cooperate with the energies of the outer planets.

Not only the Moon, but also 12th house planets and signs call for special attention, for they may operate compulsively and self-destructively if we do not remain aware of them and begin to accept them as viable and powerful parts of ourselves. We may tend to view our 12th house personalities as weak or detrimental, and in doing so block or distort their expression. But when we have experienced and accepted them, releasing the pressures they have accumulated while being pushed back into the confines of our psyche, these planets can flow more freely and become a source of strength and nourishment.[3]

Transforming Planetary Energies through Self Acceptance

This emphasis upon 12th house planets and signs is related to another important principle of depth astrology—that of transforming the expressions of our planets by cultivating an attitude of self acceptance and treating ourselves tenderly and compassionately. One of the great paradoxes of our lives is that accepting rather than rejecting qualities or behaviors in ourselves which we dislike usually leads us to become less dominated by those qualities and behaviors. If we, for example, dislike our Venus in Cancer's craving to be held and nurtured, we are not likely to give ourselves permission to be nourished by other people, or to fully enjoy all that they give us. As a result, we may feel increasingly dominated by our need for nurturance and even more judgmental of it as that need becomes more powerful. When we bind our energy by judging, resisting or otherwise battling with one of our planetary personalities, that personality is imbued with the energy of the conflict and becomes even more insistent in its demand for expression. If we do not satisfy it, its cry becomes distorted, like that of a hungry, screaming child responding to frustration and deprivation, and we fear all the more its capacity for upsetting our lives.

Every planet in our charts can operate to our advantage or disadvantage, depending upon our attitude toward it and how we channel its energy. Every planet has needs which it seeks to fulfill, and will operate destructively when we ignore those needs or do not allow ourselves to experience their satisfaction. We tend to be most often at odds with our 12th house planets and also our Moon, but we may also deny the needs of one of our planets in square or opposition when we identify too strongly and single-mindedly with the planet at the other end of the square or opposition aspect.

Whenever we feel dissatisfied or out of balance within ourselves because one of our planetary selves is being denied, or whenever we feel overcome with dislike for one of our planetary selves which seems to be operating in a twisted, destructive manner, we can turn inward and identify the source of the dissatisfaction. Which planet is creating

---

3. For more information on the 12th house, see *Your Secret Self: Illuminating the Mysteries of the Twelfth House* (Sebastopol, CA: CRCS Publications, 1989). The first section of this book was also available as a booklet, under the title *The Twelfth House*, published by Sagittarius Rising.

the problem? Which of its needs aren't being met? How can we satisfy those needs as constructively as possible without simultaneously denying all our other planets?

As we become aware of our planets as subpersonalities within us, as we hear their constant chatter within our heads and experience ourselves first becoming one and then becoming another, we can begin to enter into their dialogue. Perhaps we can be our Mars and talk to our Venus, then respond as our Venus, attempting to cooperate with Mars in resolving some of the dilemmas of our Mars/Venus square. Or we can begin as an outside observer, identifying with none of our planets but rather with the center from which all the planets emanate, and then engage one or more of our planetary selves in conversation, in order to discern why it behaves as it does and what it wants from us. Aloud or on paper or through meditation and directed fantasy, we can encounter each of our planets and allow each one to be a source of wisdom to us, telling us which of its needs aren't being met and even suggesting to us how we can begin to fulfill those needs.

Perhaps we have Venus in Cancer in the 2nd house in square to Jupiter late in the 4th. Perhaps Taurus rules our 12th house, and we are uncomfortable with the ways we experience and express our Venus personality. We want to surround ourselves with beautiful possessions; we want to be indulged and comforted by our family rather than cater to their demands. If we dislike this part of ourselves and refuse to allow it to express itself, or otherwise prevent ourselves from enjoying its expression, it may operate subconsciously and compulsively in an extreme manner. We may blow our entire paycheck on a shopping spree at Bloomingdales or eat a chocolate cake in one sitting or even retreat into bed, feigning illness so that our family will cater to us.

What if instead we dialogued with our Venus regularly and discovered what she wanted? *"I'm not getting enough,"* she might say. *"Saturn rising refuses to allow me to eat the foods I like or wear pretty clothes, and no one at home ever tells me that they appreciate me or care about how I'm feeling. I'm not getting enough nourishment,"* she may tell us, letting us know that our sometimes immoderate behavior is merely the only way we know of taking care of ourselves. The question now that we might ask Venus and our other planets is: how we can better nourish ourselves, take care of ourselves, receive love from ourselves and others? How can we become less rigid in our diet, spending habits and attire and still maintain some of our Saturn rising sense of limits? How can we best let the people around us know that we want their support and appreciation? Certainly, if we don't like the needy facets of ourselves, we are not likely to attempt to satisfy those needs or to encourage others to respond to them or to express satisfaction when they do respond. We are likely to give up some of the most extreme manifestations of our Venus/ Jupiter square when we begin to accept it as a valid part of ourselves and learn to satisfy rather than suppress its insistent cravings.

Whenever a planet is causing trouble, we can always ask what underlying need isn't being met. Perhaps our Mercury/Mars conjunction in the 5th house is provoking fights with our lover. Is our tendency to start arguments our primary problem? Or is our problem that some of our Mars/Mercury in Aquarius needs aren't being fulfilled? Perhaps our romance is becoming stale because we are no longer sharing our ideas or discovering new activities together and because our sexual relationship has become tedious. We want more stimulation; we want to awaken the excitement we once felt together. But will constant bickering bring back what we have lost? Once we know the Martian needs that aren't being met, we can begin to share them with our lover and discover mutually satisfying ways of fulfilling them.

Every planet in our charts is both positive and negative, constructive and destructive. If we ignore it or repress it or otherwise refuse to find constructive outlets for it, we are shutting off an important part of ourselves, forcing it to operate subliminally, and therefore limiting the energy that we have available to serve our conscious ends. We expect too much of ourselves when we expect ourselves to manifest healthy, virtuous, altruistic behaviors at all times. So, apart from perceiving underlying needs of planets, we can also begin to appreciate some of the qualities of our planetary selves which we have disliked by discovering how those qualities are integrally related to qualities that we do like. Our Venus square Jupiter demands for love are the other side of our capacity to give a lot of love; our Mercury conjunct Saturn tendency to withdraw into ourselves is the other side of our capacity to formulate our thoughts, to communicate effectively in our work, to write clearly and coherently.

Certainly, in the people around us, we are likely to be aware of how qualities we like and dislike manifest in the same person. We may be drawn to Scorpio men because of their depth of insight, the intensity of their feelings, their magnetism and their passion. Then we discover that when we are with them we have to cope with a certain heaviness and ruthless honesty which is the other side of their deep perceptiveness and intensity, an attractiveness to other women and a remoteness that is the other side of their magnetism, a possessiveness and constant emphasis upon sexuality which is the other side of their passion. The more extreme the Scorpio qualities we like, the more extreme may be the qualities that we dislike. In our relationships and in ourselves, we must continually remain aware of and accept the many facets of each planetary personality, understanding how they all are integrally related. We may meet a planet's underlying needs so that it becomes less destructive in its expression, but we still must come to terms with and accept its many sides, appreciating how those sides which may not at first seem particularly virtuous indeed do contribute to the sides which we most value and seek to express.

Astrology as a Path into Internal Depth

One important approach of depth astrology, related to its emphasis upon the acceptance of all our planetary selves, is that of allowing ourselves to become emotionally, creatively and spiritually involved with our birthcharts rather than merely using astrology as an intellectual exercise. The transformation that is possible within us is not likely to be positive unless we allow ourselves at times to put aside our head knowledge and really experience our feelings, experience the fear or isolation of our Saturn, the hunger of our Moon, experience the insecurity, chaos and perhaps even terror that may be unleashed within us under outer planet transits. We might experience the extreme tension, nervousness and restlessness of Uranus, the confusions and vulnerabilities of Neptune, the release of powerful emotional and sexual energy of Pluto. Our own fear of being out of control, at the mercy of our feelings, adrift in an abyss that threatens to engulf us in some unknown darkness may easily lead us to switch into our minds as soon as something new happens to us, and to attempt to interpret our experience astrologically without first fully allowing ourselves to feel what is taking place inside. Once experienced fully, the desolation of Saturn may lead to an enriching solitude and satisfying productivity; the sleep-like fogs of Neptune may awaken our creative inspiration; but unless we allow ourselves to journey deep into our own experience, for however long it takes to enlighten us, we are likely to become stuck on the periphery, afraid to go into feelings which are extremely uncomfortable, and therefore unable to discover the new and invigorating states of consciousness and activities to which they may lead.

Usually, we judge an experience as positive when it *feels* good, and consider it to be negative when it *feels* bad. But we can view our lives from a long-term perspective, in terms of the meaningfulness of each of its phases and in terms of our personal development and the aims we seek to fulfill. Then we are likely to discover that some experiences which feel good, which we consider to be positive, are actually destructive; likewise, some experiences which feel bad, which we view as negative or destructive, are actually constructive. Buying a six-course dinner at a French restaurant when we are unable to pay our rent and are 20 pounds overweight may be enjoyable but destructive; being abandoned by a lover whose insecurities have prevented us from pursuing further education may feel devastating, but may lead us to discover what we really want and to feel free to go after it. So often we struggle with transits and resist the changes they bring upon us because we are afraid of experiencing pain, anxiety, loss or fear, even though such feelings in time may lead to a deeper peace of mind, even though they allow us to leave behind people or life-styles or possessions or places which were harmful to us, and to embrace, in time, more satisfying alternatives.

In order to integrate ourselves, develop a lifestyle that constructively expresses each of our planets, and fulfill the potential of our charts, we must seek not to *feel* good all of the time, but rather to become more capable of experiencing and valuing uncomfortable feelings and states of mind—pain, isolation, nervous tension, oversensitivity, obsession—in order to fulfill aims that are far more important than momentary satisfactions. We must therefore begin to assess our experience in terms of ultimate gains, in terms of our own personal and spiritual growth and our contribution to society rather than in terms of pleasant or unpleasant feelings. One way is to consider the possible long-term influences: another way is to do all we can to deepen our faith, so that we trust that time will reveal the constructive implications. We can also develop trust in the wisdom of our subconscious and the wisdom of the universe, confident that we are being provided with experiences which will aid our soul's evolution, even though the meaning of those experiences may not be revealed to us for many years.

Astrological Awareness and the Expansion of Consciousness

One important discovery of modem physics is that the universe is a web of energy patterns in which everything is interrelated, in which the observer and the observed mutually influence each other. We already know, as students of astrology, that by changing where we stand in time and space we alter the relationship between the planets and ourselves. A decision we make at noon may be different than a decision we would make at midnight because the Moon is making different aspects to our charts at midnight, and all of the planets are influencing different houses. Living in California rather than Indiana may unfold new possibilities in our charts because the angles and houses of our charts change, particularly when we move a significant distance east or west. We know that time and space influence us, and that we can alter the effect of the planets upon us by changing our own point of reference in time and space.

What we may not be fully aware of is how we can alter the influence of the planets by altering our consciousness. The atoms, the molecules, the cells which are moving at inconceivable speeds within us are not only receiving energy from the planets, they are also discharging energy back into the universe. The energy emitted by our brain waves alone travels at such incomprehensible speeds that it may well extend far beyond our solar system. Aware that matter and energy are interchangeable and that energy can transmute itself into a variety of forms, can we not assume that our own state of mind and the collective state of mind of humanity can influence the effects of the planets upon earth? Is it not possible that by altering our state of mind, developing a deeper understanding of our relationship to the universe and expanding our consciousness, we can constructively influence the effects that our natal planets, transits and progressions have upon our lives?

Resonance is a term used in modern physics to refer to the interchange of energy that occurs between systems operating at the same frequency or at corresponding harmonics of the same frequency. When, for example, a piano tuner strikes A on a tuning fork, all the A's on a piano vibrate if they are tuned properly; they are all operating at the same resonance. In the ionosphere, which is an electrostatic field above the earth's surface where energy waves from planets and stars accumulate, the frequency of vibration is approximately 7.5 cycles per second, equivalent to the frequency of the human body in a deep state of rest, as in meditation. In other words, the body may be in resonance with the atmosphere, responding to and influencing the energy waves from all of the planets.

Most modern physicists believe that the universe is shaped like a torus, an elongated donut with a hole in the center, and that our galaxy is traveling from the dense inside center of the torus to the less dense outside, so that from our perspective space is actually expanding. This expansion of space in the outer world corresponds to the expansion of space which occurs within us, as our bodies interact with cosmic energies and absorb electrons from outer space. Electrons, being negatively charged, repel each other, which means that as electrons are absorbed into our organisms, a large amount of space is absorbed with each electron, the space whereby electrons are able to maintain their force fields and keep each other at the required distance. This space is so vast that if all the electrons in the human body were condensed, they would be no greater than a speck of dust; all else would be space—space, which we must remember is not empty, but is rather an oscillating field of energy, the activating material force that exists in the void and makes life possible.

When our bodies are in a state of deep rest, the energy level within us increases in frequency. When our energy level is high *and* when a high-speed electron from outside ourselves collides with our body, the impact causes electrons within us to be pushed to outer orbits so that a space is made vacant, and the new electron can be absorbed. As a new electron is absorbed, the space within the atom correspondingly increases. Whether or not the electron is absorbed and our inner space increases depends both upon the power of the colliding electron (consider, for example, the powerful electrons from an outer planet which is stationary, conjuncting one of our planets) and also upon the energy level within our own atoms, determined to a large extent by our state of consciousness. When we are in alpha state, when we are in harmony with ourselves and in resonance with the ionosphere, we absorb more cosmic energy and our consciousness expands. As our consciousness expands, we change; we become capable of transcending past patterns.

Saint Germain, in *Studies in Alchemy*,[4] wrote that "the concept of an expanding consciousness, simultaneously with an expanding universe, must be reckoned with if man will correctly master his affairs." What significance has this statement and the discoveries of modem physics to us as astrology students? Its significance is that we can widen our consciousness to absorb more of the universal energies into ourselves, to incorporate them into our internal experience, so that we are acting in harmony with the universe rather than experiencing the planets as outside forces controlling us. Its significance is that we are capable of attaining higher degrees of consciousness in which we identify not with the feeling of the moment or one of our planetary selves, but with our

---

4. Saint Germain, *Studies in Alchemy* (Gardiner, MT: Summit Lighthouse, 1974).

organism as a whole in its relation to the universe, thus expanding our link to the cosmos through the center of our psyche referred to as our Self. As our consciousness expands, we are able to draw upon previously inaccessible energies, to perceive new alternatives for old problems, to increase the range of our possible responses to events in our lives.

In terms of our charts, we can awaken in our planets new modes of expression, discover ways to integrate squares and oppositions, activate the channels provided by wide aspects, minor aspects, and even the subtlest of minor aspects conceivable by harmonics—energy channels which may correspond to orbs of 22½ degrees (half a semisquare) or 15 degrees (half a semisextile). What this means is that we have a full range of planetary combinations available to us and a full range of possible reactions to every experience. We develop an ability to transcend the stresses of our predominating squares and oppositions through our own enlightened insight and by channelling our energy into newly revealed modes of behavior. Our chart becomes a spectrum of colors in which we are capable of living all of the colors, a piano on which we play all of the keys, an orchestra in which every instrument is at our disposal and can cooperate like a symphony, provided that we are developing within ourselves a conductor capable of generating harmony.

The Self as Central Conductor of Planetary Energies

We are out of harmony with ourselves when we over-identify with one planet, when we allow it to dominate our lives and pursue its own ends in an extreme manner without considering the needs of our other planetary personalities. Or perhaps a planet operates subconsciously or compulsively because we do not accept it or discover viable outlets for its expression. We begin to resolve such dilemmas, as well as the conflicts of our squares and oppositions and to integrate ourselves when, through expanded consciousness, we experience our own center. Then our sense of "I" emanates from that center rather than from any one planet; and when we operate from our center, we are able to keep all facets of ourselves in our awareness and act in ways that satisfy most and hopefully all of our planets. Some of us may discover one activity that fulfills the needs of all our planets; others of us must develop a network of activities and relationships in order to satisfy and integrate all our natal planets.

Acting from our centered Self and maintaining an awareness of all parts of ourselves does not mean giving up spontaneity; rather, it helps us to develop a flexibility of consciousness, what St. Germain refers to as "a mobile and malleable consciousness," capable of shifting easily from one planetary self to another, always returning to center before allowing any one planet to take control. Under the guidance of our central conductor, we play the flutes of Mercury and then the trumpets of Mars, integrating them together into a dynamic theme as we begin to resolve our Mercury/Mars square through perhaps writing satire or organizing a sports program or starting our own radio talk show. Eventually, we integrate the harps of Venus, the violins of Neptune, the bass of Pluto and all our other planetary instruments, each one allowed a few moments of solo performance, but all of them harmonizing with each other and creating a whole, integrated piece of music, the music of our lives. We have the potential to become a living symphony, yet most of us become stuck playing the same notes repeatedly; we may respond continually to the same note from our Neptune violin with a discordant note from our Saturn bassoon, never exploring the full range of tones available on each instrument, the various harmonics of the same tone, the possible blendings of sounds, or the results of allowing other instruments to participate and round out the melody.

Becoming the conductor of our planetary orchestra is a lifelong process. It requires us, as we become aware of all of our different selves in a particular moment, to refrain from blocking the experience of one of those selves, and to experience instead their contradictions and ambiguities. We must tolerate the tension that increases within us when we do not allow one planet to run away with us or do not immediately project it onto another person. What do we do, for example, when transiting Uranus activates our Venus while transiting Saturn is activating our Mars? Do we work hard and inhibit our social and sexual desires so that we are not at the mercy of a current infatuation? Do we allow Uranus conjuncting our Venus to dominate, leading us into an unexpected love affair, although all we may want at the moment is social excitement rather than sexual involvement? If we were to tolerate the tension of these contradictory influences, experience even paralysis for a time, we might feel torn in two, but as with the *koan* of Zen meditation, the experience of that tension may lead us to a breakthrough rather than a breaking apart. Our consciousness, forced to hold within itself two paradoxical experiences, may stretch so wide that it cracks, so to speak, and lets in the light of new possibilities. Perhaps we may, to use the above example, discover a way to channel our physical energy into productive work and live the celibate lifestyle we prefer at the moment, while also exploring new and exciting possibilities in relationships. One heterosexual woman, experiencing similar planetary influences, dealt with them quite successfully by working and living for several months with a homosexual male friend.

The Self within us, as it awakens, is able to enlighten us about new possibilities and to enable us to transcend the limitations we have known. However, the Self must operate through our planets; its wisdom is vast and the energy it generates is powerful, but it cannot express itself through behaviors that are not indicated at all within our charts. We may not, if we have Jupiter rising square the Moon, fulfill our desire to become a model, even though Venus in Aries may be on our M.C., because nothing in our chart supports the physical self-control we would need in order to maintain our weight. We may not, with an afflicted Saturn in the 5th house, give birth to ten children. The Self that emanates from our center can guide and transform us in an unlimited number of ways because it transcends our planets, but it also INCLUDES our planets and urges us to explore the unknown realms of our potential as indicated by our planets—not to attempt to fulfill a potential that is beyond our own planets' capabilities.

Because the Self includes all our planets, one way to know whether or not we are operating from our center is to consult all our planetary selves and discover their reactions to a particular decision we are making. If we have dialogued with our planetary selves and begun to experience each as a subpersonality within us, this process of consultation should be easy. If we are not yet sure which part of ourselves is which planet, we may need to use our astrological expertise in order to discover how each of our planets might respond to the situation at hand.

Consider the following example. Let's assume we have an important meeting at work Thursday night, and a man who has interested us for months calls and invites us to the one and only concert of a talented folksinger. The concert is Thursday night. What should we do? Our immediate response is to say yes and ignore the voice of our conscience. But feeling intuitively that this would not be a centered decision, we tell him we'll call him back, and we begin to listen to our conflicting voices. Surveying our chart also, we discover that the excitement, the impulsive desire to say yes is the voice of Sun in Aries in the 5th house. Our romantic fantasies, not to mention our love of music, are being generated by our Venus in Pisces earlier in the 5th, who is already floating on a dream cloud. Moon in Scorpio in the 1st desires to become emotionally and sexually closer to this particular man; Mars in Taurus in the 7th for once is not at odds with Moon and has been willing to wait patiently for a new relationship to begin; Neptune in Libra in the 11th is drawn to such social events as concerts and to sensitive people who likewise appreciate good music. Why not go? Stopping a moment to listen to our nagging conscience and survey all our planets, we know that we can't say an immediate yes, that we must consider also Mercury in Aries in the 6th house and Saturn in Leo in the 10th. Mercury is really invested in attending this meeting; in fact, she has spent an entire month organizing the project that is being discussed; Saturn in the 10th is very responsible and is concerned with her reputation on the job; she knows the extent to which her chance of advancement will be threatened if she misses this meeting. Refusing to give in to the impulsive action demanded by Sun in Aries, we are now paralyzed. What should we do? How can we make a centered decision, and satisfy the needs of all of our planets?

Even if we have become deeply attuned to the Self within us, it will not always give us immediate answers. Even when it does, the answers we receive may require us to overrule one or two of our planetary voices temporarily, and satisfy them at a later date. Yet the mere act of listening to them and taking them seriously will keep us from making hasty decisions which we will later regret, and will help us to discover alternative ways of satisfying these planets.

However in the circumstance of the concert date, it is possible to satisfy all of our planets. Aware of each of their voices, we can weigh and assess the desires of each one; we can listen to our inner guidance and see what action it suggests. Recognizing that Mercury in the 6th and Saturn in the 10th are our own voices, we know that the meeting is not so much one we have to attend as one we want to attend. But we also want to date this man and go to this concert. Experiencing the tension of conflicting desires, we feel torn apart for a few minutes; then the solution to our dilemma reveals itself. We read the newspaper and discover another concert we wouldn't mind hearing a few nights later; we call him back and suggest going to the Saturday night concert. Will he be free that night? Will he want to go? He is, and does. Now, we are able to attend our meeting; now we have a date for a concert with an important new man—and the date is for Saturday night, a night we will feel free to stay up late and enjoy ourselves, knowing that we will not have to work the next morning. We have used astrology to contact our center, to consult all our planetary selves, to make the best possible decision in this particular circumstance.

Integration of Our Planetary Personalities

There are other ways of contacting our center, awakening the Self within us, integrating all our planetary personalities. We can, by dialoguing repeatedly with our planets or writing stories in which they are the main characters, begin to experience them so clearly that the center, which is indeed our observer, gains more power and begins to direct our cosmic drama. We can meditate daily and strengthen the observer within us through the detachment that meditation teaches us; such periods of inner quiet are necessary if we are to continue expanding our consciousness. We can do yoga, t'ai chi and a variety of other spiritual disciplines which help us to unify our minds and bodies and allow the cosmic energies to awaken us more fully. We can dedicate ourselves to a purpose which transcends ourselves, particularly a purpose which allows us to express all our planets; such dedication, by using and integrating all the facets of our selves while making a worthwhile contribution to society, can open that center and reward us with an influx of healing cosmic energy.

Whatever planetary positions exist in our charts, we will discover, as we become more integrated and experience more harmony with ourselves and the universe, that all our planets are one, that they are only different faces of the one Self that directs us and connects us to all other Selves. Whether through one particular activity or relationship or a series of interrelated activities and relationships, we will be living in a manner that satisfies and unifies all of our planets. Throughout each day, we will be fulfilling our Sun through expressing ourselves, strengthening our self-esteem, drawing from our inner light; our Moon, by nourishing ourselves and others; our Mercury, by processing our experience and communicating with others; our Venus, by fulfilling our deepest values and establishing loving relationships; our Mars, by releasing our energy actively and constructively; our Jupiter, by expanding our understanding and reaching out to new realms of experience; our Saturn by focusing on the important tasks before us and experiencing the sense of accomplishment which results from applying ourselves; our Uranus, by remaining attuned to our deepest intuition and by experiencing the inner freedom and transformation that results from acting independently and individualistically; our Neptune, by awakening our sources of creativity and inspiration and by feeling each day our connectedness to the universe; our Pluto, by drawing from the deepest reservoirs of our being, experiencing and channelling our inner power so that we continually regenerate not only ourselves, but also the people around us.

Even in terms of each individual planet, its most constructive expression is an expression that incorporates the needs of all of the other planets. How do we know that we are expressing our Mars constructively? Because in our actions we are considering Venus' need to remain sensitive to others and establish caring relationships; we are fulfilling Moon's need to nurture and be nurtured; we are listening to Saturn's voice and acting cautiously, focusing our energy, following through with our commitments; we are heeding Mercury's advice to plan carefully, to clearly organize and communicate our thoughts; we are responding to Neptune's request that our activities be inspiring ones which fulfill our creative and spiritual nature. The more planetary selves we express through expressing our Mars, the more constructive, the more unifying, the more satisfying will be our Martian self-assertion and activity.

Deeper Purposes of Astrological Self-Development

The aim of depth astrology is for us, as astrology students, to use our charts as guides, as maps which enable us not to arm ourselves against the future but rather to aid ourselves in our becoming, particularly in our becoming whole. But this aim, by itself, is meaningless unless we consider an even more ultimate aim to which it is subordinate. Are we to become whole for our own self-satisfaction, merely to make ourselves more comfortable, less dominated by stress? In this vast universe in which everything is interrelated, in which everything is capable of influencing and transforming everything else, are we to become whole for ourselves alone?

The more unified we become as individuals, the more capable we will become of relating harmoniously to other people, perceiving and fulfilling our tasks in society and deepening our connections with the universe. The Hopi Indians, the Dakotas, and various other cultures that we have until recently regarded as primitive have always been aware of how our states of being as individuals affect the balance of nature, and have encouraged, as their primary aim, the experience and enhancement of universal relatedness and universal harmony. We are capable individually of becoming one, of becoming unified, of becoming whole. But as a society, as a planet, as a universe, we are already one; we are all integrally related. The question is: are we as a society, as a planet, as a universe harmoniously integrated, operating from the highest Self which is the source from which the Self in each of us receives its illumination?

The final and perhaps most important principle of depth astrology is that our aim as individuals must not be merely to fulfill any of our small planetary selves or even awaken the higher Self within each of us, but rather to unify ourselves, unfold ourselves, awaken our Selves so that we may help to establish harmony within our relationships, society and environment, so that we may spread peace and love and light across the planet earth, across the solar system, across the universe.

We are in a difficult time and cannot afford to continue to waste our emotional, intellectual, physical and spiritual resources by indulging ourselves in despair and self-pity because our lives are not what we want them to be. We have a responsibility not only to ourselves but also to this planet and universe to keep our energy positive, to unify ourselves, and to dedicate ourselves to improving the quality of our own lives and the lives of others. We must all, we can all, be lightbearers.

Chapter Nine

MISUSES OF ASTROLOGY

We astrology students and astrologers tend to become overly identified with our art. Many of us are obsessive, even fanatical in
our use of the ephemeris. We define ourselves in terms of our planets;
we consult planetary positions before making decisions; we calculate
the natal charts of each person who becomes significant in our lives. We
become continually awed and excited as our minds expand and our attunement to cosmic cycles increases. Yet in spite of our growing understanding, we may also experience a growing dissatisfaction or anxiety.
Is astrology really helping us? Are we, as a result of our study, developing a greater capacity to direct our lives in accordance with our highest
values? Are we overcoming our fear and awakening a deeper trust? Are
we opening our hearts as well as our minds?

When we interpret charts, we are aligning our minds with cosmic
symbols, archetypes for the core energies within ourselves and the universe. We are dabbling in the realms of the gods. Like Icarus, we risk flying too close to the sun, singeing our wings, and plummeting to earth.
Like Eve who was tempted by the forbidden fruit, or like the builders
of the tower of Babel, each trapped within the confines of a private
language, isolated from real communication with each other as a result
of reaching for the sky, we may at times aspire too high, seek to know
too much, to be too much, and invite cosmic retribution. One cannot
play with the archetypes of the psyche without unleashing their power.
Whatever we have not faced within ourselves, whatever we have denied
or repressed or projected, is likely to come back to us.

Astrology is a powerful art, capable of enhancing our lives by enabling us to understand our own process of unfolding and how we can
cooperate with the energies within and around us. But it is also a dangerous art, and can be easily misused. We need to be painfully honest
with ourselves, highly integrated, grounded in our beings, empowered
in our actions, as well as clearly dedicated to and able to live according

to the highest within us if we are to use our astrological knowledge constructively without falling prey to many of the dangers of toying with cosmic forces. We need to be gods ourselves, and none of us are.

What then are the dangers of astrology which may have a detrimental effect upon our relationship to ourselves, to others, to reality as a whole and society at large? What unfinished business in ourselves may incline us to become victims of our art, rather than artists? What do we need to face within ourselves and in our use of astrology in order to become more conscious, more effective and certainly more humble practitioners? Only by making the unconscious conscious and orienting ourselves toward confronting those weaknesses which undermine us personally and professionally do we have any chance of becoming real helpers and healers.

Danger #1: Losing Direct Contact with Ourselves

The more we relate to ourselves and the world around us through highly abstract symbols, the more we risk diminishing our contact with our direct experience. We become less in touch with our bodies and our feelings and less capable of being fully alive and open to the present moment. As we develop our detachment, we may also increase our dissociation. As we expand our understanding, we may simultaneously contact our direct awareness of ourselves. Attempting to *gain* control over our experience through separating from it and viewing it objectively, we may paradoxically lose contact with our deepest selves and therefore *lose* control and the capacity to direct our lives.

Danger #2: Attachment to Self-Concept

We are not our self-concepts. We are who we are in each moment—feeling, thinking, acting. We are subjects, not objects; our selves exist in each experience of the "I" rather than the "me" which is the image of ourselves we hold. The experience of "I am, I feel, I want, I can, I will" operating in life and in action connects us with our core energy, whereas the concepts of "I am impulsive because I have Moon in Aries" or "I need freedom and variety in love relationships because I have Venus square Uranus" are only concepts and have nothing to do with the deep-seated experience of ourselves as alive, empowered, active individuals. Too much focus on the "me," the concepts we create to gain understanding of ourselves, may actually weaken our experience of the

"I." Our constructs are aids, but not substitutes for that sense of self which resides not in the mind but at our very core. The more fully we are connected to that core, the less we need our constructs to define ourselves. When we fully possess ourselves, when we can fully be ourselves, we are not dependent upon astrology to provide us with a self-concept. Our self-concepts are, after all, related to our egos. As we become more grounded in our beings, we become more capable of relinquishing our egos, which function best as servants rather than as masters.

Danger #3: Mistaking Knowledge for Power (Fear of Uncertainty)

Our knowledge of planetary influences can provide for us a pseudo-security, a false sense of power, a buffer against the chaos-in-here and the unknown-out-there, both of which we may fear to confront directly. Being alone in the vast universe is a terrifying experience; not knowing where we are going or what might happen is particularly frightening if we do not believe we have the resources to cope with the unexpected. Our knowledge may feel like a protection; it may deaden our anxiety to that we are not overwhelmed by it. But in doing so, it also weakens us. Only through experiencing our fear, our uncertainty, our powerlessness can we develop trust, inner certainty and inner power. Only by giving up control can we gain control; only by not knowing can we transcend the limits of knowing and align ourselves with the deeper guiding forces within us.

Danger #4: Weakening Our Intuition

When we repeatedly consult the ephemeris before making a decision and when we determine our attitude toward a particular person after calculating a chart, we weaken our trust in our own being. Instead of using and strengthening our intuitive muscles, we let them atrophy; we allow our astrological knowledge rather than our deeper internal sensing process to make choices for us. As astrology becomes a greater authority, like a god who makes judgments and proclamations and frightens us with threats of catastrophe, we lose whatever internal authority we once possessed. The power of the planets looms larger as we become smaller.

Danger #5: Mistaking the Map for Reality

The astrological chart is a map, and not reality, just as our self-concepts are concepts rather than our selves. If we are driving a car in unfamiliar territory, we consult a map, determine our route, put the map away and drive carefully and competently to our chosen destination. We arrive there not only because we have consulted the map, but also because we have been alert to the position of our feet on the accelerator and brake, and to the road ahead of us. If we were to drive with the map in front of our face, staring at the yellow and blue lines on the paper rather than looking through our windshield, we would not only fail to reach our chosen destination; we might instead arrive in a hospital or jail or end up dead and with more direct contact to the astral dimension than we had sought. Our knowledge is a boon to us when used appropriately, a burden when used inappropriately.

Danger #6: Self-Fulfilling Prophecy

Although our concepts are not reality, our concepts have the ability to influence reality. Our assumptions and beliefs lead us to act in ways which may be self-fulfilling prophecies; they influence our own behavior and the behavior of others toward us. If we expect to be rejected, we may assume an aloof and defensive manner which invites rejection; if we expect to be depressed under a Saturn transit, we may feed ourselves with negative messages which drain our energy and prevent us from involving ourselves in nourishing and revitalizing activities and interactions.

Psychologists have discovered that teachers who believe particular students to be slow or unintelligent treat those students differently than they treat students they believe to be quick and bright. As a result, the students influenced by such negative assumptions do not function as competently as those whom the teacher favored. The teacher behaves according to certain assumptions, and the students respond in a self-fulfilling manner. How important it is then for us as astrologers not only to pay attention to those beliefs, assumptions and expectations which we are consciously aware of, but also to ferret out those hidden assumptions and expectations which may manifest behaviors and events that are detrimental to ourselves and others, and may therefore become self-fulfilling prophecies.

Danger #7: Magnification of Our "Unfinished Business"

Because the planets are archetypes for our core energies, focusing upon them intensifies the patterns that are related to those energies. Our subconscious processes, our repressions, our unfinished business as related to the meanings of different planets are highlighted each time we tune into that planet, whether in our own charts or other people's charts. Symbols have an uncanny ability to concentrate and release energy buried deep within us; each time we focus upon a symbol of the psyche, we in effect stir up the energy expressed by that symbol. We invite it to play its part in the drama of our lives—creating internal experiences, external events and patterns of attraction and behavior with others.

Whatever our fears, negativities and compulsions, our focus upon the planets is likely to magnify them as well as the more positive facets of ourselves which the planets also symbolize. Certainly, focusing upon Saturn, planet of fear, may compel our fear to surface; however, paying attention to any or all of the planets is likely to intensify and activate subconscious issues and emotions, simply because we are attuning ourselves to archetypes or symbols of the subconscious. If we fear the future and are continually protecting ourselves against some unknown catastrophe, our use of astrology may magnify that fear. If we experience considerable doubt regarding our worth and keep justifying ourselves and parading our egos as a defense against our inner emptiness, our use of astrology may provide us with fuel for rationalization, support for that subconscious need to compensate for what is lacking within us. We may utilize astrology in service of our repression. Defining ourselves, for example, by our Moon in Taurus square Saturn in Leo, we may take pride in our shrewd practicality and caution, while rationalizing our unwillingness to take risks which might lead to failure.

When we reflect upon the planetary archetypes, we are focusing upon the energies within us which they represent. However, the emphasis upon the symbol enables us to make contact with those energies on a mental plane and to perceive them as outside ourselves without directly experiencing them. Whatever we have not acknowledged and accepted internally, we are therefore likely to project upon the symbol. As in most projections, we become dependent upon the object of projection because it represents to us a part of ourselves that we have denied. The more out of contact we are, the more likely we are to project; the more attention we give our object of projection, the less able we are to encounter the energies within us which we have disowned. When we have many holes in our identity and self-awareness, we are especially prone to become attached to symbols as well as to people and possessions which represent for us what we lack.

Some of us, sensing our growing dependency and loss of power, may seek to break free; we may battle with our growing obsession with astrology, or with the negativities within us which it brings to light. Like the bride of Jason, who donned a magic cloak woven for her by Medea—a cloak which burned her flesh and adhered to her more tenaciously the more she sought to cast it off—so we seek to cast off our growing dependency upon the astrological map, yet find ourselves bound even further as a result of each attempt. The danger may not be in astrology so much as in our use of it and our relationship to our own energies. The battle is resolved not by refusing to consult the ephemeris, but rather by gaining deeper contact with our own beings.

Danger #8: Powerlessness and Loss of Center

Of all our unfinished issues, probably one of the most significant for many of us is our experience of powerlessness, of not existing at the center of our selves and not feeling capable of shaping our lives according to our wills and aims. If we tend to experience ourselves as victims, as acted upon rather than as acting agents, as revolving around some known or unknown center rather than being the center of our own universe, astrology can reinforce this tendency.

In order to function competently, we need to direct our will toward the tasks in front of us—to experience "I want, I can, and I will" and to take action as a result of that internal experience. Our sense of self seems to exist most strongly as we experience and express ourselves and actively create our reality. Often we are in conflict with forces which clash with our intentions; we confront the limitations of external circumstances, unforeseen obstacles, people who oppose us. As our competence, self-respect and self-sufficiency increase we can become able to acknowledge and effectively meet most of these obstacles.

Astrology, like behavioristic psychology and deterministic philosophy, emphasizes influences operating upon us, rather than our capacity to act, operate or direct. The more attention we pay to what may be influencing us, without simultaneously experiencing control over our behavior or influence upon our environment, the more we may become disempowered. Our energy may shift from BEING (in contact with ourselves and the world) and DOING to KNOWING and BEING DONE TO. Rather than subjects, we become objects; we no longer are captains of our soul or masters of our lives. As we lose our center, the planetary influences seem to have a more pronounced effect upon us, for we exist without a central, integrating force which can effectively channel and guide our energies.

In the psychological system of psychosynthesis, founded by Roberto Assagioli, much emphasis is placed upon subpersonalities, the internal personalities within us which have specific wants and needs, often conflict with each other, and which may at times dominate our personalities. Although one aim of psychosynthesis is to contact, understand, accept, and meet the needs of each subpersonality, the overall goal is to build a center of awareness and will capable of coordinating, integrating and directing them.

Consider a play without a director, the actors each improvising according to the mood of the moment, without reference to each other; the result is likely to be uncoordinated and chaotic. Consider also a meeting without a chairperson or a class without a teacher and how little is accomplished, and how much difficulty participants or students have behaving in a unified, fulfilling and productive manner. Likewise, our personalities become strongly dysfunctional when the director or chairperson is absent. Our planetary subpersonalities may battle to meet their needs, often playing out repetitive unconscious patterns which actually sabotage all chances of satisfying needs. No central force is present to perceive the underlying issues, to signal for one subpersonality to enter and another to exit, to create a symphony out of a barrage of discordant notes.

People who possess an internal director, who experience themselves as centers of their own universe, who are in contact with their bodies and feelings and with the core of their own beings, may not be deeply influenced by the planets. They may rise above their subconscious processes. A Saturn transit experienced by an unintegrated or dissociated person as severe depression may be for an aware and integrated person a temporary flagging of emotional energy, a minor adjustment, rather than overwhelming mire.

What a vicious circle we create when, experiencing less power, we turn our attention more to the planets or our subpersonalities rather than contacting and acting from our central core. Our increased sense of powerlessness may lead us to seek even more intensively for answers which elude us because the resolution is not in our minds, not in the ephemeris, not in our knowledge and interpretation of planetary positions. It is at the base of ourselves, in our relationship to a core facet of our beings which we have disowned.

Danger #9: Alienation from Others

A final danger in our use of astrology is the effect which our astrological preoccupation may have upon relationships with other people, individually and with society at large. Certainly, our finesse with astrological jargon enables us to label and diagnose each other, to erect concepts and classifications which incline us to relate to each other through a mental barrier rather than perceiving and responding to each other directly, in all our vulnerability. How much easier, upon meeting a potential friend or lover, to calculate his chart and orient our attitudes and behaviors toward our understanding of his t-square to Pluto or his Sun conjunct Venus, rather than tuning into our own insecure perceptions and feelings with this person, without the preconceptions that astrology provides.

If we experience difficulty making real contact with people, especially sharing the depths of our feelings, needs and vulnerabilities, we can use our astrological jargon to create an illusion of intimacy which we, in fact, are not experiencing. For us to converse about "your Saturn conjunct my Moon" and "your Mars opposing my Mercury" feels a lot safer than my saying to you that, when I experience a need for comfort and reassurance, I am hurt by your tendency to withdraw, and that I often do not feel heard by you because you are frequently interrupting me when I really want to communicate. Able to express the issues between us symbolically, we may alleviate the tension of unspoken thoughts and shy away even further from establishing the real communication which makes relationships deeply fulfilling.

We may, as a result, obscure rather than reveal our actual experience, as we encounter each other through abstract symbols rather than direct communication.

Astrology is, after all, a language—a highly mystical and quite private language since such a small proportion of people are familiar with it. If we lack confidence in our worth, our social skills, and our capacity to relate in a way which evokes acceptance from others and a sense of belongingness with groups, we may subconsciously use our access to this secret language as a means of compensation. Astrology may become a way to create the inner experience of specialness and power which enables us to stand above and apart from others rather than on the same level. If we belong to the secret brotherhood and sisterhood of the mystics, and are capable of communing with the magical forces of the universe, why should we want to participate in tedious small talk with the uninitiated who are not, after all, at our "level" of consciousness? The more important our esoteric understanding becomes to us, the more unsatisfying ordinary conversation may be with those who do not share that understanding; we may forget that the deepest and most fulfilling contact between people occurs not through the mind but through our eye contact, our openness of heart, and our direct expression of and response to genuine feeling.

We may, as a result, spend much of our time with those who "speak astrology," and feel increasingly alienated with and insecure around those who are not "on our wavelength." We may become more identified with the outer fringes of society, more susceptible to rejection from people who are ignorant of or biased against the mystic arts, and more inclined to experience ourselves as separate from and sometimes superior to the common person. We may become less able to identify with, empathize with and sustain satisfying contact with those who do not share our passion than we could before we became astrology students. Ironically, our interest in astrology, the Aquarian art, which may have been motivated by our desire to experience our connection to the mysteries of the universe, may lead us away from fulfilling the ideals of Aquarius, and certainly away from integrating its opposite polarity of Leo, when we allow our preoccupation to result in experiences of increased separateness and alienation rather than togetherness and union. As our minds expand, our hearts may contract. As we become increasingly ruled by our minds and our pursuit of knowledge, we may become less willing and able to open our hearts—to pain, sadness, need and longing, and also to love.

Misuses of Authority in Astrological Counseling

These are the highly potent and often tempting dangers of studying astrology. Those of us who are astrological counselors may need to confront all of these dangers, as well as many other dangers or potential misuses which result from donning the role of professional authority. As astrological counselors, we may have a responsibility to ask ourselves, "How are we using our clients, satisfying our own unfulfilled needs rather than serving their needs? What unconscious messages are we imparting through our nonverbal or verbal messages, which may be at odds with the constructive helping philosophy we are espousing?"

All of the following personal qualities, attitudes and behaviors may undermine our effectiveness as counselors if we do not come to terms with them in ourselves and prevent them, as much as humanly possible, from interfering in our work:

1) SENSE OF SUPERIORITY: speaking from a position of complete authority about the other person, and imparting the message of "I'm better than you" or "I know more about you than you do yourself";

2) KNOW-IT-ALL ATTITUDE: acting as if we have all the answers in regard to our clients' lives, communicating our own opinions under the guise of astrological authority, or otherwise demonstrating lack of respect for our clients;

3) JUDGMENT: negatively evaluating our clients' personalities, choices and behaviors according to our own standards rather than encouraging them to be the locus of their own evaluations;

4) SEEKING ATTENTION: monologuing, showing off, sharing irrelevant personal experiences, or otherwise keeping ourselves in the center stage rather than responding to our clients' needs;

5) BOSSINESS: compulsive advice-giving or the urge to tell others how to run their lives, regardless of whether our suggestions are really useful to our clients, or respect their autonomy;

6) INTRUDING OUR OWN PHILOSOPHY: trying to convert our clients to our particular philosophy of life or spiritual outlook without due consideration for their own belief systems and needs;

7) NEEDING TO BE NEEDED: encouraging client dependency or attempting to rescue them from their problems without a high regard for their autonomy;

8) ILLUSIONS ABOUT HELPING: building our own ego satisfaction through believing we can be effective helpers and counselors by merely imparting astrological information without fully entering our clients' world and establishing a true dialogue which involves sharing feelings as well as both integrating and applying knowledge;

9) ILLUSIONS ABOUT KNOWLEDGE: placing an undue emphasis upon knowledge and abstract understanding as the key to change, without paying attention to our clients' capacity to use that knowledge;

10) IMPARTING POWERLESSNESS: undermining our clients' sense of freedom, will and motivation by focusing primarily on how the planets influence them and ignoring their capacity to actively direct their lives;

11) IMPARTING NEGATIVITY AND FEAR: making negative pronouncements or creating negative expectations for the future instead of ap-

proaching even the most difficult planets and aspects with a constructive philosophy;

12) SEEKING TO PLEASE: seeking to give clients what they want rather than what they need, or giving them temporary satisfaction or assurance at the expense of communications which may be painful to hear in the moment, but valuable from a long-range perspective;

13) INFORMATION COMPULSION: operating from a "the more the better" attitude, overloading clients with information without concern for their capacity to emotionally experience, integrate and apply their understanding;

14) USING VAGUE, UNGROUNDED GENERALITIES: operating from a level of superficial interpretation which avoids the real issues clients are struggling with in the moment and which remains safely abstract, so that the knowledge we share is of little concrete or practical use;

15) INTELLECTUALIZATION AND EMOTIONAL DISCONNECTEDNESS: communicating entirely upon an intellectual level, refusing to be emotionally engaged or to encourage our clients' emotional involvement, remaining distant rather than empathic and humanly involved;

16) CONFUSING THE MAP WITH THE CLIENT: relating to the chart rather than our clients, as if the chart has more validity than their own experience, and as if imparting information about the chart is more important than our clients' needs in the moment;

17) MYSTIFICATION: overusing astrological jargon without translating it into language understandable by our clients, and creating the illusion that we are speaking profoundly when we are merely weaving a web of astrological symbols;

18) LACK OF SELF-AWARENESS: being unable to or unwilling to acknowledge how our own conflicts and personality traits are influencing our use of astrology and leading us to project our own unresolved issues onto our clients or otherwise unconsciously use our clients to meet our needs.

Whether we are astrological students or practitioners, we may frequently fall into many of the above-mentioned traps in regard to our use of astrology. We are human beings, not gods, and can never expect to be aware enough of our actions or free enough of our vices to always use astrology constructively and wisely. We need humility and self-acceptance; we need a commitment to honesty with ourselves; we need a sense of responsibility and empowerment which will enable us to continually probe for and work at overcoming those limitations which consistently undermine our astrological study and counseling.

What can we—each of us individually and the astrological community at large—do to minimize the influence of the dangers and misuses of astrology discussed here? How can we, through courageously facing the negatives within ourselves and our art, begin to transcend them? How might we maintain and/or develop:

a) groundedness in our beings;
b) direct contact with ourselves, others and reality as a whole;
c) the capacity to confront our shadow and resolve our "unfinished business";
d) the trust capable of overcoming fear;
e) the experience of inner power;
f) the identification with the "I," the self, rather than the self-concept, with access to our central core, and
g) the will and capacity to act from that center? How might we also cultivate our desire and ability to expand our minds while simultaneously becoming more receptive and open in our hearts?

Each of us has a responsibility to ourselves and to our clients to reflect upon these questions. There are no simple answers. What answers do exist we must discover for ourselves, at the foundations of our own beings. Committing ourselves to living with the ambiguity of unresolved problems and unanswered questions while maintaining a clear and heartfelt desire to overcome our personal obstacles can lead in time to resolution. As Rainer Maria Rilke wrote in *Letters to a Young Poet*:

> I want to beg you, as much as I can, to be patient toward all that is unsolved in your heart and try to love the *questions* themselves like locked rooms and like books that are written in a very foreign tongue. Do not now seek the answers, which cannot be given you because you would not be able to live them. And the point is, to live everything. *Live* the questions now. Perhaps you will gradually, without noticing it, live along some distant day into the answers.

Chapter Ten

BEYOND FATE AND FREE WILL

Many of us, in our twenties and thirties, and even past our Uranus opposition and Pluto square Pluto in our early forties, attempt to actively shape our lives while envisioning many possible futures. Some of us, however, are knocked down by insurmountable obstacles before we reach midlife—painful losses, debilitating illness, wounded hearts, disappointed dreams—and no longer feel confident in our ability to create our own reality.

But even those of us whose lives have followed a steady course and who have been able to successfully negotiate life's roadblocks, are usually called upon, by our fifties and sixties, to come to terms with our limitations and the world's limitations, and to face the narrowing and shortening of our future life paths. We grieve then not only for loved ones lost to death, heartbreak, or divergent directions, but also for dreams that we doubt will ever materialize. We grieve for the trust we have lost in regard to the benign nature of the universe, and for the confidence we have lost that we can mold our world in accordance with our desires.

How free are we? To what extent are our lives determined by Fate, the planetary cycles, sociopolitical reality, the will of others, psychological conditioning, personal karma? To what extent are we free to shape our destinies? Is free will an illusion, or determinism a remnant of Newtonian reality soon be relegated to the past by discoveries in quantum physics, neuroscience, psychology or spiritual awakening?

I do not have the answers, and indeed do not believe that anyone does at this point in time. I only continue to explore the same questions, penetrating a little more deeply with each turn of the seasons, into the core issues, into the vast emptiness where the mind seeks but cannot find the answers—because the questions we ask are not likely to be found by seeking *or* found with the mind *or* found in the mind, *or* even found at all, but rather experienced wordlessly when we let go of seeking and finding and rest fully in the still, silent source within ourselves.

QUANTUM CONSCIOUSNESS: PART ONE

During the past eighty years, quantum physicists have been making discoveries about the unpredictable nature of electrons and protons in the world around us, our bodies and our brains. Indeed some of these discoveries help explain the synchronistic influences of the planets and the transcendent experiences of mystics throughout the ages.

We know, for example, that electrons, the negatively charged particles within atoms, are both waves and particles—waves when unobserved and particles when observed. Physicist John Bell proved the existence of "entangled particles"—electrons which have been paired or formed a connection with each other remaining part of the same system. As one alters its spin, the other likewise changes in an identical manner, even when separated by vast distances.

In the human brain, nonlocality—action at a distance—also prevails. Neurons unconnected to each other fire at the same time. Two people meditating simultaneously across the continent show coherent patterns of connection in their brain waves. If two persons engage in an emotional interaction at one location and then are separated, and one is exposed to an external stimulus, the brain pattern of the other responds in a similar manner, without the cause/effect influence of the original stimulus.

If distance is an illusion, and everything in the universe is connected, then perhaps not only our actions but also our thoughts and feelings influence external reality. Indeed, physicists may soon discover that the planets and energies far out in the solar system and galaxy are affecting our consciousness in ways that astrology has long assumed.

Scientists have known for years now that the very act of observation alters what we see. Reality crystallizes and takes form under observation. Unobserved electrons form wave packets or probability waves. When we attempt to observe an electron wave, it immediately collapses and becomes a particle. In the act of observation, the collapsing wave packet spreads into a "cloud of uncertainty" which prevents the observer from determining precisely where the electron is located. According to the Heisenberg uncertainty principle, we cannot simultaneously determine the location and the velocity of electrons; we can only guess at their probable location.

According to physicist Amit Goswami, author of the *Self-Aware Universe*, as waves materialize into particles, so the Self that is the formless ground of being may split into parts—creating the sense of a separate "I" or ego. What we experience as ourselves may be the continual process of brain waves collapsing into the "particles" of consciousness. This collapse occurs discontinuously in quantum leaps, with electrons starting in one location and ending in another without traveling in any determinable manner.

Astrology and Change

What relevance does this have to our understanding of astrology? First of all, knowing that the situation of the observer influences our experience of the world helps validate a geocentric approach to astrology since the axes and house cusps of the natal chart depend upon birthplace as well as time.

If the action of looking disturbs the object observed, if consciousness is disruptive to the object of its observation, we might wonder: Does understanding the position of the planets and their meaning in relation to our charts alter our experience of those planetary energies? In other words, would our knowledge of astrology influence the effect the planets have upon us, so that our experience differs from the experience we might have without such understanding? Does interpreting an influence in one particular way lead to different kinds of experiences than those we might have had if we held different interpretations, because of the influence of our consciousness upon reality?

Many of us, when first learning astrology, reflected upon events of our past and noticed that planetary influences were strongly affecting us before we knew our natal charts. The planets influence us whether or not we know about them, but we cannot determine if experiences we would have had before we knew astrology were any different than experiences we might have had if we had been aware of transits at earlier times.

But we do know that when we predict the future, our predictions can only be based upon what we know as a result of past experience and previously gained knowledge. We cannot predict experiences or events that are not in the realm of our experience or understanding. Nor can we predict occurrences which might result from circumstances which haven't happened yet, because the necessary experiences which would enable them to happen have not yet manifested. Who for example, could predict in 1990, that ten years later after Saturn transits a 10th house Venus in Gemini that an individual might become a successful Web designer? In 1990, we would have had no conception of the creation or impact of the World Wide Web.

Since consciousness influences reality, imposing our limited past-influenced consciousness upon our projections of the future might restrict us to experiences which are variants of the past rather than enable us to remain open-minded and allow entirely new unconditioned possibilities to manifest.

Paul Watzlawick, in his book *Change*, refers to two kinds of change. First order change is like shuffling the furniture in a room—for example, we end one relationship and start another, or switch our career from higher education to educational publishing. Second order change is more like tearing down the walls or even the foundations and building an entirely new structure—a condo complex or water park. With second order change, we might leave the educational field entirely, and, having discovered our connection to the earth, start an organic gardening business. By envisioning a first order change future, we may prevent second order change from happening.

When interpreting the influence in particular of Uranus, Neptune and Pluto, we may wish to keep our minds open and listen to the new developments occurring at the periphery of our consciousness or deep within our cells. These planets are most likely to provide opportunities for second order change to occur, and more so if we do not block the new manifestations by clinging to past-influenced interpretations.

More on the Limitations of Belief

A related and even more important influence upon our experience of planetary energies has to do with the degree to which we are identified with our beliefs. Philosopher-scientist Alfred Korzybski's well-known statement that "the map is not the territory" is of considerable significance to astrology students who drive their bodily vehicles with the astrological map in front of their eyes, blocking their direct experience of the view outside their life windshield.

The more fully we are identified with our larger Self rather than the "I" of our ego, the more capable we are of holding our beliefs loosely and interpreting them flexibly. The more we are in direct contact with the ground of our being, the more open we are to revising our beliefs, without feeling personally threatened by changes in our conceptions of reality or ourselves. Our belief systems can provide a container which helps us to make sense of the world, but they can not substitute for direct attunement to inner guidance (often resulting from keeping our attention in our heart or solar plexus) or full awareness of ourselves in the moment.

We are not our astrology charts; the self is not the self-image. We are not our beliefs, and the fullness of reality cannot be encompassed or contained in any belief system.

I have known several people who had no interest in astrology but who seemed to be deeply in touch with themselves, possessing an uncanny sense of timing in regard to making changes in their lives precisely in accord with the timing and most constructive meaning of their significant transits. My observations of these people led me to wonder if indeed we can too easily use our astrological understanding as a crutch, and listen so much to the astrological beliefs and interpretations manufactured by our minds that we fail to cultivate a deeper level of intuition and inner knowing.

The idea of not being identified with beliefs and interpretations is an alien one to many astrology students, who seek to learn about planetary cycles in order to feel more in control of their lives, especially when they lack an inner "rudder." It would have been alien to me until the early 1980s, because I had previously been identified with my 9th house stellium, which includes the South Node conjunct Saturn and Sun. At that time, while Neptune transited my Galactic Center ascendant and I was struggling with a debilitating illness, it seemed as if the ground of my being shifted. After grieving the inability of my mind to provide the answers I was seeking, I felt myself melting away and awakening then to the world in a whole new way, through nature photography, watercolors, and an opening of my heart chakra. Although this shift in consciousness was most profound during the years of my Neptune transit, I remained permanently changed by it, as if transformed at a cellular level.

My path of course is not everyone's path, and each of us needs to discover his or her own path and be true to it. But I have found sustenance in embracing the uncertainty and insubstantiality of the mind's configurations, in experiencing reality more directly through the body's inner guidance system, and far less through belief systems and mental conceptions. My own path has involved journeying from *I don't know/I don't understand* to *I need to know/understand* to *I know/I understand* back to *I don't know/I don't understand* and then finally to *I don't need to know or understand*. Now beliefs seem to me like porous nets, partially open containers in which at times I choose to rest so that I can let go of the overstimulation of thought before returning home to my essential Self.

Fate, Determinism, and Human Limitation

We are here, however, within the pages of this book, on a quest of understanding. In order to gain further insight into the relationship between freedom and determinism, fate and free will, and how astrology can relate to and transcend these polarities, we need to first explore both the limits on our freedom and our capacity for free will.

The chart on the following page summarizes personal, mental, action and spiritual/cosmic limitations upon our freedom—limitations which may influence us throughout our lifetimes, and those which we only encounter at certain life stages. I will in this chapter only address a few of these limiting factors.

THE ROLE OF FATE

"I was perfectly free to hammer on the door, but the door didn't open until fate opened it. Fate controls what is going to happen on a large scale."[1]

What is fate? Many of us may use the word *fate* to denote uncanny circumstances in our lives which appear to be synchronistic or beyond coincidence, as if some transcendent force was steering us in a predetermined direction. Some view fate as synonymous with karma; others, with destiny. Fate as karma implies that we are pushed from behind, experiencing the consequences of past actions. Fate as destiny implies rather that we are pulled from above or ahead, and have personal tasks or missions which we are here to fulfill. Fate may indeed have given us gifts which it is our destiny to cultivate and use to our best advantage.

In Greek mythology, Fate is personified as three goddesses, the Moirae or Fates, daughters of Necessity. The Fates are the ultimate power, and rule even over the gods; Zeus himself cannot alter events if the Fates decree otherwise. Clotho, the Spinner, spins the thread of life, determining our talents and deficits. Clotho also determines the time of our birth, which therefore suggests the planetary energies imprinted upon our neural net.

Lachesis, the Disposer of Lots, measures the thread of our life, determining the circumstances which we will confront during our lifetime. Atropos, the Cutter, cuts the thread of life and is therefore responsible for our time and means of dying.

---

1. Arthur Young, founder of the Institute for the Study of Consciousness, in an interview with Jeffrey Mishlove of the "Thinking Allowed" television series, http://www.intuition.org

THE LIMITS OF PERSONAL FREEDOM
Limitations in regard to the factors below may limit freedom

Personal Limitations

genetic influences	social conditioning
health and physical disability	early childhood conditioning
energy and vitality	personality disorders
socio-political factors	trauma, dissociation, repression
influence of personal relationships	personal resources, capabilities
the will or counter-influence of others	responsibilities (e.g. children)
time	money

Mental Limitations

intelligence	conscious or unconscious resistance
left brain/right brain predominance and integration	ignorance
	lack of education
belief systems	distractibility; lack of focus
over-identification with beliefs	poor judgment
over-identification with thoughts	competing intentions
self-image	invalid assumptions
over-identification with self-image	taking the wrong approach

Action Limitations

lethargy, passivity, inaction	poor timing
taking the wrong action	overextension, scattered energies
need to exert self more	need to exert self less

Cosmic/Spiritual Limitations

opposition to Fate or Destiny	obstacles indicated by natal chart
personal karma	current transits and progressions
collective karma or a nation or race	religious or spiritual dogma

Scandinavian mythology also represents the Fates as three goddesses—the Norns—who dip water from the Well of Wyrd and pour it over the roots of the World Tree, Yggdrasil. Urdh (Wyrd) rules the past and the resources we bring into each lifetime. Verdardi ("that which is becoming") determines our fate in each present moment, enabling us to use the gifts we were given in the past and uncover new resources. Skuld ("that which must be") is the inflexible death goddess.

Westerners, especially Americans, inherited the entitlement myth of Manifest Destiny (and the hubris that comes with it), as well as the individualistic pioneering spirit which is often expressed as "pull yourself up by your own bootstraps." We have tended to view fate negatively and see "her" as an obstacle to our self-ordained freedom—an obstacle which must be denied or challenged. Yet such rejection of fate can only trigger the anger of the Triple Goddess and lead to the disappointments which result from reaching too far or wide and not respecting the boundaries and limits of reality.

The Astrology of Fate and Limitation

In astrology, Saturn is often associated with fate, gifting us with the consequences of past actions, and promising us that we will eventually face the results of our present responsibility or irresponsibility. Saturn, unfortunately, is viewed as a malefic in traditional astrology, but is a friend to those who embrace her lessons.

At our first Saturn return, around age 29, we are face to face with the great Taskmaster who demands from us hard work, commitment and responsibility or plunges us into depressive free fall resulting from disappointments to our adolescent and early adult fantasies of unlimited freedom and possibility. At the second Saturn return, around age 59, we face the encroaching limitations of an aging body and the narrowing of our life path and sense of the future, but we are also given the opportunity to make a new commitment to life which may realign us to our personal destiny.

The Vertex/Antivertex axis in astrology is also associated with fate, and is likely to be of considerable importance because, as the intersection of the ecliptic with the prime vertical or I.C., it is one of the primary axes of the chart. The Vertex is often ignored by astrologers because it is flattened into insignificance on our two-dimensional chart forms, and because its common interpretation as "fate" does not lend itself to easy explanation.

SHAKESPEARE ON ASTROLOGY, FATE AND FREE WILL

This is the excellent foppery of the world, that, when we are sick in fortune,—often the surfeit of our own behavior,—we make guilty of our disasters the sun, the moon, and the stars: as if we were villains by necessity; fools by heavenly compulsion; knaves, thieves, and treachers, by spherical predominance; drunkards, liars, and adulterers, by an enforced obedience of planetary influence; and all that we are evil in, by a divine thrusting on: an admirable evasion of whoremaster man, to lay his goatish disposition to the charge of a star!

—Earl of Gloucester, *King Lear*, I, ii, 115-129.

There is a tide in the affairs of men,
Which taken at the flood, leads on to fortune;
Omitted, all the voyage of their life
Is bound in shallows and in miseries.
On such a full sea are we now afloat.

—Brutus, *Julius Caesar*, IV, 3, 218-222

Men at some time are masters of their fates:
The fault, dear Brutus, is not in our stars,
But in ourselves, that we are underlings.

—Cassius, *Julius Caesar*, I, ii, 139-141

I find my zenith doth depend upon
A most auspicious star, whose influence
If now I court not but omit, my fortunes
Will ever after droop.

—Prospero, *The Tempest*, I, ii, 26-29

You fools: I and my fellows
Are ministers of Fate. The elements,
Of whom your swords are tempered, may as well
Wound the loud winds, or with be-mocked-at stabs
Kill the still-closing waters, as diminish
One dowle that's in my plume.

—Ariel, *The Tempest*, V, ii, 70-75

What fates impose, that men must needs abide;
It boots not to resist both wind and tide.

—King Edward, *King Henry VI*, IV, iii, 59-60

Fate, show your force; ourselves we do not owe
What is decreed must be—and be this so!

—Olivia, *Twelfth Night*, I, v, 297-298

Our remedies oft in ourselves do lie,
Which we ascribe to heaven: the fated sky
Gives us free scope, only doth backward pull
Our slow designs when we ourselves are dull.

—Helena, *All's Well that Ends Well*, I, i, 209-212

Our wills and fates do so contrary run
That our devices still are overthrown;
Our thoughts are ours, their ends none of our own.

—King Claudius, *Hamlet*, III, ii, 206-208

O God! that one might read the book of fate,
And see the revolution of the times
Make mountains level, and the continent,
Weary of solid firmness, melt itself
Into the sea! and, other times, to see
The beachy girdle of the ocean
Too wide for Neptune's hips; how chances mock,
And changes fill the cup of alteration
With divers liquors!

—Henry IV, *Henry IV Part Two*, III, i, 39-46

To be, or not to be: that is the question:
Whether 'tis nobler in the mind to suffer
The slings and arrows of outrageous fortune,
Or to take arms against a sea of troubles,
And by opposing end them?

—Hamlet, *Hamlet*, III, i, 55-29

There is a divinity that shapes our ends,
Rough-hew them how we will.

—Hamlet, *Hamlet*, V, ii, 11-12

The Vertex usually occurs between the 5th and 8th houses, and is often associated with experiencing fated encounters and circumstances. Some astrologers view it as indicating the outcome of our personal karma and turning points in our lives which compel us to alter our course.

My own belief is that we all have a personal destiny, as delineated by the past push of the South Node and the future pull of the North Node, *and* we also have a cosmic destiny indicated by the Vertex/Antivertex axis. We human beings are quite self-centered in our belief that the universe views our personal destinies as consequential and in alignment with its own purpose or evolution. Might there not be a larger plan that does not serve us, but which we must serve, like cogs in the wheel of time?

The Vertex also plays a significant role in interpersonal relationships. I once had a dream in which an elderly man with a grey beard explained to me that a Vertex connection between charts means a connection which occurred *between* lifetimes, and which leads both persons to experience a deep sense of familiarity. But this previous connection is not necessarily an indicator of soulmates, for the two people may not find it easy to connect on the earth plane or through a physical relationship since their connection has been predominantly in consciousness. However, their destinies may be interwoven.

In addition to Saturn, the Vertex axis and the Nodal axis, the 12th house is also associated with the karmic dimension of fate (see my entire book on the subject, *Your Secret Self*). In our 12th house, our planetary energies take an inward direction, operating subliminally and in solitude, perhaps as a result of overuse, misuse or spiritual development in a past lifetime.

Apart from specific fate indicators in our charts, the overall chart configuration can indicate limitations upon our free will. (The freedom loving planets Jupiter and Uranus, and their signs Sagittarius and Aquarius pertain to a desire for freedom from restriction. Free will is another matter altogether).

We all differ in the degree of personal freedom or free will which we possess in our lives as a whole and in specific areas of our lives. A strong emphasis in a particular sign or house will limit our freedom to avoid expressing that energy or focus, but will also provide easy access to the resources available in regard to this sign or house. A grand trine in earth signs, for example, may enable us to at least experience a greater sense of freedom in regard to working and dealing with the physical plane, but may restrict our sense of freedom in regard to areas of life beyond the physical.

We are most likely to experience limits to our free will in areas related to our closest aspects, particularly squares and oppositions. In these cases, no matter how deeply we understand our conflicts here, we may often feel that we only make limited progress in synthesizing or overcoming the struggles we face.

Likewise, deficits in our charts, such as missing elements or empty spaces of a t-square, may continually remind us of energies which we do not feel capable of expressing or areas of life which remain blind spots that we are only occasionally able to illuminate. Fortunately transits, progressions, and synastry with people to whom we are emotionally connected may provide opportunities for us to develop weak areas of ourselves and transcend the difficulties inherent in our most exact squares and oppositions.

Psychological Limitations

Our psychological conditioning limits our free will at least as much as our genes, personality patterns, and planetary placements. We repeat learned habits of thought and action thousands of times, which become embedded into our behavior patterns, especially when reinforced by strong emotions (especially traumas) and the social pressures of our environment. Conditioned behaviors usually become so unconscious that much of the time we believe we are making free choices when we are really acting in accordance with our most embedded conditioned responses.

When our brains encounter stimuli, the neocortex replays memory associations from the past which trigger responses learned in the past. As long as we are at the mercy of conditioning, we make choices in the present which lead us to repeat past patterns, and which limit our future possibilities.

Over time, conditioned responses become unconscious. But due to repression (indicated in part by 12th house planets and signs), many of our thoughts and feelings become unconscious as well, especially those which are in conflict with our personal desires, values, or self-image, or which stir up anxiety and fear. Individuals vary in their degree of repression, but those of us who allow more of our thoughts and feelings into consciousness, and are able to integrate threatening material into our conceptions of self and reality, will experience considerably greater freedom of choice than those who don't.

The more we avoid facing and fully experiencing our feelings, the smaller and more helpless we become, and the more inclined to project our power onto other people, the government, or the planets. The smaller we become, the more we are oppressed by the demands of the world which seem infinitely larger than our capacity to cope. Indeed, the commonality of giants in fairy tales and folklore is suggestive not only of the power of the "giant" parent over the small child, but also of the imposing largeness of our own psychic contents which may occasionally threaten to erupt and overwhelm us.

Coping with Limitation and Lack of Freedom

When we fail to achieve our goals, suffer painful loss, or experience the most debilitating facets of a difficult outer planet transit, we may wonder what we have done wrong, rage at the unfairness of life, sink into depression, and/or question our belief systems regarding divine protection or a benevolent universe.

When I was in my 20's and 30's, and writing the earlier edition of this book, I believed—or wanted to believe—that if we attuned ourselves to the most constructive expression of a transit, we would cooperate with planetary cycles and minimize the negative influences. To some extent, I still believe that this is true—or at least believe that conscious *listening* to and focusing upon the highest potentials of a planetary combination will serve us. But I do now acknowledge that at times, no matter how deeply we meditate, set our intentions, and make active constructive choices, we may sometimes be creamed, blasted into bits, leveled, discombobulated, flattened, tormented, and flagellated by life circumstances.

WHY? Why do bad things happen to good people? Why do we consciously and righteously suffer when many who claw their way to the top seem to be rewarded for intemperate and callous behavior? Why, for example is our most beloved child killed by gunfire, or a lifetime of irreplaceable artwork demolished by fire? Why in recent years have thousands of innocent Iraqis died who had nothing to do with the terrorist attacks on the World Trade Center and Pentagon?

Why, I ask, did my nationally known concert pianist aunt who toured the country and delighted audiences with her music, lose six of her fingers in a car accident? Why was my mother forced to stay alive on machines for six months, her living will and wishes of her family disregarded, while she suffered in agony, as the hospital collected her six million dollar supplemental health insurance policy?

I have no idea. I've had many guesses, but I don't know and will probably never know.

We cannot know why, at least not at this point in time. But our minds often need to find reasons in order to make sense of the insensible, to provide a container to hold the pain and the terror, so we can move on and continue with our lives.

Here are some of the answers to WHY? that have helped me cope with life's most difficult circumstances (and attributing it all to personal karma is *not* one of them).

WHY? Because . . . .

- We are not doing what we are meant to be doing with our lives, and are being forced onto the right track.

- We are not who we need to be in order to have the strength of character or capacity to tackle the next task ahead, and this current circumstance will help us become who we need to become.

- We are holding onto the past, and need to let go in order to make space for the new which will soon unfold.

- Positive consequences will eventually result from this tragedy. We must trust.

- Suffering breaks us open and can lead us to open our hearts and become more compassionate and open to the grace of God.

- The universe has a plan for us, which we don't know and may never know, but in which we need to have faith.

- The universe is unpredictable (and may even be caught up in a battle between cosmic forces of good and evil, with the evil sometimes prevailing). Blips or interruptions occur in our lifeline which are not of our own choice, and not part of a divine plan, but with which we must learn to cope.

- We have been too invested in controlling our lives, and need to be humbled, to surrender and "give it to God."

Viktor Frankl, concentration camp survivor and psychologist, wrote in *Man's Search for Meaning* that although we cannot always control circumstances, we can maintain some degree of choice in regard to the meaning we attribute to them, how we respond to them, what we learn from them, and how we rebound from them to better ourselves and contribute to the world.[2]

A popular new age belief undergoing a resurgence at present due to the success of *The Secret*[3], is the idea that we create our own reality and that everything that happens to us results from our beliefs and actions. I don't fully subscribe to this notion, although I do believe that we create *much* of our reality, and that asking ourselves what we did to contribute to or cause a particular event can lead us to make more informed choices in the future. But I cannot believe that a four year old child chooses to get cancer, that a talented artist necessarily chooses to lose eyesight, or a woman walking to her car in a parking lot chooses to be raped.

We could, of course, hold that these choices are made by our larger Self, our soul, which chooses circumstances in this lifetime for a particular purpose unknown to us, and that our conscious selves or egos do not make such choices. But since most of the time we are not likely to be able to conceptualize our soul's purpose, taking this perspective can easily lead us into self-blame, guilt and helplessness.

A person who has spent years using medical, holistic, psychological and/or spiritual means to overcome a persistent illness does not need to be told that by changing his belief systems, he will overcome it (yes, some people do, but they may not necessarily have done any more inner work than the person who fails). A man who strives but does not achieve public success does not need to be told by a friend with Jupiter on his midheaven to just trust, and it will happen. In short, new age do-gooders do not necessarily possess the secret of life, and what works for us does not necessarily work for someone else.

Indeed, many of our life circumstances *do* result from our beliefs, attitudes, and actions. But at some point in our lives we may be struck down by a lightning bolt not of our own making. In these circumstances, the belief that "you create your own reality" may only irritate, masking as it sometimes does an arrogance and a desire to avoid tangling with the sometimes unexplainable cruelty of Fate.

When no matter how hard we try, we cannot find the understanding we seek, or create the change we wish to implement, then perhaps our

---

2. I have posted the conclusion to my college thesis on the Meaning of Life online at http://www.webwinds.com/frankl/meaning.htm. The understanding I gained writing it, drawing from the works of Erich Fromm, Abraham Maslow, Rollo May, Krishnamurti, Paul Tillich, Abraham Heschel, and especially Viktor Frankl, still shapes my life philosophy today.
3. *The Secret*, by Rhonda Byrne was published in 2006 by Atria Books/Beyond Words (New York). A self-help film followed in 2007. *The Secret* has helped the repopularize the ancient wisdom of the Law of Attraction.

task is to give up trying to understand and give the matter to God, or Goddess, or Providence, or whatever sustains us. At the same time, we need to be tender with ourselves and open to personal love, the beauty of nature, creative inspiration or spiritual practice, so that we may begin to rest softly within our own still center of being and reconnect with the beneficence and beauties that do illuminate our universe.

QUANTUM CONSCIOUSNESS: PART TWO

As we've previously discussed, the Heisenberg uncertainly principle tells us that we can determine the position of an electron or its velocity but cannot through observation or calculation determine both. When we attempt to observe an electron to determine its location, the electron wave collapses into a particle. We cannot precisely determine the location of that particle; its location is only *probable*. We have only partial awareness, and only partial capacity to predict reality.

Physicist Neil Bohr referred to the wavelike functions of electrons, protons and neutrons as probability waves. Nobel Prize winning physicist Richard Feynman believed that probability waves embody many possible pasts—when a wave collapses into a particle one of its probable paths materializes at a particular location, but cause and effect cannot determine which materialization will occur. We can determine the odds of a particular location, but within those odds, anything can happen.

The universe seems to be one enormous lottery. Just as one may buy a lottery ticket and have a 1-in-20 million chance of winning the jackpot, winning the jackpot *is* possible. Some people do succeed in defying seemingly impossible odds.

Anyone who has experienced winning over enormous odds might attest to uncanny transcendent forces at work. I had such an experience in my occasional escapist pastime of three deck spider solitaire, in which the odds of winning a game are supposedly 4:100. In 2006, however, I was amazed when during three days, I won sixteen games in a row. The odds of such a winning streak I calculated to be 56 quadrillion to one.

At the time of my spider solitaire winning streak, Pluto was stationary on my ascendant, Neptune was opposing my 8th house Pluto, and a lunar eclipse was occurring on my eclipsed Moon in Aries—a repeat of the eclipse at my birth. In my own experience, such doorways are more likely to open during eclipses and important Uranus, Neptune, and Pluto transits.

Despite the insignificant reality of winning a computer game, I was nonetheless left with a profound conviction that at times we can make a quantum leap beyond normal reality, and the seemingly impossible can happen. Focusing on the odds against us disempowers us. But remaining open to the impossible becoming possible may indeed open a doorway which *can* enable amazing breakthroughs. Our understanding about uncertainty and probability waves underscores our awareness, in the words of Ptolemy, that "the stars incline; they but do not compel." Interpreting the natal chart is interpreting tendencies; predicting is predicting probabilities.

Discoveries in modern physics also have an impact upon neuroscience and neuropsychology—our understanding of how the brain works and perceives reality. Neurons, the fundamental units of the nervous system, have cilia which are microtubules carrying protein while oscillating in a wavelike manner. Through "tunnelling," proteins transmit amino acids across vast distances in a quantum manner, defying cause and effect. Protein bridges create paths by which electrons disappear and appear across considerable distances without passing through intermediate space. Tunnelling allows for completely new orders and patterns to occur.

Physicist Amit Goswami, author of the *Self-Aware Universe*, and psychiatrist/physics professor Jeffrey Satinover, author of the *Quantum Brain*, have been exploring the quantum dimensions of the brain and human consciousness. The tiny quantum effects in the brain have large scale repercussions because the fractal structure of the brain allows for the change in neural pattern to be replicated elsewhere and amplified by the neural network. Both Satinover and Goswami speculate that within the quantum activities of the brain exists our capacity for free will.

This quantum brain activity is likely to be responsible for creative inspiration, mini-satoris of sudden insight, and second order change. We can only wonder if indeed Cinderella's pumpkin did transform into a carriage, and then back to a pumpkin before Cinderella shed her slipper and married her prince. "Magic" may indeed be possible.

My own belief is that the seven inner planets bounded by Saturn most influence conditioned behavior and the transpersonal planets, Uranus, Neptune, and Pluto[4] are associated with quantum experience. Significant transits of Uranus, Neptune, and Pluto often do suggest time periods in

---

4. I object to astronomers refusing to call Pluto a planet, and fear that the god Pluto is incensed that we have demoted him and has been stirring up hell through the Mideast—the meeting place of East and West, and the roots of civilization—as a result.

which we are able to shed the skin of old realities, beliefs, and behaviors and emerge into an entirely new context and way of being.

Psychologist/educator Robert Kegan presented in *The Evolving Self* a model of human behavior based upon shifts in the structure of the self. According to Kegan, individuals move through different stages of embeddedness in self-structures which encompass our world-views, desires, values, and sets of assumptions about reality. We begin in early infancy experiencing the world through the incorporative (symbiotic) self, then progress to the impulsive self, then the interpersonal self. Some of us continue to evolve to the institutional (administrative) self, and may proceed further to the interindividual self, in which the self is no longer identified with the ego, personal relationships, profession or its own system of self-government, but is truly interdependent.

Kegan views the shift from one self-structure to the next as a natural process, although, he wrote "the emergence from embeddedness involves the 'throwing away' of that in which I have been embedded."[5]

Physics professor Goswami believes that free will arises from the quantum self and that the deepest psychological breakthroughs involve "the breakdown of the boundary that is determined by one set of contexts for living to allow for an expanded set of contexts." *(Using a pen or pencil, attempt to solve the problem posed by the Awareness Exercise below; then consult the answer on page 292).*

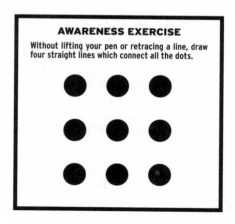

AWARENESS EXERCISE

Without lifting your pen or retracing a line, draw four straight lines which connect all the dots.

---

5. Robert Kegan, *The Evolving Self: Problem and Process in Human Development* (Cambridge, MA: Harvard University Press, 1982).

Sometimes the pressure of insurmountable problems builds up within us until a sudden—or, under Neptune, gradual—shift into a new reality brings us the solution. Other times unexpected events or encounters break open a closed mindset and enable the ground of our beings to shift to another foundation. Some shifts are small; others feel like earthquakes or tidal waves at the center of our self, and may indeed be accompanied by dreams of natural disaster.

Social conditioning, failures and successes, changes in life circumstance, significant personal relationships, and the influence of powerful transits may contribute to the internal pressure which eventually cracks the egg of old self-identifications and enables the new self to birth. Such a shift is likely to open us to a sense of larger reality and personal freedom, as if we are no longer operating at the speed of a 56k modem but have graduated to broadband, expanding the bandwidth of consciousness to cable or DSL.

I felt transformed when Neptune crossed my ascendant and I shed my identification with my 9th house stellium and belief systems as my own center of gravity shifted. Currently, I am now being transformed again by passages of Pluto over my ascendant, and although I sometimes fear I have been abducted by Pluto and am completely at the mercy of the powerful energies tearing through me, I also retain faith that in the destruction of the old, something new and substantial is transforming my very core.

Is this free will? No, for under the outer planets we may feel little choice in regard to our experience. But perhaps we do at these time periods have the freedom to transcend our conditioning and the blueprint of our birthcharts. Perhaps we need a new term for experiences which shift us out of old realities into new ones, experiences which often seem to be created by both our psyches and external forces—which may often feel fated or helped along by divine guidance, and yet which also seem to open us to a greater sense of personal freedom.[6]

---

6. I wrote the above section just before Pluto stationed on my ascendant. During the station, I had an attack of an illness I have had for 32 years, which at that time left me for the most part unconscious for four days. When I regained consciousness, I was swept away with fantasies of what I realized later was a novel I was meant to write. Ever since then, I have been well, focused on writing the novel, and in awe of the healing capacity of Pluto.

Personal Freedom and Free Will

"In order to feel its mastery in nature, the human soul must put itself into communion with the infinite and universal spirit. Its will must be one with the universal will"

—SRI AUROBINDO, *Fate and Free Will*, 1910

However powerful the restrictions of our conditioning and the demands of fate have open us, we are not completely determined. We know rather a "soft determinism" with leaks and holes within the nets of our lives, open spaces in which we may experience personal freedom and free will. Our difficulty is often knowing when and how we are limited and when, how and in what ways we might be free.

Subjectively, we experience ourselves freely making choices, but from a more "objective" standpoint, we may understand that our choices are not as free as we think they are. Choosing between Coca Cola and Pepsi is not truly a manifestation of free will, nor is choosing between a Democrat or Republican presidential candidate.

Personal freedom involves the capacity to choose between real alternatives, to determine our own response to circumstances, and to initiate actions without undue restriction. Free will however is unconditioned choice, and involves the capacity to act in opposition to habit and con-

Solution:

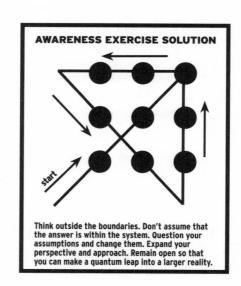

AWARENESS EXERCISE SOLUTION

start

Think outside the boundaries. Don't assume that the answer is within the system. Question your assumptions and change them. Expand your perspective and approach. Remain open so that you can make a quantum leap into a larger reality.

ditioning, step out of old systems of thought and behavior, and discover or create previously unseen alternatives and contexts.

Numerous psychological factors contribute to our personal freedom and free will. The more fully we are in touch with ourselves and able to constructively manage our feelings, the more likely we are to make wise choices, and cope with the obstacles in our paths. Knowing our values and priorities, taking responsibility for ourselves, setting our intentions, and believing that we deserve happiness, love, and prosperity all contribute to our ability to constructively shape our lives.

The table on page 294 summarizes a number of sociological, physical, psychological, and spiritual factors which can enhance our personal freedom.

When Pluto was conjuncting my Sun in the early 1970s, I was at Tufts University majoring in comparative religion, and attempting to make sense out of the chaos of my life. Fortunately, I was able to create a number of independent studies on subjects important to me. One was on the nature of the will, according to Martin Buber and Rollo May—not the willpower by which we attempt to force ourselves to do what we resist, but rather the will that arises from the central core of the self. At the time, based on understanding I had gained, I developed a personal mantra, which helped me to overcome what I experienced then as a weakness of my personal will.

The mantra is: I AM, I WANT, I CARE, I CAN, I WILL, I DARE.

For me it means:

I AM: I have to right to exist and seek satisfaction in life.

I WANT: I know my personal desires.

I CARE: I care about myself enough to commit to my wellbeing

I CAN: I have the capacities I need to fulfill my aims.

I WILL: I choose to commit myself to my goals.

I DARE: I dare to maintain my commitment despite obstacles which I face.

Another mental construct which I developed doing an independent study on the meaning of life concerns choices that are open to us, beyond the attitudes we take toward our experiences. In my view then and

---

ENHANCING PERSONAL FREEDOM
The following factors may enhance our personal freedom

Sociological/Physical Factors

Freedom from danger and physical threat
Time for activities beyond survival (e.g. earning a living)
Adequate health and mobility
A viable support system
Education; basic knowledge of psychology

Psychological Factors

Observation/attunement to external reality
Clear thinking and judgment
Awareness of our feelings; lack of repression
Awareness of our behavioral patterns
Capacity to cope with fear and soothe ourselves
Capacity to deal with frustration and conflict
Capacity to cope with failure, disappointment, loss
Willingness to face the truth about ourselves and our lives
Acceptance of our real limitations
Ability to let go of the past
Ability to learn from our mistakes
Awareness of our values and priorities
Healthy self-love and self-respect
Belief that we deserve the best
Confidence in our own capacities
Ability to love and be loved
Investment in Self rather than self-image
Willingness to take responsibility for ourselves
Desire to be the best person we can be
The ability to envision a positive future
The ability to set an intention for our future
The willingness to commit to our intentions

Spiritual Factors

Identification with our spiritual source
The capacity for inner silence
Ability to live in the now, the expanded present
Openness to grace
Ability to pray or ask for divine help
Trust that we will attract what we need
Trust in a higher power

---

now, we have three primary means of satisfaction: love, pleasure, and self-respect (the latter I have also called mastery/competence).

If at certain stages of our lives we are not able to experience love or act in a loving manner, or we do not take pleasure in our activities or relationships, then at least we can choose to focus on actions which enhance our self-esteem or demonstrate our mastery/competence. Such choices are related to choosing the mature or adult path—and acting in accordance with the lessons of Saturn. Whenever we confront unpleasant circumstances or face arduous tasks which we would prefer to avoid, choosing to fulfill the demands of Saturn and responsible adulthood may enable us to find the motivation we need to face what lies before us, and commit to the task at hand.

For many of us, a meditation practice or frequent periods of inner silence are necessary if we are to think clearly, maintain our own center of gravity, and make wise choices. In the early twentieth century, Einstein wrote, "everything is emptiness, and form is condensed emptiness." When we are in contact with the inner emptiness at the ground of our being, our intuition is awakened. We are able to hear (at least occasionally) our inner guidance, and receive insights which may transcend the programming of our conditioning and left brain thinking. The ability to observe and let go of our thoughts and feelings broadens the context of our experience, deepening our attunement to our inner space. The more frequently and the more deeply we make such contact, the more likely we are to have breakthroughs of insight, and to transcend the conflicts and polarities in our lives.

Personal growth guru Wayne Dyer, Rhonda Byrne (*The Secret*), Esther Hicks (channeler of "Abraham" and author of *The Law of Attraction*), Shakti Gawain (*Creative Visualization*) and Ramtha are only a few of a multitude of spiritual teachers who emphasize that we can attract what we want in life if we use our imagination to envision ourselves already having it. Focusing upon what we lack manifests lack, but envisioning what we wish to have and emotionally experiencing having it both send messages to our midbrains, bypassing our left brain thinking, and creating a positive magnetic field. Imagining having what we seek creates a state of emotional fulfillment and receptivity which magnifies our power of attraction.

Such thinking is viewed as new age hogwash by many, and indeed is no magic sesame which opens Aladdin's cave and reveals the treasures hidden there. We will not attract what we seek if the universe has other plans for us, if the timing is not right, if our will interferes with the paths of others, and if we have other conscious or unconscious needs or desires which take precedence. But creating a regular routine in which we clearly envision our future—especially in a manner related to the positions of our natal Neptune and our Neptune transits—usually does have positive consequences, and increases our experience of personal freedom.

Often, asking the universe in general rather than in specific terms for whatever furthers our greater wellbeing and that of others is most advantageous under outer planet transits. When we envision a specific aim, we may be projecting thought-forms based upon past experiences and understanding. However, under Uranus, Neptune, and Pluto, we have the opportunity to transcend past conditioning. We are then most likely to benefit if we let go of specific agendas and allow the new energies impacting us to guide us in previously unforeseen directions.

When are emotionally close to other people, the energy exchange we experience, reflected in the synastry between our charts, also awakens us to new possibilities of expression and manifestation.

The North Node of the Moon is also associated with receiving guidance from higher sources. Transits and progressions conjuncting our North Nodes, and transits of the North Node itself signify time periods in which we can best receive help from the universe. On a daily basis, the twelve-minute interval in which the transiting North Node crosses the ascendant in our locality is a particularly fruitful time for being receptive to internal and external guidance.

Clarifying Beliefs and Affirmations

Previously, I warned against over-identification with belief systems. I do not mean to imply that we don't benefit from clarifying our beliefs, for indeed we do. But this clarifying process does not mean *only* changing the mental constructs of which we are conscious. We also need to ferret out the unconscious beliefs and assumptions which may be influencing, and sometimes sabotaging, our intentions and actions.

Sometimes, we can determine these unconscious constructs by stating the opposite of the beliefs with which are consciously identifying. Our 12th house planets and signs may give us clues to these unconscious influences.

For example, if we have a 2nd house Neptune in Sagittarius, we may be motivated by a social service ethic, and choose to work at low wages teaching English to the urban poor because we believe in the value of helping the disadvantaged. But our 12th house Pluto may alert

ECLIPSE & LUNATION TABLES
BY ZODIACAL DEGREE

LUNATIONS BY SIGN 1960 TO 1995

from 0° Aries to 17° Cancer

DEGREE	DATE	Lunation	DEGREE	DATE	Lunation	DEGREE	DATE	Lunation	DEGREE	DATE	Lunation
00♈14	9/23/72	Full	26♈34	4/16/69	New	23♉50	5/14/80	New	20Ⅱ38	6/11/72	New
00 24	9/23/91	Full	26 43	4/16/88	New	23 50	11/16/86	Full	20 38	12/12/89	Full
00 49	3/21/85	New	27 49	10/21/64	Full	24 09	11/17/67	Full	21 02	6/12/91	New
01 07	3/22/66	New	27 56	10/22/83	Full	25 16	5/15/88	New	21 57	6/13/61	New
01 11	9/24/61	Full	28 17	4/18/77	New*	25 17	5/16/69	New	22 00	6/12/80	New
01 35	9/24/80	Full	29 15	10/22/72	Full	25 42	11/18/94	Full*	22 10	12/14/78	Full
02 35	9/25/69	Full*	29 33	10/23/91	Full	25 58	11/18/75	Full	23 32	6/14/88	New
02 40	3/23/93	New	00♉05	4/20/85	New	27 03	5/18/77	New	23 41	6/14/69	New
02 52	3/23/74	New	00 14	10/23/61	Full	27 21	11/19/64	Full	24 01	12/16/86	Full
02 55	9/25/88	Full	00 18	4/20/66	New	27 37	11/20/83	Full	24 19	12/16/67	Full
04 07	9/27/77	Full*	00 36	10/23/80	Full	28 44	11/20/72	Full	25 28	6/16/77	New
04 08	3/25/63	New	01 46	10/25/69	Full	28 50	5/19/85	New*	25 55	12/17/94	Full
04 26	3/25/82	New	01 52	4/21/93	New	28 55	5/20/66	New*	26 03	12/18/75	Full
05 29	3/26/71	New	01 55	4/22/74	New	29 08	11/21/91	Full	27 07	6/18/66	New
05 48	9/29/85	Full	01 59	10/25/88	Full	29 51	11/22/61	Full	27 11	6/18/85	New
05 53	3/26/90	New	02 58	4/23/63	New	00Ⅱ07	11/22/80	Full	27 14	12/19/64	Full*
06 05	9/29/66	Full	03 21	4/23/82	New	00 24	5/21/74	New	27 36	12/20/83	Full*
06 39	3/27/60	New*	03 27	10/26/77	Full	00 31	5/21/93	New*	28 30	6/20/74	New*
06 51	3/28/79	New	04 19	4/25/71	New	01 19	5/23/63	New	28 37	12/20/72	Full
07 37	9/30/93	Full	04 43	4/25/90	New	01 32	11/23/69	Full	29 03	12/21/91	Full*
07 52	10/01/74	New	05 15	10/28/85	Full*	01 35	11/23/88	Full	29 23	6/21/63	New
08 18	3/29/87	New*	05 32	10/29/66	Full*	01 44	5/23/82	New	29 47	6/21/82	New
08 19	3/28/68	New*	05 40	4/25/60	New	02 42	5/24/71	New	29 56	12/22/61	Full
09 15	10/03/63	Full	05 43	4/26/79	New	03 03	5/24/90	New	00♋03	12/21/80	Full
09 30	10/03/82	Full	07 06	10/30/93	Full	03 21	11/25/77	Full	00 49	6/22/71	New
09 54	3/30/95	New	07 14	10/31/74	Full	04 10	5/26/79	New	01 05	6/22/90	New
10 07	3/30/76	New	07 15	4/28/87	New	04 17	5/25/60	New	01 37	12/23/88	Full
10 37	10/04/71	Full	07 25	4/27/68	New	05 13	11/27/85	Full	01 44	12/23/69	Full
11 00	10/04/90	Full	08 25	11/01/63	Full	05 25	11/26/66	Full	02 23	6/24/79	New
11 41	10/04/60	Full	08 46	11/01/82	Full	05 49	5/27/87	New	02 28	12/24/92	New*
11 57	4/01/84	New	08 56	4/29/95	New*	06 04	5/27/68	New	02 37	6/24/60	New
11 58	10/05/79	Full	09 13	4/29/76	New*	07 01	11/29/74	Full*	03 37	12/25/77	Full
12 03	4/02/65	New	09 48	11/02/71	Full	07 03	11/29/93	Full*	04 07	6/26/87	New
13 17	10/06/68	Full*	10 13	11/02/90	Full	07 34	5/29/95	New	04 23	6/25/68	New
13 22	10/07/87	Full*	10 53	5/01/65	New	07 49	5/29/76	New	05 00	5/27/91	Full*
13 35	4/03/73	New	10 57	5/01/84	New	08 03	11/30/63	Full	05 29	12/27/85	Full
13 42	4/03/92	New	11 04	11/03/60	Full	08 28	12/01/82	Full	05 32	12/27/66	Full
14 33	4/04/62	New	11 13	11/04/79	Full	09 13	5/30/65	New*	05 54	6/28/95	New
14 54	10/08/95	Full*	12 18	5/02/73	New	09 26	5/30/84	New*	06 04	6/27/76	New
14 58	4/04/81	New	12 34	5/02/92	New	09 28	12/02/71	Full	07 02	12/29/74	Full
15 02	10/08/76	Full	12 44	11/05/87	Full	09 52	12/02/90	Full	07 14	6/29/65	New
15 57	4/06/70	New	12 49	11/05/68	Full	10 33	6/01/73	New	07 34	6/29/84	New
16 19	4/06/89	New	13 14	5/04/62	New	10 55	6/01/92	New	08 01	12/30/63	Full*
16 52	10/09/84	Full	13 37	5/04/81	New	10 59	12/03/79	Full	08 27	12/30/82	Full*
17 04	10/10/65	Full	14 24	11/07/95	Full	11 01	12/03/60	Full	08 32	6/30/73	New*
17 27	4/07/78	New*	14 41	5/05/70	New	11 32	6/02/62	New	09 30	12/31/71	Full
18 39	10/12/73	Full	14 41	11/06/76	Full*	11 50	6/02/81	New	09 38	7/01/62	New
18 40	10/11/92	Full	14 57	5/05/89	New	12 38	12/05/87	Full	09 50	7/01/81	New
19 06	4/09/86	New*	16 17	5/07/78	New	12 53	12/04/68	Full	09 50	12/31/90	Full
19 22	4/09/67	New	16 30	11/08/84	Full*	13 04	6/04/70	New	11 07	1/02/80	Full
19 42	10/13/62	Full	16 33	11/09/65	Full	13 12	6/03/89	New	11 15	7/03/89	New
20 06	10/13/81	Full	18 01	5/08/86	New	14 27	12/06/95	New	11 16	7/03/70	New
20 53	4/10/94	New	18 03	11/10/73	Full	14 45	6/05/78	New	11 19	1/01/61	Full
21 04	10/14/70	Full	18 14	11/10/92	Full	14 46	12/06/76	Full	12 02	7/03/93	Full
21 10	4/11/75	New	18 18	5/09/67	New*	16 25	12/08/65	Full*	12 54	1/04/88	Full
21 28	10/14/89	Full	19 02	11/11/62	Full	16 32	12/08/84	Full	13 01	7/05/78	New
22 32	10/16/78	Full	19 27	11/11/81	Full	16 32	6/07/86	New	13 13	1/03/69	Full
22 38	4/12/64	New	19 48	5/10/94	New*	16 44	6/08/67	New	13 51	1/04/92	New*
22 50	4/13/83	New	19 59	5/11/75	New*	17 51	12/10/71	Full*	14 48	7/07/86	New
24 00	4/13/72	New	20 30	11/13/70	Full	18 10	12/09/92	Full*	14 53	7/07/67	New
24 07	10/17/86	Full*	20 50	11/13/89	Full	18 17	6/09/94	New	15 03	1/05/77	Full
24 21	10/18/67	Full*	21 10	5/11/64	New	18 19	6/09/75	New	16 21	7/09/75	New
24 21	4/14/91	New	21 30	5/12/83	New	18 52	12/11/63	Full	16 28	1/07/66	Full
25 01	4/15/61	New	22 06	11/14/78	Full	19 13	12/11/81	Full	16 29	7/08/94	New
25 20	4/15/80	New	22 30	5/13/72	New	19 19	6/10/64	New*	16 44	1/07/85	Full
25 53	10/19/94	Full	22 54	5/14/91	New	19 43	6/11/83	New*	17 16	7/09/64	New*
26 11	10/20/75	Full	23 38	5/14/61	New	20 26	12/12/70	Full	17 41	7/10/83	New

*indicates an eclipse.

us to the rage we feel at sacrificing ourselves for those of our clientele who are unwilling to help themselves. In time, we may need to redefine our beliefs and values in order clarify for ourselves those people whom we truly wish to help, and those for whom we are not willing to expend our energy.

One way to begin altering our beliefs about ourselves is through defining the beliefs we wish to have, and creating affirmations to reinforce them. However, affirmations are useless, and indeed counter-productive, if we cannot believe them, and if they provide only a thin veneer over life experiences of beliefs and actions which belie them.

For affirmations to be effective, we must be able to recall experiences we have had which reveal to us the validity of the affirmation about ourselves which we wish to reinforce (e.g., that we are capable of maintaining an exercise regime). We must be able to envision ourselves engaged in the action in question, and *believe* that we can do so. Otherwise, our affirmations will not only be impotent; they will stir up and activate our resistance, and our negative beliefs about ourselves.

This surfacing of the counter-belief is frequently a necessary stage in learning to create and use affirmations effectively. It is an indicator that we need to take time to come to terms with and disempower the negative thought-forms, and to revise our affirmation in a manner which takes into consideration other "planetary selves" and the real, limiting factors in our lives.

Let's consider, for example, that we have Uranus in Virgo rising, ruling our 6th house, and that too often, we have forfeited work references and financial stability because we suddenly walked out of a job without giving notice. Creating the affirmation, "I will make a long-term commitment to my next job" may be unrealistic, given our Uranus. A more realistic affirmation, taking into consideration the financial goals of our 9th house Saturn in Taurus might be: "I can and will give two weeks notice on my next job when and if I choose to quit."

CONCLUSION

All of our planets have lessons to teach us, as does every transit and progression. The transits and progressions of the five outer planets in particular are guides to "the next step in our becoming," and therefore deserve our greatest attention.

- Under Jupiter, we might ask ourselves: How may I expand in this area of my life, be open to new opportunities, and develop my understanding?

- Saturn asks us to finish the unfinished, to commit to tasks or persons important to us, to persevere, to act responsibly, and to demonstrate our ability to cope with obstacles.

- When we experience a Uranus transit, we need to create space to prepare for the unexpected, to embrace dramatic change, to open ourselves to more radical modes of thinking, and to dare to be fully who we are.

- Neptune asks us to surrender to the flow of life, to open to our vulnerability and compassion, and to awaken our creativity and spirituality. In enriching our imagination, Neptune contributes to our capacity to envision a more satisfying future. We most befriend Neptune when we learn to "go where the clarity is" and follow our Muse.

- Pluto, in contrast, asks us to "go where the energy is"—the energy of our aliveness and passion. Pluto enables us to unleash the energy trapped at the core of ourselves in order to transform and heal. Where we have been powerless, we can become empowered, but first we may need to come to terms with our rage and our shadow selves.

The planets are not merely outside us; they are also within us. As we become capable of listening to their messages, we become freer to discover and fulfill our personal destinies.

If you see the path before you too clearly, it may be path carved from your past. Keep looking; keep listening.

If the path is barely discernible, but the step before you is visible and clear—and when you set your foot upon it, the next step appears—move forward.

If further ahead all you discern is dark empty space, do not be afraid. It may be a quantum space, over which you may leap, and which will propel you into another reality, another future, much larger and more resplendent than the one you have known. Trust.

You are not in control of your life, nor are you a passive victim of circumstance. You are a co-creator, capable of living in harmony with your planetary selves, and co-creating your life with the universe.

ELEMENTAL

HAIKUS, BY TRACY MARKS

The four elements:
Fire, earth, air and water.
Let them be your guides.

FIRE

Singed by light and fire?
Like a moth drawn to the flame?
Then let the past burn.

Craving heat and warmth?
Fleeing from winter's cold? Wrap
Yourself in blankets.

EARTH

Hemmed in by steep walls?
Locked doors? Wait. Look toward the roof.
There is a ladder.

Buried underground?
Weighted down by life's demands?
Dig roots into soil.

AIR

Scattered by the wind?
Let yourself be blown apart.
You will become whole.

Flying far too high?
Lost sight of the earth? Glide on.
Wing your way toward God.

WATER

Battling with fog?
Do not resist. Cling to the
Ground or soar above.

Dragged underwater?
Sink deep. Surrender to grief.
You will rise again.

LUNATIONS BY SIGN 1960 TO 1995

from 17° Cancer to 6° Scorpio											
Degree	**Date**	**Lunation**	**Degree**	**Date**	**Lunation**	**Degree**	**Date**	**Lunation**	**Degree**	**Date**	**Lunation**
17♋51	1/08/84	Full	15♌40	8/08/83	New	12♍58	9/05/94	New	09♎56	10/03/67	New
18 37	7/10/72	New*	16 24	2/05/66	Fun	13 18	3/03/88	Full*	10 16	10/03/86	New*
18 59	1/09/63	Fun*	16 43	8/09/72	New	13 28	3/04/69	Full	11 03	3/31/80	Full
19 14	1/09/82	Full*	16 47	2/05/85	Full	13 36	9/06/64	New	11 16	10/05/75	New
20 04	7/12/80	New	16 59	8/10/91	New	13 55	9/07/83	New	11 16	4/01/61	Fun
20 10	7/12/61	New	17 48	2/06/74	Full	15 01	3/05/77	Full	11 41	10/04/94	New
20 40	1/11/71	Full	18 13	8/11/71	Full	15 10	9/07/72	New	12 27	10/05/64	New
20 42	1/11/90	Full	18 17	8/10/80	New*	15 18	9/08/91	New	12 38	10/06/83	New
21 41	7/13/88	New	18 31	8/11/61	New*	16 02	3/07/66	Full	12 51	4/02/69	Full*
21 56	7/14/69	New	19 08	2/08/63	Full	16 27	3/07/85	Full	12 51	4/02/88	Full
22 30	1/13/79	Full	19 14	2/08/82	Full	16 52	9/09/80	New	14 09	10/07/72	New
22 34	7/14/92	Fun	20 00	8/12/88	New	17 10	9/10/61	New	14 17	4/04/77	Full*
22 49	1/13/60	Full	20 17	8/13/69	New	17 27	3/08/84	Full	14 17	10/07/91	New
23 42	7/16/77	New	20 47	2/09/90	Full*	17 50	3/08/93	Full	15 13	4/05/66	Full
24 24	1/15/87	Fun	20 55	2/10/71	Full*	18 40	9/11/88	New*	15 38	4/05/85	Fun
24 35	1/15/68	Fun	21 58	8/14/77	New	18 53	9/11/69	New*	15 58	10/09/80	New
25 07	7/18/66	New	22 47	2/12/79	Full	18 57	3/09/82	Full	16 14	10/09/61	New
25 19	7/17/85	New	23 01	2/12/60	Full	19 01	3/10/63	Full	16 41	4/06/74	Full
25 20	1/15/91	New*	23 10	8/16/66	New	20 29	9/13/77	New	16 58	4/06/93	Full
26 12	1/17/76	Full	23 29	8/16/85	New	20 37	3/11/90	Full	17 48	10/10/88	New
26 15	1/16/95	Full	24 29	8/17/74	New	20 52	3/12/71	Full	17 54	10/11/69	Full
26 27	7/19/74	New	24 37	2/13/87	Full	21 31	9/14/66	New	18 15	4/08/82	Full
27 15	1/17/65	Full	24 38	2/14/68	Full	21 55	9/14/85	New	18 28	4/09/63	Full
27 24	7/20/63	New*	24 53	8/17/93	New	22 42	3/13/79	Full*	19 24	10/12/77	New*
27 40	1/lfi/84	Full	25 37	8/19/63	New	22 47	3/13/60	Full*	20 00	4/10/90	Full
27 43	7/20/82	New*	25 48	8/19/82	New	22 52	9/16/74	New	20 18	4/10/71	Full
28 40	1/18/73	Full*	26 08	2/15/76	Full	23 16	9/15/93	New	20 21	10/14/66	New
28 56	7/22/71	New*	26 21	2/15/95	Full	24 14	9/17/63	New	20 47	10/14/85	New
29 04	7/22/90	New*	27 08	2/16/65	Full	24 16	3/14/68	Full	21 46	10/15/74	New
00♌10	1/20/81	Full*	27 15	8/20/71	New*	24 16	9/17/82	New	21 57	4/11/60	Full
00 14	1/20/62	Full	27 15	8/20/90	New	24 25	3/15/87	Full	22 02	4/12/79	Full
00 36	7/24/79	New	27 32	2/17/84	Full	25 39	3/16/76	Fun	22 08	10/15/93	New
00 52	7/23/60	New	28 37	2/17/73	Full	25 59	3/16/95	Fun	23 18	10/17/82	New
01 50	1/21/89	Full	28 55	2/18/92	Full	25 50	9/19/90	New	23 20	4/13/68	Full*
02 06	1/22/70	Full	29 01	8/22/79	New*	26 00	9/19/71	New	23 25	10/17/63	New
02 22	7/25/87	New	29 16	8/22/60	New	26 40	3/17/65	Full	23 38	4/14/87	Full*
02 35	7/25/68	New	00♍13	2/18/81	Full	27 01	3/17/84	Full	24 39	4/14/76	Full
03 59	1/24/78	Full	00 25	2/19/62	Full*	27 49	9/21/79	New	25 00	10/18/90	New
04 08	7/27/95	New	00 48	8/24/87	New	27 58	9/20/60	New*	25 04	4/15/95	Full
04 09	7/27/76	New	00 53	8/23/68	New	28 14	3/18/73	Full	25 17	10/19/71	New
05 10	7/28/65	New	01 59	2/20/89	Full*	28 24	3/18/92	Full	25 45	4/15/65	New
05 34	7/28/84	New	02 18	2/21/70	Full*	29 30	9/22/68	New*	26 00	4/15/84	Full
05 37	1/26/67	Full	02 22	8/25/76	New	29 34	9/23/87	New*	27 06	10/20/60	New
05 45	1/26/86	Full	02 29	8/26/95	New	29 56	3/20/81	Full	27 06	10/21/79	New
06 30	7/29/73	New	03 18	8/26/65	New	00♎13	3/21/62	Full	27 25	4/17/73	Full
06 54	7/29/92	New	03 43	8/26/84	New	00 54	9/23/76	New	27 26	4/17/92	Full
07 03	1/27/75	Full	04 04	2/23/78	Full	01 10	9/24/95	New	28 33	10/21/68	New
07 23	1/27/94	Full	04 41	8/28/73	New	01 45	3/22/89	Full	28 46	10/22/87	New
07 49	7/31/62	New*	05 03	8/27/92	New	01 51	9/25/65	New	29 10	4/19/81	Full
07 51	7/31/81	New*	05 26	2/24/67	Full	02 01	3/23/70	Full	29 28	4/20/62	Fun
08 05	1/28/64	Full	05 43	2/24/86	Full	02 14	9/25/84	New	29 55	10/23/76	New*
08 26	1/28/83	Full	06 10	8/29/81	New	03 20	9/26/73	New	00♏18	10/24/95	New*
09 22	8/01/89	New	06 16	8/30/62	New	03 35	9/26/92	New	00 57	10/24/65	New
09 32	8/02/70	New	06 49	2/26/75	Full	03 40	3/24/78	Full*	01 00	4/21/89	Full
09 39	1/30/72	Full*	07 13	2/25/94	Full	04 47	3/26/67	Full	01 09	4/21/70	Full
09 51	1/30/91	Full*	07 48	8/31/89	New*	04 57	9/28/81	New	01 16	10/24/84	New
11 19	8/04/78	New	07 57	2/27/64	Full	05 10	3/26/86	Full	02 34	10/26/73	New
11 22	2/01/80	Full	08 04	8/31/70	New*	05 12	9/28/62	New	02 39	4/23/78	Full
11 41	1/31/61	Full	08 12	2/27/83	Full	06 08	3/27/75	Full	02 41	10/25/92	New
12 58	8/06/67	New	09 39	2/29/72	Full	06 33	3/27/94	Full	03 37	4/24/67	Full*
13 02	8/05/86	New	09 40	2/28/91	Full	06 43	9/29/89	New	04 03	4/24/86	Full*
13 14	2/02/88	Full	09 50	9/02/78	New	07 01	9/30/70	New	04 19	10/27/81	New
13 31	2/02/69	Full	11 15	9/04/67	New	07 27	3/28/64	Full	04 38	10/28/62	New
14 22	8/07/75	New	11 26	3/01/80	Full*	07 33	3/28/83	Full	04 59	4/25/75	Full
14 38	8/07/94	New	11 28	9/04/86	New	08 43	10/02/78	New*	05 22	4/25/94	Full
15 14	2/04/77	Full	11 45	3/02/61	Full*	09 05	3/30/91	Full	06 11	10/29/89	New
15 17	8/07/64	New	12 36	9/05/75	New	09 14	3/29/72	Full	06 25	10/30/70	New

*indicates an eclipse.

LUNATIONS BY SIGN 1960 TO 1995

from 6° Scorpio to 23° Aquarius											
Degree	Date	Lunation	Degree	Date	Lunation	Degree	Date	Lunation	Degree	Date	Lunation
06♏26	4/28/83	Full	03♐25	5/25/75	Full*	00♑06	6/22/67	Fun	26♑55	1/17/80	New
06 31	4/26/64	Full	03 45	5/24/94	Full*	00 27	6/22/86	Fun	27 04	7/20/78	Full
08 03	10/31/78	New	04 16	11/26/81	New	00 49	12/22/65	New	27 56	1/18/69	New
08 04	4/28/91	Full	04 32	11/27/62	New	00 49	12/22/84	New	28 09	7/21/67	Full
08 19	4/28/72	Full	04 57	5/26/83	Full	01 36	6/23/75	Full	28 21	1/19/88	New
09 07	11/02/67	New*	05 09	5/26/64	Full	01 47	6/23/94	Full	28 23	7/21/86	Full
09 31	11/02/86	New*	06 08	11/28/89	New	02 40	12/24/73	New*	29 24	1/19/77	New
10 06	4/30/80	Full	06 14	11/28/70	New	02 28	12/23/92	New*	29 46	7/23/75	Full
10 10	4/30/61	Full	06 39	5/28/91	Full	03 14	6/25/83	Full*	01♒00	1/21/85	New
10 29	11/03/75	New*	06 56	5/28/72	Full	03 30	6/25/64	Full*	01 10	1/21/66	New
10 54	11/03/94	New	07 46	11/30/78	New	04 33	12/26/81	New	01 29	7/24/83	Full
11 37	5/02/69	Full	08 32	5/30/61	Full	04 42	12/26/62	New	01 45	7/24/64	Full
11 48	5/01/88	Full	08 38	5/29/80	Full	05 00	6/26/91	Full*	02 46	1/22/93	New
11 54	11/04/64	New	08 47	12/01/67	New	05 14	6/26/72	Full	03 04	1/23/74	New
11 56	11/04/83	New	09 12	12/01/86	New	06 17	12/28/70	New	03 16	8/26/91	Full*
12 58	5/03/77	Full	09 54	5/31/69	Full	06 22	12/28/89	New	03 24	7/26/72	Full*
13 32	11/06/91	New	10 12	5/31/88	Full	06 34	6/28/61	Full	04 31	7/27/61	Full
13 44	11/06/72	New	10 13	12/03/75	New	06 48	6/28/80	Full	04 52	7/27/80	Full*
13 56	5/04/66	Full*	10 35	12/02/94	New	07 44	12/29/78	New	04 52	1/25/63	New*
14 17	5/04/85	Full*	11 13	6/01/77	Full	07 52	6/29/69	Full	04 54	1/25/82	New*
15 27	5/06/74	Full	11 47	12/04/83	New*	08 15	6/29/88	Full	05 49	7/29/69	Full
15 36	11/07/80	New	11 56	12/04/64	New*	08 46	12/31/67	New	06 14	7/29/88	Full
15 38	5/06/93	Full	12 28	6/03/66	Full	09 08	12/31/86	New	06 21	1/26/71	New
15 46	11/08/61	New	12 31	6/03/85	Full	09 11	7/01/77	Full	06 35	1/26/90	New*
17 07	5/08/82	Full	13 31	12/06/91	New	10 19	1/01/76	New	07 09	7/30/77	Full
17 21	11/09/69	New	13 49	12/05/72	New	10 27	7/02/66	Full	07 20	1/28/60	New
17 24	5/08/63	Full	13 54	6/04/74	Full*	10 33	7/02/85	Full	07 44	1/28/79	New
17 24	11/09/88	New	13 55	6/04/93	Full*	10 33	1/01/95	New	08 36	7/31/85	Full
18 47	5/11/77	New	15 37	6/06/82	Full	12 00	1/03/84	New	08 40	8/01/66	Full
18 54	5/09/90	Full	15 39	12/07/61	New	12 02	7/03/93	New	08 50	1/29/68	New
19 10	5/10/71	Full	15 40	12/07/80	New	12 10	7/04/74	Full	09 07	1/29/87	New
19 45	11/12/66	New*	15 53	6/07/63	Full	12 17	1/02/65	New	10 12	8/02/93	Full
20 09	11/12/85	New*	17 09	12/09/69	New	13 51	1/04/92	New*	10 27	8/03/74	Full
20 32	5/11/60	Full	17 22	12/09/88	New	13 55	7/06/82	Full	10 30	1/31/76	New
20 46	5/12/79	Full	17 24	6/08/90	Full	14 06	7/06/63	Full*	10 35	1/30/95	New
21 16	11/14/74	New	17 32	6/09/71	Full	14 10	1/04/73	New*	12 12	8/04/82	Full
21 32	11/13/93	New*	18 33	12/10/77	New	15 38	7/08/71	Full	12 15	8/05/63	Full
21 51	5/12/68	Full	18 40	6/09/60	Full	15 39	7/08/90	Full	12 19	2/01/84	New
22 14	5/13/87	Full	19 01	6/10/79	Full	15 43	1/06/62	New	12 38	2/01/65	New
22 56	11/15/82	New	19 38	12/12/66	New	15 54	1/06/81	New	13 41	8/06/71	Full*
23 10	5/13/76	Full*	19 59	12/12/85	New	16 36	7/08/60	Full	13 52	8/06/90	Full*
23 11	11/16/63	New	19 59	6/10/68	Full	17 01	7/09/79	Full	14 12	2/03/92	New
23 35	5/14/95	Full	20 24	6/11/87	Full	17 09	1/07/70	New	14 25	2/03/73	New
24 26	5/15/65	Full	21 17	12/13/74	New*	17 29	1/07/89	New	14 35	8/07/60	Full
24 31	5/15/84	Full*	21 19	6/12/76	Full	17 55	7/10/68	Full	15 00	8/08/79	Full
24 45	11/17/90	New	21 23	12/13/93	New	18 20	7/11/87	Full	15 43	2/05/62	New*
25 03	11/18/71	New	21 42	5/13/95	Full	18 32	1/09/78	New	15 58	8/08/68	Full
26 01	5/16/92	Full	22 45	6/13/84	Full*	19 20	7/11/76	Full	16 02	2/04/81	New*
26 09	5/17/73	Full	22 48	6/14/65	Full*	19 38	7/12/95	Full	16 19	8/09/87	Full
26 39	11/18/60	New	23 04	12/15/82	New*	19 49	1/10/67	New	17 05	2/06/70	New
26 48	11/19/79	New	23 23	12/16/63	New	19 58	1/10/86	New	17 29	8/09/76	Full
27 56	5/19/81	Full	24 20	6/15/92	Full*	20 52	7/13/84	Full	17 30	2/06/89	New
28 04	11/20/68	New	24 35	6/15/73	Full*	21 04	7/13/65	Full	17 39	8/10/95	Full
28 08	5/19/62	Full	24 58	12/17/90	New	21 31	1/11/94	New	18 29	2/07/78	New
28 24	11/21/87	New	25 11	12/17/71	New	21 35	1/12/75	New	19 08	8/11/84	Full
29 27	11/21/76	New	26 19	6/17/81	Full	22 34	7/14/92	Full	19 24	8/12/65	Full
29 41	5/21/70	Full	26 22	6/18/62	Full	22 51	7/15/73	Full*	19 58	2/09/86	New
29 42	5/20/89	Full	26 32	12/18/60	New	23 27	1/14/83	New	20 00	2/09/67	New
29 52	11/22/95	New	26 50	12/19/79	New	23 43	1/14/64	New*	20 55	8/13/92	Full
00♐40	11/23/65	New*	27 27	6/19/70	Full	24 25	7/17/92	Full*	21 09	8/14/73	Full
00 50	1/22/84	New*	27 56	12/19/68	New	24 31	7/17/81	Full*	21 38	1/10/94	New
01 05	5/22/78	Full	27 59	6/19/89	Full	25 20	1/15/91	New*	21 51	2/11/75	New
02 00	5/23/67	Full	28 20	12/20/87	New	25 25	1/16/72	New*	22 30	8/15/62	Full*
02 21	11/24/92	New	29 08	6/20/78	Full	25 46	7/18/70	Full	22 45	8/15/81	Full
02 24	11/24/73	New	29 21	12/21/76	New	26 04	7/18/89	Full	23 44	2/13/83	New
02 25	5/23/86	Full	29 45	12/21/95	New	26 32	1/16/61	New	23 49	8/17/70	Fun*

*indicates an eclipse.

LUNATIONS BY SIGN 1960 TO 1995

from 23° Aquarius to 29° Pisces

Degree	Date	Lunation	Degree	Date	Lunation	Degree	Date	Lunation	Degree	Date	Lunation
23♒52	2/13/64	New	03♓33	8/26/80	Full*	12♓15	9/05/90	Full	20♓62	9/14/62	Full
24 12	8/17/89	Full*	03 13	2/22/74	New	12 22	3/02/84	New	21 13	9/14/81	Full
25 07	8/18/78	Full	03 58	8/27/69	Full*	12 37	3/03/65	New	21 29	3/12/94	New
25 26	2/15/72	New	04 23	8/27/88	Full*	12 53	9/05/60	Full*	21 47	3/12/75	New
25 31	2/15/91	New	04 45	2/24/63	New	13 16	9/06/79	Full*	22 12	9/15/70	Full*
26 24	8/20/67	Full	04 56	2/23/82	New	14 14	3/04/92	New	22 37	9/15/89	Full
26 25	2/15/61	New*	05 24	8/28/77	Full	14 17	3/05/73	New	23 32	3/14/64	New
26 29	8/19/86	Full	06 09	2/25/71	New*	14 21	9/06/68	Full	23 33	9/16/78	Full*
26 50	2/16/80	New*	06 30	2/25/90	New	14 35	9/07/87	Full	23 35	3/14/83	New
27 50	2/16/69	New*	06 57	8/30/85	Full	15 23	3/06/62	New	25 00	3/15/72	New
28 00	8/21/94	Full	07 09	8/31/66	Full	15 46	3/06/81	New	25 01	9/18/86	Full
28 08	8/21/75	Full	07 10	2/26/60	New	15 59	9/08/76	Full	25 05	9/18/67	Full
28 12	2/17/88	New	07 29	2/26/79	New*	16 00	9/09/95	Full	25 14	3/16/91	New
29 22	2/18/77	New	08 41	9/01/93	Full	16 44	3/04/70	New*	25 57	3/16/61	New
29 55	8/23/83	Full	08 45	2/28/68	New	17 10	3/07/89	New*	26 21	3/16/80	New
00♓06	8/23/64	Full	08 54	2/28/87	New	17 45	9/10/84	Full	26 39	9/19/94	Full
01 05	2/19/85	New	08 58	9/01/74	Full	18 01	9/10/65	Fun	26 54	9/20/75	Full
01 21	2/20/66	New	10 25	3/01/95	New	18 10	3/09/78	New	27 25	3/18/69	New*
01 40	8/24/72	Full	10 31	2/29/76	New	19 34	9/12/92	Full	27 42	3/18/88	New*
01 41	8/25/91	Full	10 34	9/03/63	Full	19 42	9/12/73	Full	28 42	9/22/83	Full
02 39	8/26/61	Full*	10 41	9/03/82	Full	19 44	3/10/86	New	28 45	9/21/64	Full
02 55	2/21/93	New	11 57	9/05/71	Full	19 55	3/11/67	New	29 02	3/19/77	New

*indicates an eclipse.

LUNATIONS BY SIGN 1996 TO 2015

from 00° Aries to 29° Gemini								
ARIES			**TAURUS**			**GEMINI**		
Degree	Date	Lunation	Degree	Date	Lunation	Degree	Date	Lunation
00:15	10/23/10	Full	01:10	10/24/99	Full	00:21	5/20/12	New*
00:39	03/20/04	New	01:35	04/21/12	New	00:32	11/23/99	Full
01:56	09/25/99	Full	02:23	10/26/07	Full	01:55	11/24/07	Full
02:22	03/22/12	New	03:21	10/26/96	Full	02:03	05/23/01	New
03:20	09/26/07	Full	03:22	04/23/01	New	03:10	11/25/96	Full
04:17	09/27/96	Full**	03:45	10/27/15	Full	03:20	11/25/15	Full
04:25	03/25/01	New	05:02	10/28/04	Full**	03:28	05/24/09	New
04:40	09/28/15	Full**	05:04	04/25/09	New	04:23	05/25/98	New
05:45	09/28/04	Full	06:03	04/26/98	New	04:55	11/26/04	Full
06:08	03/26/09	New	06:06	10/29/12	Full	05:48	05/27/06	New
07:15	03/28/98	New	07:24	04/27/06	New	06:47	11/28/12	Full**
07:22	09/30/12	Full	08:52	11/01/01	Full	07:21	05/28/14	New
08:35	03/29/06	Full**	08:52	04/29/14	New*	08:43	11/30/01	Full
09:26	10/02/01	Full				09:20	05/31/03	New*
09:59	03/30/14	New	10:30	11/09/09	Full	10:15	12/02/09	Full
			10:43	05/01/03	New	11:02	06/01/11	New*
11:10	10/04/09	Full	11:35	11/04/98	Full	11:15	12/03/98	Full
11:39	04/01/03	New	12:31	05/03/11	New	12:15	06/02/00	New
12:23	10/05/98	Full	12:58	11/05/06	Full	12:43	12/06/06	Full
12:58	11/05/06	Full	14:01	05/05/00	New	13:34	06/03/08	New
13:30	04/03/11	New	14:26	11/06/14	Full	14:18	12/06/14	Full
13:43	10/07/06	Full	15:22	05/05/08	New	14:40	06/05/97	New
15:05	10/08/14	Full**	16:13	11/09/03	Full**	16:16	06/06/05	New
15:16	04/04/00	New	16:21	05/06/97	New	16:20	12/08/03	Full
16:35	10/10/03	Full	17:52	05/08/05	New	18:01	06/08/13	New
16:44	04/06/08	New	18:05	11/10/11	Full	18:11	12/10/11	Full**
17:40	04/07/97	New	19:31	05/10/13	New*	19:38	12/11/00	Full
18:24	10/12/11	Full	19:47	11/11/00	Full	19:54	06/10/02	New*
19:06	04/08/05	New*						
20:19	10/13/00	Full	21:15	11/13/08	Full	21:02	12/12/08	Full
20:41	04/10/13	New	21:32	05/12/02	New	21:24	06/12/10	New
21:51	10/14/08	Full	22:15	11/14/97	Full	22:08	12/14/97	Full
22:42	04/12/02	New	23:09	05/14/10	New	22:20	06/13/99	New
22:49	10/16/97	Full	23:46	11/16/05	Full	23:41	06/15/07	New
24:13	10/17/05	Full**	24:14	05/15/99	New	23:48	12/15/05	Full
24:27	04/14/10	New	25:26	11/17/13	Full	25:07	06/16/15	New
25:45	04/16/99	New	25:33	05/16/07	New	25:12	06/16/96	New
25:45	10/18/13	Full*	26:51	05/17/96	New	25:36	12/17/13	Full
27:05	04/17/07	New	26:56	05/18/15	New	26:57	06/17/04	New
27:43	10/21/02	Full	27:33	11/20/02	Full**	27:42	12/19/02	Full
028:15	04/17/96	New*	28:33	05/19/04	New	28:43	06/19/12	New
28:25	04/18/15	New	29:18	11/21/10	Full	29:21	12/21/10	Full**
29:33	10/23/10	Full						
29:49	04/19/04	New*						

*indicates a New Moon (solar) eclipse.

**indicates a Full Moon (lunar) eclipse.

LUNATIONS BY SIGN 1996 TO 2015

from 00° Cancer to 29° Virgo

CANCER			LEO			VIRGO		
Degree	Date	Lunation	Degree	Date	Lunation	Degree	Date	Lunation
0:10	06/21/01	New*	0:26	01/21/00	Full**	00:20	02/19/00	full**
0:25	12/22/99	Full	0:31	07/23/98	New	00:31	08/23/06	New
01:30	06/22/09	New	01:54	01/22/08	Full	01:53	02/21/08	Full**
01:50	12/24/07	Full	02:07	07/25/06	New	02:19	08/25/14	New
02:27	06/24/98	New	03:40	01/23/97	Full	03:51	02/22/97	Full
03:20	12/24/96	Full	03:52	07/26/14	New	04:02	08/27/03	New
03:20	12/25/15	Full	05:34	01/25/05	Full	05:27	08/29/11	New
03:58	06/25/06	New	05:46	07/29/03	New	05:41	02/24/05	Full
05:12	12/26/04	Full	07:16	07/30/11	New	06:23	08/29/00	New
05:37	6/27/14	New	07:24	01/27/13	Full	07:24	02/25/13	Full
07:06	12/28/12	Full	08:01	07/31/00	New*	07:48	08/30/08	New
07:37	06/29/03	New	08:51	01/28/02	Full	08:36	02/27/02	Full
08:48	12/30/01	Full**	09:32	08/01/08	New*	09:34	09/01/97	New*
09:12	07/01/11	New*				09:59	02/28/10	Full
10:14	07/01/00	New*	10:15	01/30/10	Full			
10:15	12/31/09	Full**	11:02	08/03/97	New	11:15	03/02/99	Full
11:15	01/02/99	Full	11:20	01/31/99	Full**	11:21	09/03/05	New
11:32	07/03/08	New	12:48	08/05/05	New	13:00	03/03/07	Full**
12:48	07/04/97	New	12:59	02/02/07	Full	13:04	09/05/13	New
12:48	01/03/07	Full	14:35	08/06/13	New	14:20	09/07/02	New
14:31	07/06/05	New	14:48	02/03/15	Full	14:50	03/05/15	Full
14:31	07/05/15	New	15:07	02/04/96	Full	15:06	03/05/96	Full
14:48	01/05/96	Full	16:04	08/08/02	New	15:41	09/08/10	New
16:18	07/08/13	New	16:54	02/06/04	Full	16:43	03/06/04	Full
16:40	01/07/04	Full	17:25	08/10/10	New	16:47	09/09/99	New
18:00	07/10/02	New	18:21	08/11/99	New*	18:13	03/08/12	Full
18:26	01/09/12	Full	18:32	02/07/12	Full	18:25	09/11/07	New*
19:24	07/11/10	New*	19:35	02/08/01	Full	19:12	03/09/01	Full
19:39	01/09/01	Full**	19:51	08/12/07	New	19:17	09/12/11	New
20:17	07/13/99	New						
21:02	01/11/09	Full	20:41	08/13/11	New	20:10	09/13/15	New
21:41	07/14/07	New	21:00	02/09/09	Full**	20:27	09/12/96	New
22:28	01/12/98	Full	21:31	08/14/15	New	20:40	03/11/09	Full
23:14	07/16/15	New	21:47	08/14/96	New	22:06	09/14/04	New
23:26	07/05/96	New	22:29	02/11/98	Full	22:24	03/13/98	Full**
24:05	01/14/06	Full	23:31	08/16/04	New	23:37	09/16/12	New
25:13	07/17/04	New	24:20	02/13/06	Full	24:15	03/14/06	Full**
25:58	01/16/14	Full	25:08	08/17/12	New	24:36	09/17/01	New
26:55	07/19/12	New	26:12	08/19/01	New	25:59	09/18/09	New
27:55	01/18/03	Full	26:13	02/14/14	Full	26:02	03/16/14	Full
28:09	07/20/01	New	27:32	08/20/09	New	27:25	03/18/03	Full
29:27	07/22/09	New*	27:54	02/16/03	Full	27:32	09/20/98	New
29:27	01/19/11	Full	28:48	08/22/98	New*	28:48	03/19/11	Full
			29:20	02/18/11	Full	29:20	09/22/06	New*
						29:53	03/20/00	Full

*indicates a New Moon (solar) eclipse.
**indicates a Full Moon (lunar) eclipse.

LUNATIONS BY SIGN 1996 TO 2015

from 1° Libra to 29° Sagittarius

LIBRA			SCORPIO			SAGITTARIUS		
Degree	Date	Lunation	Degree	Date	Lunation	Degree	Date	Lunation
01:08	09/24/14	New	00:25	10/23/14	New	00:07	11/22/14	New
01:31	03/21/08	Full	00:43	04/20/08	Full	01:14	11/23/03	New*
02:38	09/26/03	New	01:41	10/25/03	New	01:19	05/22/97	Full
03:35	03/24/97	Full**	02:45	04/22/97	Full	02:27	11/25/11	New*
04:00	9/27/11	New	03:03	10/26/11	New	02:47	05/23/05	Full
05:00	09/27/00	New	04:12	10/27/00	New	04:00	11/25/00	New
05:18	03/25/05	Full	04:20	04/24/05	Full**	04:08	05/25/13	Full**
06:33	09/29/08	New	05:54	10/28/08	New	05:04	05/26/02	Full**
06:52	03/27/13	Full	06:41	04/27/02	Full	05:49	11/27/08	New
07:54	03/28/02	Full	08:01	10/31/97	New	06:33	05/27/10	Full
08:33	10/01/97	New	08:07	04/28/10	Full	7:54	11/30/97	New
09:17	03/30/10	Full	09:43	11/02/05	New	8:26	05/30/99	Full
10:19	03/31/99	Full	09:49	04/30/99	Full	09:31	12/01/05	New
10:19	10/03/05	New*						
10:46	03/31/99	Full	11:16	11/03/13	New*	10:12	06/01/07	Full
11:56	10/05/13	New	11:38	05/02/07	Full	10:59	12/03/13	New
12:35	04/02/07	Full	12:15	11/04/02	New	11:37	06/01/96	Full
13:02	10/06/02	New	13:19	05/03/96	Full	11:49	06/02/15	Full
13:04	09/05/13	New	13:23	05/04/15	Full	11:58	12/04/02	New*
14:24	10/07/10	New	13:40	11/06/10	New	12:56	06/03/04	Full
14:24	04/04/15	Full**	14:42	05/04/04	Full**	13:29	12/05/10	New
14:31	04/04/96	Full**	15:17	11/08/99	New	14:14	06/04/12	Full**
15:44	10/9/99	New	16:01	05/06/12	Full	15:22	12/07/99	New
16:00	04/05/04	Full	17:04	05/07/01	Full	15:26	06/06/01	Full
17:23	04/06/12	Full	17:10	11/09/07	New	17:07	06/07/09	Full
17:30	10/11/07	New	18:41	05/09/09	Full	17:16	12/09/07	New
18:22	04/08/01	Full	19:01	11/11/15	New	18:56	12/10/96	New
19:20	10/13/15	New	19:03	11/11/96	New	19:03	12/11/15	New
19:32	10/12/96	New*				19:06	06/10/98	Full
19:53	04/09/09	Full	20:33	11/12/04	New			
			20:42	05/11/98	Full	20:22	12/12/04	New
21:06	10/14/04	New	21:57	11/13/12	New*	20:41	06/11/06	Full
21:49	04/11/98	Full	22:23	05/13/06	Full	21:45	12/13/12	New
22:32	10/15/12	New	22:58	11/15/01	New	22:06	06/13/14	Full
23:30	10/16/01	New	23:55	05/14/14	Full	22:56	12/14/01	New*
23:37	04/13/06	Full	24:34	11/16/09	New	23:00	06/14/03	Full
24:59	10/18/09	New	24:53	05/16/03	Full**	24:23	06/15/11	Full**
25:16	04/15/14	Full**	26:13	05/17/11	Full	24:40	12/16/09	New
26:24	04/16/03	Full	26:38	11/19/98	New	26:03	06/16/00	Full
26:49	10/20/98	New	27:40	05/18/00	Full	26:48	12/18/98	New
27:44	04/18/11	Full	28:27	11/20/06	New	27:50	06/18/08	Full
28:40	10/22/06	New	29:27	05/20/08	Full	28:33	12/20/06	New
28:59	04/18/00	Full				29:29	06/20/97	Full

*indicates a New Moon (solar) eclipse.
**indicates a Full Moon (lunar) eclipse.

LUNATIONS BY SIGN 1996 TO 2015

from 00° Capricorn to 29° Pisces

CAPRICORN			AQUARIUS			PISCES		
Degree	Date	Lunation	Degree	Date	Lunation	Degree	Date	Lunation
00:06	12/22/14	New	00:06	07/22/13	Full	00:00	02/18/15	New
00:51	06/22/05	Full	00:09	01/20/15	New	01:04	02/20/04	New
01:08	12/30/03	New	01:10	01/21/04	New	01:24	08/24/10	Full
02:10	06/23/13	Full	01:18	07/24/02	Full	02:42	02/21/12	New
02:34	12/24/11	New	02:42	01/23/12	New	03:17	08/26/99	Full
03:11	06/24/02	Full**	03:00	07/26/10	Full	04:37	02/23/01	New
04:14	12/25/00	New*	04:37	01/24/01	New	04:46	08/28/07	Full**
04:46	06/26/10	Full**	04:58	07/28/99	Full**	05:41	08/28/96	Full
06:08	12/27/08	New	06:30	01/26/09	New*	06:06	08/29/15	Full
06:45	06/28/99	Full	06:31	07/30/07	Full	06:35	02/25/09	New
08:01	12/29/97	New	07:32	07/30/96	Full	07:30	08/30/04	Full
08:25	06/30/07	Full	07:56	07/31/15	Full	07:55	02/26/98	New*
09:32	12/31/05	New	08:06	01/28/98	New	08:34	08/31/12	Full
09:36	07/01/96	Full	08:51	07/31/04	Full	09:16	02/28/06	New
09:55	07/02/15	Full	09:32	01/29/06	New			
10:54	07/02/04	Full				10:28	09/02/01	Full
10:57	01/01/14	New	10:15	08/02/12	Full	10:39	03/01/14	New
12:01	01/02/03	New	10:55	01/30/14	New	12:06	03/03/03	New
12:14	07/03/12	Full	11:58	08/04/01	Full	12:15	09/04/09	Full
13:31	07/05/01	Full**	12:09	02/01/03	New	13:40	09/06/98	Full**
13:39	01/04/11	New*	13:43	08/06/09	Full**	13:56	03/04/11	New
15:24	07/07/09	Full**	13:54	02/03/11	New	15:00	09/07/06	Full**
15:44	01/06/00	New	15:21	08/08/98	Full	15:56	03/06/00	New
17:15	07/09/98	Full	16:02	02/05/00	New*	16:19	09/09/14	Full
17:33	01/08/08	New	16:44	08/09/06	Full	17:31	03/07/08	New
18:42	07/11/06	Full	17:44	02/07/08	New*	17:34	09/10/03	Full
18:57	01/09/97	New	18:02	08/10/14	Full	18:31	03/09/97	New*
20:03	07/12/14	Full	18:53	02/07/97	New			
20:21	01/10/05	New	19:05	08/12/03	Full	19:17	09/12/11	Full
20:59	07/13/03	Full				19:24	03/10/05	New
21:46	01/11/13	New	20:16	02/08/05	New	21:18	09/13/00	Full
22:48	07/15/11	Full	20:41	08/13/11	Full	21:24	03/11/13	New
23:11	01/13/02	New	21:43	02/10/13	New	22:54	09/15/08	Full
24:19	07/16/00	Full	22:21	08/15/00	Full	23:19	03/14/02	New
25:01	01/15/10	New*	23:25	02/12/02	New	23:56	09/16/97	Full**
26:04	07/18/08	Full	24:21	08/16/08	Full**	25:10	03/15/10	New
27:05	01/17/99	New	25:18	02/14/10	New	25:16	09/18/05	Full
27:28	07/20/97	Full	25:32	08/18/97	Full	26:41	09/19/13	Full
28:41	01/19/07	New	26:50	08/19/05	Full	26:44	03/17/99	New
28:47	07/21/05	Full	27:08	02/16/99	New*	28:07	03/19/07	New*
29:45	01/20/96	New	28:11	08/21/13	Full	28:25	09/21/02	Full
29:45	01/20/96	New	28:37	02/17/07	New	29:07	03/19/96	New
			29:36	02/18/96	New	29:27	03/20/15	New*
			29:39	08/22/02	Full			
			29:60	02/18/15	New			

*indicates a New Moon (solar) eclipse.
**indicates a Full Moon (lunar) eclipse.

SOLAR AND LUNAR ECLIPSES BY DEGREE

January 1980 to December 2015 (New/Solar and Full/Lunar)

DEGREE	DATE	ECLIPSE	DEGREE	DATE	ECLIPSE	DEGREE	DATE	ECLIPSE
ARIES			**LEO**			**SAGITTARIUS**		
04:17	9/26/96	Full	00:10	1/20/81	Full	00:50	11/22/84	New
04:40	9/28/15	Full	00:26	1/20/00	Full	01:14	11/23/03	New
08:18	3/29/87	New	07:51	7/31/81	New	02:37	11/25/11	New
08:35	3/29/05	New	08:11	7/30/00	New	03:43	5/24/94	Full
13:22	10/07/87	Full	09:32	8/1/08	New	03:59	5/25/13	Full
14:54	10/08/95	Full	09:51	1/30/91	Full	05:04	5/26/02	Full
15:05	10/08/14	Full	11:20	1/31/99	Full	11:47	12/04/83	New
19:06	4/09/86	New	18:17	8/10/80	New	11:58	11/04/02	New
19:06	4/08/05	New	18:21	8/11/99	New	14:14	6/04/12	Full
24:07	10/17/86	Full	20:47	2/09/90	Full	18:55	6/4/93	Full
24:13	10/17/05	Full	21:00	2/09/09	Full	22:45	6/13/84	Full
25:45	10/18/13	Full	28:38	08/21/98	New	22:56	12/14/01	New
28:12	4/17/96	New				23:04	12/15/82	New
29:49	4/19/04	New				24:02	6/14/92	Full
						24:23	6/15/11	Full
TAURUS			**VIRGO**			**CAPRICORN**		
05:02	10/27/04	Full	01:53	2/21/08	Full	02:28	12/23/92	New
05:15	10/28/85	Full	01:59	2/20/89	Full	03:11	6/24/02	Full
08:52	4/29/14	New	07:48	8/31/89	New	03:14	6/25/83	Full
08:56	4/29/95	New	09:34	9/1/97	New	04:14	12/25/00	New
16:13	11/08/03	Full	11:26	3/11/80	Full	04:50	6/26/10	Full
16:30	11/08/84	Full	13:00	3/3/07	Full	05:00	6/26/91	Full
19:31	5/9/13	New	13:18	3/03/88	Full	13:39	1/04/11	New
19:48	5/10/94	New	18:25	9/11/07	New	13:39	7/05/01	Full
25:43	11/18/94	Full	18:40	9/11/88	New	13:51	1/04/92	New
27:33	11/19/02	Full	20:10	9/13/15	New	13:55	7/06/82	Full
28:50	5/19/85	New	22:34	3/12/98	Full	15:24	7/07/09	Full
			24:15	3/14/06	Full	24:19	7/16/00	Full
			29:20	9/22/06	New	24:31	7/17/81	Full
			29:34	9/23/87	New	25:01	1/15/10	New
						25:20	1/15/91	New
GEMINI			**LIBRA**			**AQUARIUS**		
00:06	5/20/12	New	03:35	3/23/97	Full	03:16	7/29/91	Full
00:31	5/21/93	New	10:16	10/03/86	New	04:52	7/27/80	Full
06:47	11/28/12	Full	10:19	10/03/05	New	04:54	1/25/82	New
07:03	11/29/93	Full	14:24	4/04/15	Full	04:58	7/28/99	Full
09:02	5/30/03	New	14:31	4/3/96	Full	06:30	1/26/09	New
09:26	5/30/84	New	19:32	10/12/96	New	06:35	1/26/90	New
11:02	6/01/11	New	21:06	10/13/04	New	13:43	8/06/09	Full
18:10	12/9/92	Full	23:38	4/14/87	Full	13:52	8/06/90	Full
18:11	12/10/11	Full	25:04	4/15/95	Full	15:21	8/7/98	Full
19:43	6/11/83	New	25:16	4/15/14	Full	16:02	2/04/81	New
19:54	6/10/02	New				16:02	2/05/00	New
27:36	12/20/83	Full				17:44	2/06/08	New
29:03	12/21/91	Full				24:12	8/17/89	Full
29:23	12/21/10	Full				24:21	8/16/08	Full
29:47	6/21/82	New				26:50	2/16/80	New
						27:08	2/16/99	New
CANCER			**SCORPIO**			**PISCES**		
00:10	6/21/01	New	00:18	10/23/95	New	03:03	8/26/80	Full
08:27	12/30/82	Full	00:25	10/23/14	New	04:23	8/27/88	Full
08:48	12/30/01	Full	04:03	4/24/86	Full	04:46	8/28/07	Full
08:57	6/30/92	New	04:20	4/24/05	Full	07:55	2/26/98	New
9:12	7/01/11	New	05:46	4/25/13	Full	13:40	9/06/98	Full
10:14	7/01/00	New	10:54	11/03/94	New	15:00	9/07/06	Full
10:15	12/31/09	Full	11:16	11/03/13	New	17:10	3/07/89	New
18:59	7/11/91	New	14:17	5/04/85	Full	18:31	3/08/97	New
19:14	1/09/82	Full	14:42	5/04/04	Full	23:56	9/16/97	Full
19:24	7/11/10	New	19:31	5/10/13	Full	27:42	3/18/88	New
19:39	1/09/01	Full	20:09	11/12/85	New	28:07	3/19/07	New
27:43	7/20/82	New	21:32	11/13/93	New	29:27	3/20/15	New
29:04	7/22/90	New	21:57	11/13/12	New			
29:27	7/21/09	New	24:31	5/15/84	Full			
			24:53	5/15/03	Full			

SELECTED BIBLIOGRAPHY

Assagioli, Roberto. *Psychosynthesis: A Manual of Principles and Techniques.* New York: Viking Press, 1965.

Byrne, Rhonda. *The Secret.* New York: Atria Books, 2006.

Frank, Victor. *Man's Search for Meaning.* New York: Washington Square Press, 1967.

Goswami, Amit. *The Self-Aware Universe.* New York: Jeremy Tarcher, 1995.

Greene, Brian. *The Fabric of the Cosmos.* New York: Knopf, 2004.

Grof, Stanislav and Christina. *Beyond Death: The Gates of Consciousness.* London: Thames & Hudson, 1980.

Harding, Esther. *Woman's Mysteries: Ancient and Modern—A Psychological Interpretation of the Feminine Principle As Portrayed in Myth, Story, and Dreams.* New York: Bantam Books, 1973.

Hicks, Esther and Jerry. *The Law of Attraction.* Carlsbad, CA: Hay House, 2006.

Kegan, Robert. *The Evolving Self: Problem and Process in Human Development.* Cambridge, MA: Harvard University Press, 1982.

Marks, Tracy. *The Art of Chart Interpretation: A Step-by-Step Method of Analyzing, Synthesizing & Understanding the Birth Chart.* Sebastopol, CA: CRCS Publications, 1987. New edition to be published by Ibis Press/Nicolas Hays, Lake Worth, FL, fall 2009.

———. *Planetary Aspects: From Conflict to Cooperation.* Sebastopol, CA: CRCS Publications, 1987. (A revised edition of *How to Handle Your T-Square,* Sagittarius Rising, 1979).

———. *The Square Aspect.* Arlington, MA: Sagittarius Rising, 1981.

———. *Your Secret Self: Illuminating the Mysteries of the Twelfth House.* Sebastopol, CA: CRCS Publications, 1989. (An expanded edition of *The Twelfth House,* published by Sagittarius Rising, Arlington, MA 1978.)

Rilke, Rainer Maria. *Letters to a Young Poet.* Trans. M.D. Herter Norton. New York: W.W. Norton and Company, 1962.

Rudhyar, Dane. *An Astrological Mandala.* New York: Vintage Books, 1974.

Satinover, Jeffrey. *The Quantum Brain.* New York: John Wiley and Sons, 2001.

Schulman, Martin. *Karmic Astrology: The Moon's Nodes and Reincarnation.* Newburyport, MA: Weiser Books, 1975.

Van Toen, Donna. *The Astrologer's Node Book.* Newburyport, MA: Weiser Books, 1981.

Watzlawick, Paul. *Change.* New York: W.W. Norton, 1974.

Wilhelm, Richard. Trans. *The I Ching or Book of Changes.* Trans. Cary F. Baynes. Princeton: Princeton University Press, 1950, 1967.

Wolinsky, Stephen. *Quantum Consciousness.* Las Vegas: Bramble Books, 1993.

ABOUT THE AUTHOR

Tracy Marks, M.A., L.M.H.C., is an Arlington, Massachusetts, psychotherapist, astrologer, writer, nature photographer and instructor of Adobe Photoshop and English literature. Her transformational astrology books, *The Astrology of Self-Discovery*, *The Art of Chart Interpretation*, *Planetary Aspects* (originally titled *How to Handle Your T-square*) and *Your Secret Self: Illuminating the Mysteries of the Twelfth House*, have been translated into nine languages and have sold over 150,000 copies. Originally published by Sagittarius Rising and CRCS Publications, they are currently being republished in revised editions.

Tracy was born September 26, 1950, in Miami, Florida, and moved to Boston in 1968, where she received her bachelors degree in religion and masters degree in education at Tufts University. She also completed postgraduate training in clinical psychology and social work, participated in training programs in alternative psychotherapies such as psychosynthesis, and became a licensed mental health counselor. She has been practicing psychotherapy since 1985.

Tracy was born under a lunar eclipse, with Sun in Libra opposing Moon in Aries in exact t-square to Uranus. She has a 9th house Virgo/ Libra stellium, with Sun and Neptune straddling the Midheaven, and 27 degrees Sagittarius rising.

Currently, Tracy Marks maintains a psychotherapy and astrology practice, and teaches in continuing education programs in the Boston area. She is available for both counseling and astrology consultations, and may be contacted at tracy@marks.net.

Her websites include:
http://www.windweaver.com, *http://www.webwinds.com*, and *http://tracymar.smugmug.com*. Astrological articles are posted at *http://www.windweaver.com/astrology*.